Francis Walkingame, William Taylor

The Tutor's Assistant

Being a Compendium of Arithmetic

Francis Walkingame, William Taylor

The Tutor's Assistant
Being a Compendium of Arithmetic

ISBN/EAN: 9783337138479

Printed in Europe, USA, Canada, Australia, Japan

Cover: Foto ©ninafisch / pixelio.de

More available books at **www.hansebooks.com**

THE
TUTOR's ASSISTANT;
BEING
A COMPENDIUM of ARITHMETIC,
AND
A Complete Question-Book:
CONTAINING,

I. *Arithmetic* in Whole Numbers; being a brief Explanation of all its Rules, in a new and more concise Method than any hitherto published; with an *Application* to each Rule, consisting of a large Variety of Questions in real Business, with their Answers annexed.

II. *Vulgar Fractions*, which are treated with a great deal of Plainness and Perspicuity.

III. *Decimals*, with the *Extraction* of the *Square*, *Cube*, and *Biquadrate* Roots, after a very plain and familiar Manner; in which are set down *Rules* for the easy Calculation of *Interest*, *Annuities*, and Pensions in *Arrears*, the present Worth of Annuities, &c. either by Simple or Compound Interest.

IV. *Duodecimals*, or *Multiplication* of Feet and Inches, with Examples applied to measuring and working by Multiplication, Practice, and Decimals.

V. The *Mensuration* of *Circles*, &c.

VI. A *Collection* of *Questions* set down promiscuously, for the greater Trial of the foregoing *Rules*.

VII. A *Course* of *Book-Keeping*, according to the method of *Single Entry*; with a description of the Books, and directions for using them.

TO WHICH ARE ADDED,

A new and very short Method of extracting the CUBE ROOT, *and a* GENERAL TABLE *for the ready calculating the* INTEREST *of any Sum of Money, at any Rate per Cent. likewise* Rents, Salaries, &c.

The Whole adapted as a QUESTION-BOOK for Schools, or REMEMBRANCER and INSTRUCTOR to such as have some Knowledge therein.

This Work having been perused by several Eminent MATHEMATICIANS *and* ACCOMPTANTS, *is recommended as the best* COMPENDIUM *hitherto published, for the Use of* SCHOOLS, *or for* PRIVATE PERSONS.

By *FRANCIS WALKINGAME,*
WRITING-MASTER & ACCOMPTANT.

A NEW EDITION,
With the Addition of Book-Keeping by Single Entry.
Carefully Revised, and every Question wrought anew,
By *WILLIAM TAYLOR*;
Author of a Complete System of Arithmetic; the Measurer's Assistant, Trader's Sure Guide, &c.

BIRMINGHAM:
Printed for the Editor, and sold by SWINNEY & WALKER, in the HIGH-STREET, and all other BOOKSELLERS, M,DCC,XCII.

PREFACE.

THE Public, no doubt, will be furprized to find there is another attempt made to publifh a Book of ARITHMETIC, when there are fuch numbers already extant on the fame Subject, and feveral of them that have fo lately made their appearance in the World; but, I flatter myfelf, that the following reafons which induced me to compile it, the Method, and the Concifenefs of the Rules, which are laid down in fo plain and familiar a manner, will have fome weight towards its having a favourable reception.

Having fome time ago drawn up a Set of Rules, and proper Queftions, with their Anfwers annexed, for the ufe of my own School, and divided them into feveral Books, as well for more eafe to myfelf, as the readier improvement of my Scholars, I found them, by experience, of infinite ufe; for when a mafter takes upon him that laborious (though unneceffary) method of writing out the Rules and Queftions in the childrens books, he muft either be toiling and flaving

PREFACE.

slaving himself after the fatigue of the School is over, to get ready the books for the next day, or else must lose that time which would be much better spent in instructing and opening the minds of his Pupils. There was, however, still an inconvenience which hindered them from giving me the Satisfaction I at first expected; *i. e.* where there are several boys in a class, some one or other must wait till the boy who first has the book, finishes the writing out of those rules or questions he wants; which detains the others from making that progress they otherwise might, had they a proper Book of Rules and Examples for each; to remedy which, I was prompted to compile one, in order to have it printed, that might not only be of use to my own School, but to such others as would have their Scholars make a quick progress. It will also be of great use to such Gentlemen as have acquired some knowledge of numbers at School, to make them the more perfect; likewise to such as have completed themselves therein, it will prove after an impartial perusal, on account of its great variety and brevity, a most agreeable and entertaining Exercise Book. I shall not presume to say any thing more in favour of this Work, but beg leave to refer the unprejudiced reader to the remark of a certain Author*, concerning compositions of this nature. His words are as follow:

"And now, after all, it is possible that some "who like best to tread the old beaten path, "and

* Dilworth.

PREFACE.

" and to sweat at their business, when they may
" do it with pleasure, may start an objection
" against the use of this well-intended ASSIST-
" ANT, because the course of ARITHMETIC is
" always the same; and therefore say, *That*
" *some boys lazily inclined, when they see another*
" *at work upon the same Question, will be apt to*
" *make his operation pass for their own.* But these
" little forgeries are soon detected, by the dili-
" gence of the TUTOR: therefore, as different
" questions to different boys do not in the least
" promote their improvement, so neither do the
" questions hinder it. Neither is it in the power
" of any Master (in the course of his business)
" how full of spirits so ever he be, to frame new
" questions at pleasure, in any Rule; but the
" same question will frequently occur in the
" same Rule, notwithstanding his greatest care
" and skill to the contrary.

" It may also be further objected, *That to*
" *teach by a printed Book is an argument of Igno-*
" *rance and incapacity;* which is no less trifling
" than the former. He, indeed, (if any such
" there be) who is afraid his Scholars will im-
" prove too fast, will, undoubtedly, decry this
" method: But that Master's ignorance can
" never be brought in question, who can begin
" and end it readily; and, most certainly, that
" scholar's non-improvement can be as little
" questioned, who makes a much greater pro-
" gress by this than by the common method."

PREFACE.

To enter into a long detail of every Rule, would tire the reader, and swell the Preface to an unusual length; I shall, therefore, only give a general idea of the method of proceeding, and leave the rest to speak for itself; which, I hope, the kind reader will find to answer the title, and the recommendation given it. As to the Rules, they follow in the same manner as the Table of Contents specifies, and in much the same order as they are generally taught in Schools. I have gone through the four fundamental Rules in integers first, before those of the several denominations: In order that they being well understood, the latter will be performed with much more ease and dispatch, according to the rules shewn, than by the customary method of dotting. In Multiplication I have shewn both the beauty and use of that excellent Rule, in resolving most Questions that occur in merchandizing; and have prefixed before Reduction, several bills of Parcels, which are applicable to real business. In working Interest by Decimals, I have added Tables to the Rules, for the readier calculating Annuities, &c. and have not only shewn the use, but the method of making them. I have also added to this *Edition* a NEW RULE for extracting the *Cube Root*, being a much shorter way than any that is already published; as likewise an Interest Table, calculated for the easier finding the Interest of any Sum of money at any Rate *per Cent.* by Multiplication and Addition only; it is also useful in calculating Rates, Incomes, and Servants Wages, for any number of Months, Weeks, or Days; and I may venture to say, I have gone through the whole

PREFACE.

whole with so much plainness and perspicuity, that there is none better extant.

I have nothing further to add, but a return of my sincere thanks to all those Gentlemen, Schoolmasters, and others, whose kind approbation and encouragement hath now established the use of this book in almost every School of eminence throughout the Kingdom: But I think my gratitude more especially due to those who have favoured me with their remarks; though, I must still beg of every cand'd and judicious Reader, that if he should, by chance, find a transposition of a Letter, or a false Figure, to excuse it; for, notwithstanding there has been great care taken in correcting, yet errors of the Press will inevitably creep in; and some may also have slipped my observation: In either of which cases, the Admonition of a good-natured Reader will be very acceptable to his

    Much obliged,

      And most obedient

        Humble Servant,

          F. WALKINGAME.

Just published, by SWINNEY & WALKER, *Birmingham,*

THE SCHOOL and FAMILY
NEW TESTAMENT:
Containing the Life of our Lord and Saviour
JESUS CHRIST:
WITH
NOTES and ILLUSTRATIONS.

To which is prefixed, A DICTIONARY of SCRIPTURE NAMES, difficult of Pronunciation, copiously explained, properly divided into Syllables, and accented.

AND

A COLLECTION OF ENGLISH WORDS, which agree in Sound, yet differ in Sense.

The whole adapted to the Use of Schools and Families; to give Youth a more intelligible Idea of the Holy Scriptures, in which mankind are so deeply interested.

By a Clergyman of the Church of England.

Carefully Revised and Corrected

By THOMAS FEARNLEY, *Schoolmaster.*

(Price One Shilling and Sixpence, neatly Bound.)

ALSO,

DIVINE SONGS,
FOR THE USE OF
CHILDREN.
By J. Watts, D. D.—Price Sixpence.

CONTENTS.

PART I.

ARITHMETIC in WHOLE NUMBERS.

	Page.		Page
*I*NTRODUCTION	1	Purchasing of Stocks	61
Numeration	2	Brokage	63
Integers, Addition	3	Compound Interest	68
———— Subtraction	4	Rebate or Discount	69
———— Multiplication	5	Equation of Payments	70
———— Division	7	Barter	72
Tables	9	Profit and Loss	73
Addition of several Denominations	16	Fellowship	75
		———— with Time	77
———— Subtraction	21	Alligation Medial	78
———— Multiplication	25	———— Alternate	80
———— Division	29	Position, or Rule of False	84
Bills of Parcels	32	———— Double	85
Reduction	35	Exchange	87
Single Rule of Three Direct	45	Comparison of Weights and Measures	91
———— Inverse	49		
Double Rule of Three	51	Conjoined Proportion	92
Practice	52	Progression Arithmetical	93
Simple Interest	60	———— Geometrical	96
Commission	61	Permutation	100

PART

PART II.
VULGAR FRACTIONS.

	Page		Page
Reduction	102	Division	110
Addition	108	The Rule of Three Direct	111
Subtraction	ib.	———— Inverse	112
Multiplication	109	The Double Rule of Three	ib.

PART III.
DECIMALS.

	Page		Page
Numeration	113	A general Rule for extracting the Roots of all Powers	135
Addition	114		
Subtraction	115	Simple Interest	137
Multiplication	ib.	———— for Days	138
Contracted Multiplication	116	Annuities and Pensions, &c. in Arrears	141
Division	117		
———— Contracted	118	Present worth of Annuities	144
Reduction	119	Annuities, &c. in Reversion	147
Decimal Tables of Coin, Weights and Measures	122	Rebate or Discount	149
The Rule of Three	125	Equation of Payments	151
Extraction of the Square Root	126	Compound Interest	152
		Annuities, &c. in Arrears	155
———— Vulgar Fractions	127	Present Worth of Annuities	159
———— Mixed Numbers	ib.	Annuities, &c. in Reversion	160
Extraction of the Cube Root	131	Purchasing Freehold or Real Estates	162
———— Vulgar Fractions	133		
———— Mixed Numbers	ib.	———— in Reversion	163
———— Biquadrate Root	135	Rebate or Discount	164

PART.

CONTENTS.

PART IV.
DUODECIMALS.

	Page		Page
Multiplication of Feet and Inches	167	Measuring by the Square of 100 Feet	170
Measuring by the Foot Square	169	Measuring by the Rod	171
Measuring by the Yard Square	ib.	Multiplying several Figures by several, and the Operation in one Line only	173

PART V.
The MENSURATION of CIRCLES, &c.

PART VI.
QUESTIONS.

	Page		Page
A Collection of Questions set down promiscuously, for the greater Trial of the foregoing Rules	178	A general Table for calculating Interests, Rents, Incomes, and Servants Wages	187

PART VII.
A COURSE OF BOOK-KEEPING,

According to the method of Single Entry; with a description of the Books, and directions for using them.   193

Explanation *of the* Characters *made use of in this* Compendium.

= *Equal.* The Sign of Equality; as, 4 qrs. = 1 cwt. signifies, that 4 qrs. are equal to 1 cwt.

— *Minus or Less.* The Sign of Subtraction; as, 8−2=6, that is, 8 lessened by 2 is equal to 6.

+ *Plus or more.* The Sign of Addition; as, 4+4=8, that is, 4 added to 4 more is equal to 8.

× *Multiplied by.* The Sign of Multiplication; as, 4×6=24, that is, 4 multiplied by 6 is equal to 24.

÷ *Divided by.* The Sign of Division; as, 8÷2=4, that is, 8 divided by 2 is equal to 4.

$\frac{2357}{63}$ Numbers placed like a Fraction do likewise denote Division; the upper number being the Dividend and the lower the Divisor.

∷ *So is.* The Sign of Proportion; as, 2:4∷8:16, that is, as 2 is to 4, so is 8 to 16.

$\overline{7-2+5}=10.$ Shews that the difference between 2 and 7 added to 5 is equal to 10.

$9-\overline{2+5}=2.$ Signifies that the Sum of 2 and 5 taken from 9, is equal to 2.

$\sqrt{}$ Prefixed to any number, signifies the Square Root of that number is required.

$\sqrt{}^{3}$ Signifies the Cube, or Third Power.

$\sqrt{}^{4}$ Denotes the Biquadrate, or the Fourth Power, &c.

i.e. *id est,* that is.

THE TUTOR's ASSISTANT;

BEING A COMPENDIUM OF ARITHMETIC.

PART I.

Arithmetic in Whole Numbers.

THE INTRODUCTION.

ARITHMETIC is the Art or Science of Computing by Numbers, and confifts both in Theory and Practice.

The Theory confiders the Nature and Quality of Numbers, and demonftrates the Reafon of Practical Operations.

The Practice is that which fhews the method of working by Numbers, fo as to be the moft ufeful and expeditious for Bufinefs, and has five principal or fundamental Rules for the Operations : *viz.*

NOTATION or NUMERATION, ADDITION, SUBTRACTION, MULTIPLICATION, and DIVISION.

NUMERATION

TEACHETH the different Value of Figures by their different Places, and to read and write any Sum or Number.

Numeration.

The TABLE.

C Millions	X Millions	Millions	C Thousands	X Thousands	Thousands	Hundreds	Tens	Units
9	8	7	6	5	4	3	2	1
9	0	0	0	0	0	0	0	0
	8	0	0	0	0	0	0	0
		7	0	0	0	0	0	0
			6	0	0	0	0	0
				5	0	0	0	0
					4	0	0	0
						3	0	0
							2	0
								1

RULE. There are three Periods; the first on the Right Hand, Units; the Second, Thousands; and the Third, Millions; each consisting of Three Figures, or Places. Reckon the first Figure of each from the Left Hand as so many Hundreds, the next as Tens, and the Third as so many single Ones of what is written over them: As the first Period on the Left Hand is read thus, Nine Hundred Eighty-seven Millions; and so on for any of the rest.

The APPLICATION.

Write down in proper Figures the following Numbers:

Twenty-three.

Two Hundred and Fifty-four.

Three Thousand Two Hundred and Four.

Twenty-five thousand, Eight Hundred Fifty-six.

One Hundred Thirty-two Thousand, Two Hundred Forty-five.

Four Millions, Nine Hundred Forty-one Thousand, Four Hundred.

Twenty-seven Millions, One Hundred Fifty-seven Thousand, Eight Hundred Thirty-two.

Seven Hundred Twenty-two Millions, Two Hundred Thirty-one Thousand, Five Hundred and Four.

Six Hundred Two Millions, Two Hundred Ten Thousand, Five Hundred.

Write down in Words at Length the following Numbers:

35	2017	519007	5207054	65700047
59	5201	750058	2071909	900061057
172	20760	5900630	70054008	201900790

Notation by ROMAN *Letters.*

I One.
II Two.
III Three.
IV Four.
V Five.
VI Six.
VII Seven.
VIII Eight,
IX Nine.
X Ten.
XI Eleven.
XII Twelve.
XIII Thirteen.
XIV Fourteen.
XV Fifteen.
XVI Sixteen.
XVII Seventeen.
XVIII Eighteen.
XIX Nineteen.
XX Twenty.

XXX Thirty.
XL Forty.
L Fifty.
LX Sixty.
LXX Seventy.
LXXX Eighty.
XC Ninety.
C Hundred.
CC Two Hundred.
CCC Three Hundred.
CCCC Four Hundred.
D Five Hundred.
DC Six Hundred.
DCC Seven Hundred.
DCCC Eight Hundred.
DCCCC Nine Hundred.
M One Thousand.
MDCCXCII One Thousand Seven Hundred and Ninety two.

INTEGERS.

ADDITION

TEACHETH to add two or more Sums together, to make one whole or total Sum.

RULE. There must be due Regard had in placing the Figures one under the other, *i. e.* Units under Units, Tens under Tens, &c. then beginning with the first Row of Units, add them up to the Top; when done, set down the Units, and carry the Tens to the next, and so on; continuing to the last Row, at which set down the total Amount.

PROOF. Begin at the Top of the Sum, and reckon the Figures downwards, the same as you added them up; and, if the same as the first, the Sum is supposed to be right.

Addition and Subtraction TABLE.

1	2	3	4	5	6	7	8	9
2	4	5	6	7	8	9	10	11
3	5	6	7	8	9	10	11	12
4	6	7	8	9	10	11	12	13
5	7	8	9	10	11	12	13	14
6	8	9	10	11	12	13	14	15
7	9	10	11	12	13	14	15	16
8	10	11	12	13	14	15	16	17
9	11	12	13	14	15	16	17	18

£.	Cwt.	Qrs.	Months.	£.	Years.
2	27	275	1234	7524	27104
5	35	110	7098	3750	32547
7	47	473	8314	9147	10758
9	35	354	6732	3214	62590
2	41	271	2546	4725	75408
5	36	352	3709	2147	27973
4	59	471	4152	3254	85421
3	37	310	3705	2716	12706
7	14	473	1076	1047	10471
44	331				

SUBTRACTION

TEACHETH to take a lefs Number from a greater, and fhews the Remainder, or Difference.

RULE. This being the Reverfe of Addition, you muft borrow here (if it requires) what you ftopped at there, always remembering to pay it to the next.

PROOF. Add the Remainder and lefs Line together, and if the fame as the greater, it is right.

From 271	4754	42087	452705	271508	3750215
Take 154	2725	34096	327616	152471	2150874
Rem. 117					
Proof. 271					

MULTIPLICATION

MULTIPLICATION

TEACHETH how to increase the greater of two Numbers given, as often as, there are Units in the less; and compendiously performs the Office of many Additions:

To this Rule belong three principal Members: viz.
1, The Multiplicand, or Number to be multiplied:
2, The Multiplier, or Number by which you multiply:
3, The Product, or Number produced by multiplying.

RULE. Begin with that Figure that stands in the Unit's Place of the Multiplier, and with it multiply the first Figure in the Unit's Place of the Multiplicand. Set down the Units, and carry the Tens in Mind, till you have multiplied the next Figure in the Multiplicand by the same Figure in the Multiplier; to the Product of which add the Tens you kept in Mind, setting down the Units, and proceed as before, till the whole Line is multiplied.

PROOF. The usual Way of proving Multiplication is, by casting out the Nines from the Multiplicand and Multiplier: the Remainders put on each Side of a Cross; multiply the Figures on each Side together, cast the Nines from the Product, and put the Overplus at Top; then cast out the Nines from the Product of the Multiplication, and its Remainder place at the Bottom; if it agree with the Top, the Work is supposed right. But the surest Way is, to divide the Product by the Multiplicand, and the Quotient will be the same as the Multiplier.

MULTIPLICATION and DIVISION TABLE.

1	2	3	4	5	6	7	8	9	10	11	12
2	4	6	8	10	12	14	16	18	20	22	24
3	—	9	12	15	18	21	24	27	30	33	36
4	—	—	16	20	24	28	32	36	40	44	48
5	—	—	—	25	30	35	40	45	50	55	60
6	—	—	—	—	36	42	48	54	60	66	72
7	—	—	—	—	—	49	56	63	70	77	84
8	—	—	—	—	—	—	64	72	80	88	96
9	—	—	—	—	—	—	—	81	90	99	108
10	—	—	—	—	—	—	—	—	100	110	120
11	—	—	—	—	—	—	—	—	—	121	132
12	—	—	—	—	—	—	—	—	—	—	144

Multiplication of Integers.

Multiplicand	25104736	52471021	7925437521
Multiplier	2	3	4
Product	50209472		

27104107	231047	7092516	3725104
5	6	7	8

4215406	2701057	31040171	35210472
9	10	11	12

When the Multiplier is more than 12, and lefs than 20, multiply the Unit Figure in the Multiplier, adding to the Product the back Figure to that you multiplied.

5710592	5107252	7653210	92057165
13	14	15	16

6251721	9215324	2571341	3592104
17	18	19	19

When the Multiplier confifts of feveral Figures, there muft be as many Products as there are Figures in the Multiplier, obferving to put the firft Figure of every Product under that Figure you multiply by. Add the feveral Products together, and their Sum will be the total Product.

	271041	32104	2710432	27501976
6+0	27	25	375	271
	1897287	802600	10164120000	7453035496
	542082			
	7318107			

When Cyphers are placed between the fignificant Figures in the Multiplier, they may be omitted; but great Care muft be taken that the next Figure muft be put one Place more to the Left Hand, i. e. under the Figure you multiply by.

571204

571204	7104325	5271094
27009	57020	590030
15427648836	405038611500	3110103592820

When there are Cyphers at the End of the Multiplicand or Multiplier, they may be omitted, by only multiplying by the rest of the Figures, and setting down on the right Hand of the total product as many Cyphers as were omitted.

27100	379500	265000	574000
52600	274000	7200	630
1425460000	103983000000	1908000000	361620000

When the Multiplier is a composite Number, i. e. if any two Figures, being multiplied together, will make that Number, then multiply by one of those Figures, and that Product by the other will give the Answer.

771039 by 35	921563 by 32	715241 by 56
26986365	29490016	40053496

DIVISION

TEACHETH to find how often one Number is contained in another; or to divide any Number into what Parts you please.

In this Rule there are three Numbers real, and a fourth accidental: viz.

1, The Dividend, or Number to be divided:

2, The Divisor, or Number by which you Divide:

3, The Quotient, or Number that shews how often the Divisor is contained in the Dividend:

4th, or accidental Number, is what remains when the Work is finished, and is of the same Name as the Dividend.

RULE. When the Divisor is less than 12, find how often it is contained in the first Figure of the Dividend: set it down under the Figure you divided, and carry the Overplus (if any) to the next in the Dividend, as so many Tens; then find how often the Divisor is contained therein, set it down, and continue the same till you have gone through the

8 · *Division of Integers.* *The* TUTOR's

the Line: But when the Divisor is more than 12, multiply it by the Quotient Figure; the Product subtract from the Dividend, and to the Remainder bring down the next Figure in the Dividend, and proceed as before, till the Figures are all brought down.

PROOF. Multiply the Divisor and Quotient together, adding the Remainder (if any) and the Product will be the same as the Dividend.

	Dividend. Rem.		
Divisor	2)725107(1	3)7210472(	4)7210416(
Quotient	362553		
	2		
		5)7203287(	6)5231037(
Proof	725107		
	7)2532701(	8)2547325(	9)2504730C(
	10)2750012(	11)2710513(	12)27100732(

Divisor. Dividend. Quotient.
29)4172377(143575
   29   29
——
127   37)7210473(194877
116   1294875   473)2104721(4449
—— 287750   275)3720147(13527
.112   2 Rem. 3701)73109521(1943
 87   3576)72104726(20163
——   4172377 Proof. 2510)63210476(25183
.253   25204)321047217(12737
232   31700)521047321(16432
——   270234)7210472532(2669
.217   210472)352107193214(1672040
203   3721071)21071921473(5662
——
.147
145
——
Rem. ..2

When

When there are Cyphers at the End of the Divisor, they may be cut off, and as many places from off the Dividend, but must be annexed to the Remainder at last.

27|00)25473|2|21(939   572|00)725347|2|16(1267
373|000)75247|3|719(2017   215|000)632510|4|997(29419

When the Divisor is a composite Number (i. e. if any two Figures being multiplied together, will make that Number) then, by dividing the Dividend by one of those Figures, and that Quotient by the other, it will give the Quotient required. But as it sometimes happens that there is a remainder to each of the Quotients, and neither of them the true one, it may be found by this

RULE. Multiply the first Divisor into the last Remainder, to that Product add the first Remainder, which will give the true one.

Div. 3210473 by 27   7210473 by 35   6251043 by 42   5761034 by 54

118906. 11 Rem.   205013. 18 Rem.   148834. 15 Rem.   106685. 44 Rem.

MONEY.

Marked		Marked.
¼ Farthing,	4 Farthings make 1	Penny. - d.
½ Halfpenny.	12 Pence - 1	Shilling. - s.
¾ Three Farthings.	20 Shillings - 1	Pound. - l.
Farthings.		

```
   4 =   1 Penny.
  48 =  12 =  1 Shilling.
 960 = 240 = 20 = 1 Pound.
```

SHILLINGS.   PENCE TABLE.

s.	l.	s.	d.	s.	d.	d.	s.	d.
20	- 1 : 0	20	- 1 : 8	90	- 7 : 6
30	- 1 : 10	24	- 2 : 0	96	- 8 : 0
40	- 2 : 0	30	- 2 : 6	100	- 8 : 4
50	- 2 : 10	36	- 3 : 0	108	- 9 : 0
60	- 3 : 0	40	- 3 : 4	110	- 9 : 2
70	- 3 : 10	48 is 4 : 0	120 is 10 : 0
80	- 4 : 0	50	- 4 : 2	130	- 10 : 10
90	- 4 : 10	60	- 5 : 0	132	- 11 : 0
100	- 5 : 0	70	- 5 : 10	140	- 11 : 8
110	- 5 : 10	72	- 6 : 0	144	- 12 : 0
120	- 6 : 0	80	- 6 : 8	150	- 12 : 6
130	- 6 : 10	84	- 7 : 0	160	- 13 : 4

TROY

TROY WEIGHT.

		Marked
24 Grains - make - 1 Pennyweight.		gr.
20 Pennyweights - - - 1 Ounce. -	-	dwt. oz.
12 Ounces - - - - - 1 Pound.	-	lb.

Grains.
24 = 1 Pennyweight.
480 = 20 = 1 Ounce.
5760 = 240 = 12 = 1 Pound.

By this Weight are weighed Gold, Silver, Jewels, Electuaries, and all Liquors.

N. B. The Standard for Gold Coin is 22 Carats of fine Gold, and 2 Carats of Copper, melted together. For Silver, is 11 oz. 2 dwts of fine Silver, and 18 dwts. of Copper. 25 lb. is a quarter of an *cwt.* 100 lb. 1 *cwt.*
20 *cwt.* 1 Ton of Gold or Silver.

AVOIRDUPOISE WEIGHT.

		Marked
16 Drams - make - 1 Ounce	-	dr. oz.
16 Ounces - - 1 Pound	-	lb.
28 Pounds - - - 1 Quarter	-	qrs.
4 Quarters, or 112 *lb.* - 1 Hundred Weight		cwt.
20 Hundred Weight - 1 Ton	-	Ton.

Drams
16 = 1 Ounce,
256 = 16 = 1 Pound.
7168 = 448 = 28 = 1 Quarter.
28672 = 1792 = 112 = 4 = 1 Hund. Weight.
573440 = 35840 = 2240 = 80 = 20 = 1 Ton.

There are several other Denominations in this Weight, that are used in some particular Goods : *viz.*

	lb.		*lb.*
A Firkin of Butter -	56	A Stone of Iron, Shot or Horseman's wt.	14
Soap -	94		
A Barrel of Anchovies	30	Butcher's Meat	8
Soap -	256	A Gallon of Train Oil	7½
Raisins -	112	A Truss of Straw	36
A Puncheon of Prunes	1120	New Hay	60
A Fother of Lead, 19 *cwt.*		Old Hay	56
2 *qrs.*		36 Trusses a Load.	

Cheese

Cheese and Butter.

A Clove, or Half Stone, 8 lb.

	lb.		lb.
A Wey in Suffolk, 32 Cloves, or	256	A Wey in Essex, 42 Cloves, or	336

Wool.

	lb.		lb.
A Clove	7	A Wey is 6 Tod and 1 Stone, or	182
A Stone	14	A Sack is 2 Weys, or	364
A Tod	28	A Last is 12 Sacks, or	4368

By this Weight is weighed any thing of a coarse or drossy Nature; as all Grocery and Chandlery Wares: Bread, and all Metals but Silver and Gold.

Note, 1 Pound Avoirdupoise is equal to 14 *oz.* 11 *dwts.* 15 *grs.* ¼ Troy.

APOTHECARIES WEIGHT.

			Marked
20 Grains make	1 Scruple	-	℈
3 Scruples	1 Dram	-	ʒ
8 Drams	1 Ounce	-	℥
12 Ounces	1 Pound	-	℔

Grains
  20 = 1 Scruple.
  60 = 3 = 1 Dram.
 480 = 24 = 8 = 1 Ounce.
5760 = 288 = 96 = 12 = 1 Pound.

Note, The Apothecaries mix their Medicines by this Rule, but buy and sell their Commodities by Avoirdupoise Weight.

The Apothecaries Pound and Ounce, and the Pound and Ounce Troy, are the same, only differently divided and subdivided.

CLOTH MEASURE.

			Marked
4 Nails make	1 Quarter of a Yard		{ *n.* qrs.
3 Quarters	1 Flemish Ell	-	F. E.
4 Quarters	1 Yard	-	yd.
5 Quarters	1 English Ell	-	E. E.
6 Quarters	1 French Ell	-	Fr. E.

Inches.

Table of Measures

Inches.
- 2¼ = 1 Nail.
- 9 = 4 = 1 Quarter.
- 36 = 16 = 4 = 1 Yard.
- 27 = 12 = 3 = 1 Flemish Ell.
- 45 = 20 = 5 = 1 English Ell.

LONG MEASURE.

		Marked
3 Barley Corns make	1 Inch	bar. in.
12 Inches	1 Foot	feet.
3 Feet	1 Yard	yd.
6 Feet	1 Fathom	fth.
5½ Yards	1 Rod, Pole, or Perch	rod. p.
40 Poles	1 Furlong	fur.
8 Furlongs	1 Mile	mile.
3 Miles	1 League	lea.
60 Miles	1 Degree	deg.

Barley Corns.
- 3 = 1 Inch.
- 36 = 12 = 1 Foot.
- 108 = 36 = 3 = 1 Yard.
- 594 = 198 = 16½ = 5½ = 1 Pole.
- 23760 = 7920 = 660 = 220 = 40 = 1 Furlong.
- 190080 = 63360 = 5280 = 1760 = 320 = 8 = 1 Mile.

N. B. A Degree is 69 Miles, 4 Furlongs, nearly, though commonly reckoned but 60 miles.

This Measure is used to Measure Distance of Places, or any thing else that hath Length only.

WINE MEASURE.

		Marked
2 Pints make	1 Quart	pt. qts.
4 Quarts	1 Gallon	gal.
10 Gallons	1 Anchor of Brandy	anc.
18 Gallons	1 Rundlet	run.
31½ Gallons	Half an Hogshead	½hhd.
42 Gallons	1 Tierce	tierce
63 Gallons	1 Hogshead	hhd.
2 Hogsheads	1 Pipe or Butt	P. or *Butt.*
2 Pipes or 4 Hogsheads	1 Tun	tun.

Inches.

ASSISTANT.   *Tables of Measures.*   13

Inches.
  $28\frac{7}{8}$ =   1 Pint.
  $57\frac{3}{4}$ =   2 =   1 Quart.
  231 =   8 =   4 = 1 Gallon.
  9702 = 336 = 168 = 42 = 1 Tierce.
  14553 = 504 = 252 = 63 = $1\frac{1}{2}$ = 1 Hogshead.
  19404 = 672 = 336 = 84 = 2 = $1\frac{1}{3}$ = 1 Puncheon.
  29106 = 1008 = 504 = 126 = 3 = 2 = $1\frac{1}{2}$ = 1 Pipe.
  58212 = 2016 = 1008 = 252 = 6 = 4 = 3 = 2 = 1 Tn.

All brandies, spirits, perry, cyder, mead, vinegar, honey, and oil, are measured by this measure; as also milk: not by law, but custom only.

ALE *and* BEER MEASURE.

2 Pints	make	1 Quart	Pts. Qts.
4 Quarts	-	1 Gallon	Gal.
8 Gallons	-	1 Firkin of Ale	A. fir.
9 Gallons	-	1 Firkin of Beer	B. fir.
2 Firkins	-	1 Kilderkin	Kil.
4 Firkins, or 2 Kilderkins	-	1 Barrel	Bar.
1 Barrel and $\frac{1}{2}$, or 54 Gal.		1 Hogshead of Beer	Hhd.
2 Barrels	-	1 Puncheon	Pun.
3 Barrels, or 2 Hogsheads	-	1 Butt	Butt.

BEER.

Cubic Inches.
  $35\frac{1}{4}$ = 1 Pint.
  $70\frac{1}{2}$ = 2 = 1 Quart.
  282 = 8 = 4 = 1 Gallon.
  2538 = 72 = 36 = 9 = 1 Firkin.
  5076 = 144 = 72 = 18 = 2 = 1 Kilderkin.
  10152 = 288 = 144 = 36 = 4 = 2 = 1 Barrel.
  15228 = 432 = 216 = 54 = 6 = 3 = $1\frac{1}{2}$ = 1 Hogshead.
  20304 = 576 = 288 = 72 = 8 = 4 = 2 = 1 Puncheon.
  30456 = 864 = 432 = 108 = 12 = 6 = 3 = 2 = 1 Butt.

ALE.

Cubic Inches.
  $35\frac{1}{4}$ = 1 Pint.
  $70\frac{1}{2}$ = 2 = 1 Quart.
  282 = 8 = 4 = 1 Gallon.
  2256 = 64 = 32 = 8 = 1 Firkin.
  4512 = 128 = 64 = 16 = 2 = 1 Kilderkin.
  9024 = 256 = 128 = 32 = 4 = 2 = 1 Barrel.
  13536 = 384 = 192 = 48 = 6 = 3 = $1\frac{1}{2}$ = 1 Hogshead.

In *London* they compute but 8 gallons to the firkin of ale, and 32 to the barrel; but in all other parts of England, for ale, strong beer, and small, 34 gallons to the barrel, and 8 gallons and $\frac{1}{2}$ to the firkin.

N. B.	A barrel of salmon or eels is	-	42 gallons.
	A barrel of herrings	- -	32 gallons.
	A keg of sturgeon	- -	4 or 5 gallons.
	A firkin of soap	- -	8 gallons.

DRY MEASURE.

					Marked
2 Pints	-	make	-	1 Quart -	*pts.* / *qts.*
2 Quarts	-	-	-	1 Pottle -	*pot.*
2 Pottles	-	-	-	1 Gallon -	*gal.*
2 Gallons	-	-	-	1 Peck -	*pk.*
4 Pecks	-	-	-	1 Bushel -	*bu.*
2 Bushels	-	-	-	1 Strike -	*strike*
4 Bushels	-	-	-	1 Coom -	*coom.*
2 Cooms, or 8 Bushels			-	1 Quarter -	*qr.*
4 Quarters			-	1 Chaldron	*chal.*
5 Quarters		-	-	1 Wey -	*wey.*
2 Weys		-	-	1 Last -	*last.*

In *London* 36 bushels make a chaldron.

Solid Inches.

$268\frac{4}{5}$ = 1 Gallon.
$537\frac{3}{5}$ = 2 = 1 Peck.
$2150\frac{2}{5}$ = 8 = 4 = 1 Bushel.
$4300\frac{4}{5}$ = 16 = 8 = 2 = 1 Strike.
$8601\frac{3}{5}$ = 32 = 16 = 4 = 2 = 1 Coom.
$17203\frac{1}{5}$ = 64 = 32 = 8 = 4 = 2 = 1 Quarter.
86016 = 320 = 160 = 40 = 20 = 10 = 5 = 1 Wey.
172032 = 640 = 320 = 80 = 40 = 20 = 10 = 2 = 1 Last.

The bushel in *Water Measure* is 5 Pecks.

A score of coals	is	21 chaldron.
A sack of coals	-	3 bushels.
A chaldron of coals	-	12 sacks.
A load of corn	- - -	5 bushels.
A cart load of ditto	-	43 bushels.

This measure is applied to all dry goods.

The standard bushel is 18 inches and $\frac{1}{2}$ wide, and 8 inches deep.

TIME.

TIME.

			Marked
60 Seconds	make	1 Minute	"
60 Minutes	-	1 Hour	m.
			hour.
24 Hours	-	1 Day	day.
7 Days	-	1 Week	week.
4 Weeks	-	1 Month	mo.
13 Months, 1 day, 6 hours	1 Julian year	yr.

Seconds.
```
      60 =     1 Minute.
    3600 =    60 =    1 Hour.
   86400 =  1440 =   24 = 1 Day.
  604800 = 10080 =  168 =  7 = 1 Week.
 2419200 = 40320 =  672 = 28 = 4 = 1 Month.
                           d    h   w  d  h
31557600 = 525960 = 8766 = 365.6 = 52.1.6 = 1 Julian year.
                           d    h   m.  "
31556937 = 525948 = 8765 = 365.5.48.57 = 1 Solar year.
```

To know the days in each month, observe,

Thirty days hath September,
April, June, and November:
February hath twenty-eight alone,
All the rest have thirty and one;
Except in Leap-Year, and then's the time,
February's days are twenty and nine.

SQUARE MEASURE.

144 Inches	make	-	1 Foot.
9 Feet	-	-	1 Yard.
100 Feet	-	-	1 Square of flooring.
272¼ Feet	-	-	1 Rod.
40 Rods	-	-	1 Rood.
4 Roods, or 160 Rods, or 4840 yds.			1 Acre of land.
640 Acres	-	-	1 Square mile.
30 Acres	-	-	1 Yard of land.
100 Acres	-	-	1 Hide of land.

Inches.

Inches.

144 =	1 Foot.					
1296 =	9 =	1 Yard.				
39204 =	272¼ =	30¼ =	1 Pole.			
1568160 =	10890 =	1210 =	40 =	1 Rood.		
6272640 =	43560 =	4840 =	160 =	4 =	1 Acre.	

By this meaſure are meaſured all things that have length and breadth; ſuch as land, painting, plaſtering, flooring, thatching, plumbing, glazing, &c.

SOLID MEASURE.

1728 Inches	make	1 Solid Foot.
27 Feet	-	1 Yard, or load of earth.
40 Feet of round timber }	is 1 Ton or load.	
Or, 50 Feet of hewn timber }		

108 ſolid feet, *i. e.* 12 feet in length, 3 feet in breadth, and 3 deep, or, commonly, 14 feet long, 3 feet 1 inch broad, and 3 feet 1 inch deep, is a ſtack of wood.

128 ſolid feet, *i. e.* 8 feet long, 4 feet broad, and 4 feet deep, is a cord of wood.

By this meaſure are meaſured all things that have length, breadth, and depth.

ADDITION *of* MONEY, WEIGHTS, *and* MEASURES.

RULE. Add the firſt row or denomination together as in integers; then divide the ſum by as many of the ſame denomination as makes one of the next greater, ſetting down the remainder under the row added, and carry the quotient to the next ſuperior denomination, continuing the ſame to the laſt, which add as in ſimple Addition.

MONEY.

£.	s.	d.	£.	s.	d.	£.	s.	d.	£.	s.	d.
2	13	5½	27	7	2	35	17	3	75	3	7
7	9	4¼	34	14	7¼	59	14	7½	54	17	1½
5	15	4½	57	19	2¼	97	13	5¼	91	15	4¼
9	17	6¼	91	16	1	37	16	8¼	35	16	5¾
7	16	3	75	18	7¾	97	15	7	29	19	7¼
5	14	7¾	97	13	5	59	16	5½	91	17	3¼
39	6	7¼									

MONEY.

ASSISTANT.   *Addition of Weights.*   17

MONEY.

£.	s.	d.	£.	s.	d.	£.	s.	d.	£.	s.	d.
257	1	5½	525	2	4¼	21	14	7¼	73	2	1½
734	3	7¼	179	3	5	75	16	0	25	12	7
595	5	3	250	4	7¼	79	2	4¼	96	13	5¼
159	14	7½	975	3	5¼	57	16	5¼	76	17	3¼
207	5	4	254	5	7	26	13	8¼	97	11	1
798	16	7¼	379	4	5¼	54	2	7	54	11	7¼

127	4	7½	261	17	1½	31	1	1½	27	13	5
525	3	5	379	13	5	75	13	1	16	7	9¼
271	0	5	257	16	7¼	39	19	7¼	9	15	3
524	9	1	184	13	5	97	17	3¼	15	2	7¼
379	4	3¼	725	2	3¼	36	13	5	37	19	1
215	5	8¼	359	6	5	24	16	3¼	56	19	1¼

TROY WEIGHT.

oz.	dwt.	gr.	oz.	dwt.	gr.	lb.	oz.	dwt.	lb.	oz.	dwt.
7	15	21	5	11	4	7	1	2	5	2	15
8	17	6	7	19	21	3	2	17	3	11	17
2	5	15	3	15	14	5	1	15	3	7	15
3	16	19	7	19	22	7	10	11	9	1	13
9	18	23	9	18	15	2	7	13	3	9	7
7	15	14	8	13	12	3	11	16	5	2	15

AVOIRDUPOISE WEIGHT.

lb.	oz.	dr.	lb.	oz.	dr.	cwt.	qrs.	lb.	t.	cwt.	qrs.
152	15	15	17	12	3	25	1	17	7	17	2
272	14	10	23	15	6	72	3	26	5	5	3
803	15	11	31	11	14	54	1	16	2	4	1
255	10	4	97	0	9	24	1	16	3	18	2
173	6	2	48	7	15	17	0	19	7	9	3
635	13	13	79	10	6	55	2	16	8	5	1

APOTHE-

Addition of Measures.

APOTHECARIES WEIGHT.

ʒ	Ə	gr.	℥	ʒ	Ə	gr.	℔	℥	ʒ	Ə	℔	℥	ʒ	Ə
7	1	17	9	2	0	17	7	10	7	1	7	2	1	0
3	0	18	3	5	2	19	9	5	2	2	3	1	7	1
6	2	16	9	2	1	14	7	11	1	2	9	10	2	0
5	1	15	3	5	0	18	9	5	6	1	7	5	7	1
7	0	18	7	7	2	15	7	10	5	2	3	9	5	2
3	1	9	3	3	0		9		7	0	7	1	4	1

CLOTH MEASURE.

FF.	qrs.	n.	yds.	qrs.	n.	yds.	qrs.	n.	EE.	qrs.	n.
27	2	1	35	3	3	73	3	2	72	2	1
15	1	3	70	2	2	97	1	3	52	1	2
37	0	2	95	3	0	54	0	2	79	0	1
52	1	3	76	1	3	76	2	0	56	2	0
76	2	1	26	0	1	59	1	3	79	3	1
97	1	3	79	2	1	76	2	2	54	2	1

LONG MEASURE.

feet.	in.	bar.	yds.	feet.	in.	m.	fur.	p.	lea.	m.	fur.
27	9	2	25	1	9	35	7	3	72	2	1
35	10	1	71	0	3	27	5	27	27	1	7
17	2	0	52	2	3	52	0	35	35	2	5
85	11	1	97	0	10	97	1	17	79	0	6
97	2	2	54	2	7	56	7	18	51	1	6
54	8	1	37	1	4	91	5	27	72	0	5

LAND MEASURE.

a.	r.	p.	a.	r.	p.	a.	r.	p.	a.	r.	p.
75	3	27	27	1	35	26	1	31	32	1	14
36	2	15	29	2	19	19	2	17	27	0	19
97	1	16	37	1	15	55	3	14	31	2	15
35	2	15	95	2	27	79	1	21	19	1	18
27	1	14	62	0	13	95	2	14	59	2	17

WINE

ASSISTANT.   *Addition of Measures.*   19

WINE MEASURE.

run.	gal.	qts.	tier.	gal.	qts.	hhds.	gal.	qts.	T.	hhds.	gal.
27	17	2	25	36	2	31	57	1	14	3	27
35	15	3	75	41	2	97	18	2	19	2	56
56	14	1	62	15	1	76	13	1	17	0	39
97	10	3	94	13	2	55	46	2	75	2	16
92	15	—	15	14	3	87	38	3	54	1	19
79	3	1	19	17	1	55	17	1	97	3	54

ALE and BEER MEASURE.

A.B.	fir.	gal.	B.B.	fir.	gal.	hhd.	gal.	qt.	hhd.	gal.	qt.
25	2	7	37	2	8	76	51	2	76	2	1
17	3	5	54	1	7	57	3	3	95	35	2
96	2	6	97	3	8	97	27	3	57	16	3
75	1	4	78	2	5	22	17	2	22	14	1
96	3	7	47	0	7	32	19	3	32	37	3
75	0	5	35	2	5	55	38	0	55	16	1

DRY MEASURE.

qr.	bu.	p.	qr.	bu.	p.	ch.	bu.	p.	ch.	bu.	p.
75	7	2	36	2	1	75	27	2	73	2	1
37	2	3	71	0	3	57	3	1	41	24	1
51	2	0	53	6	0	95	25	3	92	16	1
79	7	1	82	4	1	76	35	2	70	13	2
55	0	3	95	3	3	97	25	1	54	17	3
96	2	1	78	2	1	75	16	3	79	25	1

TIME.

hs.	m.	".	d.	h.	m.	w.	d.	h.	w.	d.	h.
52	57	35	72	23	27	71	3	11	57	2	15
97	16	27	54	15	35	51	2	9	95	3	21
16	51	54	67	13	31	76	0	21	76	0	15
96	18	31	58	21	45	95	3	21	53	2	21
75	35	21	96	20	48	79	1	15	98	2	18

Subtraction.

The Application.

1. A man born in the year 1750, when will he be 47 years of age? *Anf.* 1797

2. A, B, C, D, went partners in the purchafe of a quantity of goods; A laid out £7. half a guinea and a crown, B 49s. C 54s. 6d. and D 87d. What was laid out in all?
Anf. £13..6..3.

3. A man lent his friend at different times thefe feveral fums, viz. £63, £25..15, £32..7, £15..14..10, and fourfcore and nineteen pounds, half a guinea and a fhilling. How much did he lend in all? *Anf.* £236..8..4.

4. What's the eftate worth *per annum*, when the taxes are 21 guineas, the neat income 8 fcore, and £19..14?
Anf. £201..15.

5. There are three numbers; the firft 215, the fecond 519, and the third is as much as the other two. What is the fum of them all? *Anf.* 1468.

6. Bought a parcel of goods, for which I paid £54..17, for packing 13s. 8d. carriage £1..5..4, and fpent about the bargain 14s. 3d. What do thefe goods ftand me in?
Anf. £57..10..3.

7. There are two numbers, the leaft whereof is 40, their difference 14. I defire to know what is the greater number, and the fum of both? *Anf.* 54 greater number, 94 fum.

8. A gentleman left his eldeft daughter £1500 more than the youngeft, and her fortune was 11 thoufand, 11 hundred and £11. What was the eldeft fifter's fortune, and what did the father leave them?
Anf. Eldeft fifter's fortune £13611. Father left them £25722.

9. A nobleman, before he went out of town, was defirous of paying all his tradefmens bills, and upon enquiry he found, that he owed 82 guineas for rent; to his wine-merchant £72..5; to his confectioner £12..13..4; to his draper £47..13..2; to his taylor £110..15..6; to his coach-maker £157..8; to his tallow-chandler £8..17..9; to his cornchandler £170..6..8; to his brewer £52..17; to his butcher £122..11..5; to his baker £37..9..5; and to his fervants for wages £53..18. I defire to know what money he had to raife in the whole, when we add to the above fums £100. which he wifhed to take with him? *Anf.* £1037..17..3.

10. A father was 24 years of age, (allowing 13 months to a year, and 28 days to a month) when his firft child was born; between the eldeft and next born was 1 year, 11 months, and 14 days; between the fecond and third were 2

years, 1 month, and 15 days; between the third and fourth were two years, 10 months, and 25 days; when the fourth was 27 years, 9 months, and 12 days old, how old was the father? *Anſ. Years* 58..7..10.

11. A banker's clerk, having been out with bills, brings home an account, that A paid him £7..5..2 B £15..18..6¼. C £150..13..2¼ D £17..6..8. E 5 guineas, 2 crown pieces, 4 half crowns, and 4s. and 2d. F paid him only 20 groats, G £76..15..9¼. and H £121..12..4. I defire to know how much the whole amounted to that he had to pay?
Anſ. £396..7..6¼.

12. A nobleman had a ſervice of plate, which confifted of twenty diſhes, weighing 203 oz. 8 *dwts.*; thirty-fix plates, weighing 408 oz. 9 *dwts.*; five dozen of ſpoons, weighing 112 oz. 7 *dwts.*; fix ſalts and fix pepper-boxes, weighing 71 oz. 8 *dwts.*; knives and forks, weighing 73 oz. 5 *dwts.*; two large cups, a tankard, and a mug, weighing 121 oz. 4 *dwts.*; a tea-kettle and lamp, weighing 131 oz. 7 *dwts.*; together with ſundry other ſmall articles, weighing 105 oz. 5 *dwts.* I defire to know the weight of the whole?
Anſ. 102 lb. 2 oz. 18 *dwts.*

13. A hop-merchant buys five bags of hops, of which the firſt weighed 2 *Cwt.* 3 *qrs.* 13 lb.; the ſecond 2 *Cwt.* 2 *qrs.* 11 lb.; the third 2 *Cwt.* 3 *qrs.* 5 lb.; the fourth 2 *Cwt.* 3 *qrs.* 12 lb.; the fifth 2 *Cwt.* 3 *qrs.* 15 lb. Befides theſe, he purchafed two pockets, each weighing 84 lb. I defire to know the weight of the whole? *Anſ.* 15 *Cwt.* 2 *qrs.*

14. A, of Vienna, owes to B, of Liverpool, for goods received in January, the ſum of £103..12..2.; for goods received in February, £93..3..4.; for goods received in March £121..17.; for goods received in April £142..15..4; for goods received in May £171..15..10.; for goods received in June £142..12..6.; but the latter fix months of the year, owing to the falling off in the demands for the articles in which he dealt, amounted to the ſum only of £205..7..2.. I defire to know the amount of the whole year's bill? *Anſ.* £981..3..4.

SUBTRACTION *of* MONEY, WEIGHTS, *and* MEASURES.

RULE. Subtract as in Integers: only when any of the lower denominations are greater than the upper, borrow as many of that as make one of the next ſuperior, adding it to the upper, from which take the leſs; ſet down the difference, and carry 1 to the next higher denomination for what you borrowed.

PROOF. As in Integers. MONEY.

MONEY.

	£.	s.	d.		£.	s.	d.
Borrowed	715	2	7¼	Lent	316	3	5½
Paid	476	3	8½	Received	218	2	1¼
Remains to pay	238	18	10¾				
Proof	715	2	7¼				

£.	s.	d.	£.	s.	d.	£.	s.	d.	£.	s.	d.
87	2	10	3	15	1½	25	2	5¼	37	3	4¼
79	3	7½	1	14	7	17	9	8½	25	5	2¾

£.	s.	d.	£.	s.	d.	£.	s.	d.	£.	s.	d.
821	17	1½	59	15	3¼	71	2	4	527	3	5¼
257	14	7	36	17	2½	19	13	7¾	189	5	7½

	£.	s.	d.		£.	s.	d.
Borrowed	25107	15	7	Lent	250156	1	6
Paid at different times	375	5	5¼	Received at ſeveral payments	271	13	7¼
	259	2	7½		359	15	3
	359	13	4¼		475	13	9½
	523	17	8		527	15	3¾
	274	15	7¼		272	16	5
	325	13	5		150	—	0
Paid in all							
Remains to pay							

TROY WEIGHT.

	oz.	dt.	gr.	oz.	dt.	gr.	lb.	oz.	dt.	gr.	lb.	oz.	d.	gr.
Bought	27	15	2	7	5	15	52	1	7	2	7	2	2	5
Sold	21	14	7	6	7	14	39	0	15	7	5	7	1	7
Unſold														

AVOIRDUPOISE WEIGHT.

lb.	oz.	dr.	lb.	oz.	dr.	cwt.	qrs.	lb.	T.	cwt.	qrs.	lb.
25	11	15	35	10	5	35	1	21	21	1	2	7
17	9	13	29	12	7	25	1	20	9	1	3	5

APOTHE-

APOTHECARIES WEIGHT.

℈	ʒ	℈ gr.	ʒ	ʒ	℈gr.	℔	ʒ	ʒ	℈	℔	ʒ	ʒ	℈
27 .. 1 .. 0 .. 1			3 .. 1 .. 2 .. 4			5 .. 2 .. 1 .. 0				9 .. 7 .. 2 .. 1			
15 .. 2 .. 0 .. 7			1 .. 0 .. 0 .. 7			2 .. 5 .. 2 .. 1				5 .. 7 .. 3 .. 1			

CLOTH MEASURE.

EF	qrs.	n.	yds.	f.	in.	yds.	qrs.	n.	EE.	qrs.	n.
35	2	2	47	1	0	71	1	2	35	2	1
17	2	1	35	2	2	3	2	1	14	3	2

LONG MEASURE.

f.	in.	bar.	yds.	f.	in.	m.	fur.	p.	L.	m.	f.	p.
25	1	0	37	2	1	52	1	27	71	1	7	—
17	0	2	15	2	7	25	7	34	50	0	3	27

LAND MEASURE.

a.	r.	p.	a.	r.	p.	a.	r.	p.	a.	r.	p.
75	1	27	37	1	27	25	0	1	325	2	1
59	0	27	35	2	15	17	1	0	279	3	5

WINE MEASURE.

tun.	gal.	qts.	tier.	gal.	qts.	hhd.	gal.	qts.	hhd.	gal.	qts.
72	1	1	27	27	1	75	57	1	79	2	14
35	1	2	19	35	2	57	59	1	35	5	27

ALE and BEER MEASURE.

| 25 .. 1 .. 2 | 37 .. 2 .. 1 | 27 .. 27 .. 1 | 709 .. 2 .. 1 |
| 21 .. 1 .. 5 | 25 .. 1 .. 7 | 12 .. 50 .. 2 | 157 .. 2 .. 2 |

DRY MEASURE.

qu.	bu.	p.	qu.	bu.	p.	ch.	bu.	p.	ch.	bu.	p.
72	1	2	65	2	1	79	3	0	35	3	3
35	2	3	57	2	3	54	7	1	23	5	1

TIME.

h.	m.	".	d.	h.	m.	m.	w.	d.	m.	w.	d.
75	1	27	72	1	51	35	2	1	65	2	1
52	7	31	36	3	27	17	3	5	14	1	1

The Application.

1. A man born in the year 1723, what was his age in the year 1781? *Anſ.* 58.

2. What is the difference between the age of a man born in 1710, and another born in 1766? *Anſ.* 56.

3. A merchant had five debtors, A, B, C, D, and E; which together owed him £1156; B, C, D, and E, owed him £737. What was A's debt? *Anſ.* £419.

4. When an eſtate of £300 *per annum* is reduced, on paying of taxes, to 12 ſcore and £14..6: What is the tax? *Anſ.* £45..14.

5. What is the difference between 9154, and the amount of 754 added to 305. *Anſ.* 8095.

6. A horſe in his furniture is worth £37..5; out of it, 14 guineas: How much does the price of the furniture exceed that of the horſe? *Anſ.* £7..17.

7. A merchant, at his out-ſetting in trade, owed £750; he had in caſh, commodities, the ſtocks, and good debts, £12510..7; he cleared the firſt year by commerce, £452..3..6: What is the neat balance at the 12 months end? *Anſ.* £12212..10..6.

8. A gentleman dying left £45247, between two daughters; the youngeſt was to have 15 thouſand, 15 hundred, and twice £15: What was the eldeſt ſiſter's fortune? *Anſ.* £28717.

9. A, B, C, and D, ſent their money to the bankers, and drew upon them in this manner: Jan. 3, 1788, A ſent in £152..12; B had £132..15..2 good in the bankers' hands, and on the 10th ſent in £52..12..6 more; C, after taking out £100. found he had left in the bankers' hands £173..8..4, and on the 6th added £175 to his ſtock. The day following, D made up his ſtock £172..12..6, and on the 10th drew for £121..6..2. On the 12th A drew for £119..12..3, and ſent in good bills to the amount of £171..11..5. The ſame day B drew for £142..14..6, as did C for £205..10. On the 20th D ſent in £128..12..4, and the next day drew for £93..15..2. On the 30th they drew 20 guineas each, and in the afternoon ſent in 30 guineas each. I deſire to know how their accounts ſtood ſeparately with the bankers.

Anſ. A had left in the bankers' hands £215..1..2. B £53..3..2. C £153..8..4. D £96..13..6.

10. A tradeſman happening to fail in buſineſs, called all his

his creditors together, and found he owed to A £53..7..6; to B £105..10; to C £34..5..2; to D £28..16..5; to E £14..15..8; to F £112..9; and to G £143..12..9. His creditors found the value of his stock to be £212..6; and that he had owing him in good book debts £112..8..3; besides £21..10..5, money in hand. As his creditors took all his effects into their hands, I desire to know, whether they were losers or gainers, and how much?

Ans. The creditors lost £146..1..10.

11. My correspondent at Seville, in Spain, sends me the following account of money received at different sales for goods sent him by me, viz. Bees-wax to the value of £37..15..4: stockings £37..6..7; tobacco £125..11..6; linen cloth £112..14..8; tin £115..10..5. My correspondent at the same time informs me, that he has shipped, agreeable to my order, wines to the value of £250..15; fruit to the value of £51..12..6; figs 19..17..6; oil £19..12..4; and Spanish wool to the value of £115..15..6. I desire to know how the account stands between us, and who is the debtor?

Ans. Due to my Spanish correspondent £26..14..4.

12. My grandfather is 112 years of age, and my father just 64. I am not so old as my grandfather by 82 years. What is the difference in years between me and my father?

Ans. 34 Years.

13. What is the difference between the ages of A, born in the year 1693, and B, who will be born 15 years hence, the question being put in 1788? *Ans.* 110 years.

MULTIPLICATION *of several* DENOMINATIONS.

RULE. Multiply the first denomination by the quantity given, dividing the product by as many of that as make one of the next, setting down the remainder, and add the quotient to the next superior, after it is multiplied.

If the given quantity is above 12, multiply by any two numbers, which multiplied together, will make the same number; but if no two numbers multiplied together will make the exact number, then multiply the top line by as many as is wanting, adding it to the last product.

PROOF. By Division.

£. s. d.	£. s. d.	£. s. d.	£. s. d.
35..12..7¼	75..13..1½	62..5..4¼	57..2..4¼
2	3	4	5
71..5..2½			

D

26 *Multiplication.* The TUTOR's

lb. oz. dwts. gr.	ton, cwt. qrs. lb.	yds. qrs. n.	m. fur. p.
8..5..17..4	25..7..2..1	76..1..2	36..7..5
7	8	2	5

a. r. p.	A.B. fir. gal.	B.B. fir. gal.	m. fur. p.
7..2..1	32..1..7	26..2..7	54..2..1
9	7	3	5

1. 18 yds. of cloth at 9s. 6d. per yd.
$9 \times 2 = 18$

```
            9
         ———
        4..5..6
            2
         ———
        8..11..0
```

2. 26 lb. of tea, at £1..2..6 per lb.
$8 \times 3 + 2 = 26$

```
            8
         ———
        9..0..0
            3
         ———
       27..0..0
Top line × 2   2..5..0
              ———
              29..5..0
```

3. 21 ells of holland, at 7s. 8d½ per ell.
        Facit £ 8 .. 1 .. 10½

4. 85 firkins of butter, at 15s. 3d¼ per firkin.
        Facit £ 26 .. 15 .. 2¼

5. 75 lb. of nutmegs, at 7s. 2d¼ per lb.
        Facit £27 .. 2 .. 2¼

6. 37 yards of tabby, at 9s. 7d. per yard.
        Facit £17 .. 14 .. 7

7. 97 cwt. of cheese, at 1l. 5s. 3d. per cwt.
        Facit £122 .. 9 .. 3

8. 43 dozen of candles, at 6s. 4d. per dozen.
        Facit £13 .. 12 .. 4

9. 127 lb. of bohea tea, at 12s. 3d. per lb.
        Facit £77 .. 15 .. 9

10. 135 gallons of rum, at 7s. 5d. per gallon.
        Facit £50 .. 1 .. 3

11. 74 ells of diaper, at 1s. 4d½ per ell.
        Facit £ 5 .. 1 .. 9

12. 6 dozen pair of gloves, at 1s. 10d. per pair.
        Facit £ 6 .. 12 .. 0

When the given quantity consists of ½, ¼, divide the price by ½, ¼; when ¾, divide the price by ½, and that quotient by ½; which add to the product of the quantity given.

13. 25½ ells of holland, at 3*s.* 4½*d per.* ell.

5	5½ × 5 + ½ = 25½
16 .. 10½	
5	
4 .. 4 .. 4½ = 25	
0 .. 1 .. 8¼ = ½	
4 .. 6 .. 0¾ = 25½	

14. 75½ ells of diaper, at 1*s.* 3*d. per* ell.
Facit £4 .. 14 .. 4½.

15. 19½ ells of damask, at 4*s.* 3*d. per* ell.
Facit £4 .. 2 .. 10½.

16. 35½ ells of dowlas, at 1*s.* 4*d. per* ell.
Facit £2 .. 7 .. 4.

17. 7¼ cwt. of Malaga raisins, at 1*l.* 1*s.* 6*d. per* cwt.
Facit £7 .. 15 .. 10½.

18. 6½ barrels of herrings, at 3*l.* 15*s.* 7*d. per* barrel.
Facit £24 .. 11 .. 3½.

19. 35½ cwt. of double refined sugar, at 4*l.* 15*s.* 6*d. per* cwt.
Facit £169 .. 10 .. 3.

20. 154½ cwt. of tobacco, at 4*l.* 17*s.* 10*d. per* cwt.
Facit £755 .. 15 .. 3.

21. 117¼ gallons of arrack, at 12*s.* 6*d. per* gallon.
Facit £73 .. 5 .. 7½.

22. 85¾ cwt. of cheese, at 1*l.* 7*s.* 8*d. per* cwt.
Facit £118 .. 12 .. 5.

23. 29¼ lb. of fine Hyson tea, at 1*l.* 3*s.* 6*d. per* lb.
Facit £34 .. 7 .. 4½.

24. 17¾ yards of superfine scarlet drab, at 1*l.* 3*s.* 6*d. per* yd.
Facit £20 .. 17 .. 1½.

25. 37½ yards of rich brocaded silk, at 12*s.* 4*d. per* yard.
Facit £23 .. 2 .. 6.

26. 56¾ cwt. of sugar, at 2*l.* 18*s.* 7*d. per* cwt.
Facit £166 .. 4 .. 7¼.

27. 96½ cwt. of currants, at 2*l.* 15*s.* 6*d. per* cwt.
Facit £267 .. 15 .. 9.

28. 45¾ lb. of Belladine silk, at 18*s.* 6*d. per* lb.
Facit £42 .. 6 .. 4½.

29. 87¼ bushels of wheat, at 4*s.* 3*d. per* bushel.
Facit £18 .. 12 .. 11¾.

30. 120¾ cwt. of hops, at 4*l.* 7*s.* 6*d. per* cwt.
Facit £528 .. 5 .. 7½.

Compound Multiplication.   The Tutor's

The Application.

1. What sum of money must be divided amongst 18 men, so that each may receive £14..6..8½?
Ans. £258..0..9.

2. A privateer of 250 men took a prize, which amounted to £125..15..6 to each man, what was the value of the prize?
Ans. £31443..15..0.

3. What is the difference between six dozen dozen and half a dozen dozen; and what is their sum and product?
Ans. 792 Diff. Sum 936, Product 62208.

4. What difference is there between twice eight and fifty, and twice fifty-eight, and what's their product?
Ans. 50 Diff. 7656 Prod.

5. There are two numbers, the greater of them is 37 times 45, and their difference 19 times 4; their sum and product are required?
Ans. 3254 Sum, 2645685 Prod.

6. The sum of two numbers is 360, the less of them 144; what is their product, and the square of their difference?
Ans. 31104 Product, 5184 Square of their difference.

7. In an army, consisting of 187 squadrons of horse, each 157 men, and 207 battalions, each 560 men, how many effective soldiers, supposing that in seven hospitals there are 473 sick?
Ans. 144806.

8. What sum did that gentleman receive in dowry with his wife, whose fortune was her wedding suit: her petticoat having two rows of furbelows, each furbelow 87 quills, and in each quill 21 Guineas?
Ans. £3836..14..0.

9. A merchant had £19118 to begin trade with; for 5 years together he cleared £1086 a year; the next 4 years he made good £2715..10..6 a year; but the last 3 years he was in trade had the misfortune to lose, one year with another, £475..4..6 a year; what was his real fortune at 12 years end?
Ans. 33984..8..6.

10. In some parts of the kingdom they weigh their coals by a machine, in the nature of a steelyard, waggon and all. Three of these draughts together amount to 137 cwt. 2 qrs. 10 lb. and the tare or weight of the waggon 13 cwt. 1 qr. How many coals had the customer in twelve such draughts?
Ans. 391 cwt. 1 qr. 12 lb.

11. A

11. A certain gentleman lays up every year £294..12..6. and spends daily £1..12..6. I desire to know what is his annual income? *Ans.* £887..15.

12. A tradesman gave to his daughter as a marriage portion a scrutore, in which were twelve drawers, in each drawer were six divisions, and in each division there were £50. four crown pieces, and eight half crowns pieces. How much had she to her fortune? *Ans.* £3744.

13. Admitting that I pay eight guineas and half a crown for a quarter's rent, and am allowed quarterly 15s. for trifling repairs, what does my apartment cost me annually, and how much in seven years?
Ans. In one year £31..2. In seven £217..14.

14. A robbery being committed on the highway, an assessment was made on a neighbouring hundred for the sum of £386..15..6. of which four parishes paid each £37..14..2. four hamlets £31..4..2. each, and the four townships £18..12..6. each. How much was the deficiency?
Ans. £36..12..2.

15. A gentleman at his decease left his widow £4560.; to a public charity he bequeathed £572..10. to each of his four nephews £750..10.; to each of his four nieces £375..12..6.; to 30 poor housekeepers ten guineas each, and 150 guineas to his executor. What sum must he have been possessed of at the time of his death to answer all these legacies? *Ans.* £10107..10.

16. Admit 20 to be remainder of a division sum, 423 the quotient, the division the sum of both, and 19 more. What was the number of the dividend? *Ans.* 195446.

DIVISION of *several* DENOMINATIONS.

RULE. Divide the first Denomination on the left hand; and, if any remains, multiply them by as many of the next less as make one of that, which add to the next, and divide as before.

PROOF. By Multiplication.

£. s. d.	£. s. d.	£. s. d.	£. s. d.
2)25 .. 2 .. 4	3)37 .. 7 .. 7	4)57..5..7	5)52..7..0

lb. oz. dwt. gr.	lb. oz. dr.	T. cwt. qrs. lb.
7)75..3..7..5	8)35..14..13	6)5..10..1..13
yds. qrs. n.	m. f. p.	yds. ft. inch.
11)35..1..3	9(76..3..27	12)75..2..9
A.B. fir. gal.	A.B. fir. gal.	ch. bu. pk.
12)35..2..5	9)55..3..7	11)357..2..1

The Application.

1. If a man spends £257::2::5 in 12 month's time, what is that *per* month?   Ans. £21..8..6¼.

2. The cloathing of 35 charity boys came to £57..3..7. What is the expence of each?   Ans. £1..12..8.

3. If I give £37::6::4¼ for nine pieces of cloth, what did I give *per* piece?   Ans. £4..2..11.

4. If 20 cwt of tobacco came to £27::5::4½, at what rate is that *per* cwt?   Ans. £1..7..3.

5. What is the value of 1 hogshead of beer, when 120 are sold for £154::17::10?   Ans. £1..5..9¼.

6 Bought 72 yards of cloth for £85::6::0, I desire to know at what rate *per* yard?   Ans. £1..3..8¼.

7. Gave £275::3::4 for 36 bales of cloth. What is that for 2 bales?   Ans. £15..5..8¼.

8. A prize of £7257::3::6, is to be equally divided amongst 500 sailors. What is each man's share?   Ans. £14..10..3¾.

9. There are 2545 bullocks to be divided among 509 men. I desire to know how many each man had, and the value of each man's share, supposing every bullock worth £9..14..6?   Ans. 5 bullocks each man, £48..12..6 each share.

10. A gentleman has a garden walled in, containing 9625 yards; the breadth was 35 yards. What was the length?   Ans. 275.

11. A club in London, consisting of 25 gentlemen, joined for a lottery ticket of £10. value, which came up a prize of £4000. I desire to know what each man contributed, and what each man's share came to?   Ans. each contributed 8s. each share £160.

12. A trader cleared £1156, equally in 17 years. How much did he lay by in a year?   Ans. £68.

13 Another cleared £2805, in 7½ years. What was his yearly increase of fortune?   Ans. £374.

14. What

14. What number added to the 43 part of 4429 will raile it to 240? *Anf.* 137.

15. Divide 20s. between A, B, and C, in such sort that A may have 2s. less than B, and C 2s. more than B.
Anf. A 4s. 8d. B 6s. 8d. C 8s. 8d.

16. If there are a 1000 men to a regiment, and but 50 officers, how many private men are there to one officer?
Anf. 19.

17. What number is that which multiplied by 7847 will make the product 3013248? *Anf.* 384.

18. The quotient is 1083, the divisor 28604, what was the dividend, if the remainder came out 1788? *Anf.* 30979920.

19. An army, consisting of 20,000 men, took and plundered a city of 12,000l. What was each man's share, the whole being equally divided among them? *Anf.* 12s.

20. My purse and money, said Dick to Harry, are worth 12s. 8d. but the money is worth seven times the purse. What did the purse contain? *Anf.* 11s. 1d.

21. A merchant bought two lots of tobacco, which weighed 12cwt. 3qrs. 15lb. for 14l. 15s. 6d. Their difference in point of weight was 1cwt. 2qrs. 13lb. and of price 7l. 15s. 6d. I desire to know their respective weights and value?
Anf. Lesser weight 5cwt. 2qrs. 15lb. Price 53l. 10s.
Greater weight 7cwt. 1qr. Price 61l. 5s. 6d.

22. The Spectator mentions a club of fat people, whose number was only fifteen, and yet weighed no less than three tons. What was the weight of each person? *Anf.* 4cwt.

23. Five auditors in a public office receive ten pounds a quarter, for which they attend seven times during that period; but, if one more of them be absent at any time, then the absent persons shares are divided among those who attend. A and B never miss attendance on these occasions; but C and D are generally absent twice in a quarter, and E once. When the payment comes due, I wish to know what each has to receive?
Anf. A £2::9::0$\frac{4}{7}$. B £2::9::0$\frac{2}{7}$. C £1::10::0.
D £1::10::0. E £2::1::10$\frac{6}{7}$.

24. Divide 1000 crowns in such a manner between A, B, and C, that A may receive 129 more than B, and B 178 less than C. *Anf.* A 360, B 231, C, 409.

25. A young fellow owed his guardian £74::18::2 on balance. He paid off £41::14::8 and then declared that his sister owed the gentleman half as much again as himself.
Being

Being told of this circumstance, she pays off in part £13::12::10, and gives out that her uncle Joseph was not less in arrears than her brother and she together. In consequence of this the uncle pays in £24::7::3, and then the uncle's brother, who by the bye, was not the uncle of those children, for £150 undertakes to set them all clear, and has £35::15::5 to spare, according to his account. I desire to know whether this be true or not?

26. Three boys met a servant maid carrying apples to the market. The first took half what she had, but returned her ten; the second took one third, but returned two; and the third took away half those she had left, but returned her one. She had then twelve apples left: how many had she at first? *Ans.* 40.

BILLS of PARCELS.

Hosier's.

Mr. John Thomas,
   Bought of Samuel Green, March 7, 1792.
        s. d.

8 Pair of worsted stockings, at 4 :: 6 *per* pair, £
5 Pair of thread ditto - at 3 :: 2 - -
3 Pair of black silk ditto at 14 :: 0 - -
6 Pair of milled hose - at 4 :: 2 - -
4 Pair of cotton ditto - at 7 :: 6 - -
2 Yards of fine flannel   at 1 :: 8 - -

           £ 7 :: 12 :: 2

Mercer's.

Mr. Isaac Grant,
   Bought of John Sims, March 7, 1792.
        s. d.

15 Yards of satin,   at 9 :: 6 *per* yard £
18 Yards of flowered silk, at 17 :: 4 - -
12 Yards of rich brocade, at 19 :: 8 - -
16 Yards of sarsenet,   at 8 :: 2 - -
13 Yards of Genoa Velvet at 27 :: 6 - -
23 Yards of lutestring, at 6 :; 3 - -

         £. 62 :: 5 :: 2.

ASSISTANT. *Bills of Parcels.*

LINEN-DRAPER'S.

Mr. Simon Surety,
  Bought of Josiah Short, March 27, 1792.

                        s. d.
4 Yards of cambrick - at 12..6 *per* yard £.
12 Yards of muslin   - at 8..3
15 Yards of printed linen at 5..4
2 Dozen of napkins - at 2..3 each
14 Ells of diaper   - at 1..7 *per* ell
35 Ells of dowlas   - at 1..1½

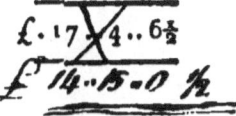

MILLINER'S.

Mrs. Bright,
  Bought of Lucy Brown, April 5, 1792.

                        l. s. d.
18 Yards of fine lace - at 0..12..3 *per* yard £.
5 Pair of fine kid gloves at 0..2..2 *per* pair
12 Fans of French mounts at 0..3..6 each
2 Fine laced tippets   at 3..8..0
4 Dozen Irish lamb   at 0..1..3 *per* pair
6 Sets of knots   - at 0..2..6 *per* set

                                   £. 23..14..4

WOOLLEN-DRAPER'S.

Mr. Thomas Sage,
  Bought of Ellis Smith, April 7, 1792.

                        l. s. d.
17 Yards of fine serge - at 0..3..9 *per* yard £.
18 Yards of drugget - at 0..9..0
15 Yards of superfine scarlet at 1..2..0
16 Yards of black   - at 0..18..0
25 Yards of shalloon - at 0..1..9
17 Yards of drab   - at 0..17..6

                                    £. 59..5..0

LEATHER-SELLER'S.

Mr. Giles Harris,
>Bought of Abel Smith, April 15, 1792.

		s.	d.	
27 Calf skins	at	3	9	per skin £.
75 Sheep ditto	at	1	7	
36 Coloured ditto	at	1	8	
15 Buck ditto	at	11	6	
17 Russia hides	at	10	7	
120 Lamb-skins	at	1	2½	

£. 38 .. 17 .. 5

GROCER'S.

Mr. Richard Groves,
>Bought of Francis Elliot, April 21, 1792.

		s.	d.	
25 lb. of lump sugar	at	0	6½	per lb. £
2 loaves of double refined, weight 15 lb.	at	0	11¾	
14 lb. of rice	at	0	3	
28 lb. of Malaga raisins	at	0	5	
15 lb. of currants	at	0	5¾	
7 lb. of black pepper	at	1	10	

£. 3 .. 2 .. 9½

CHEESEMONGER'S.

Mr. Charles Crofs,
>Bought of Samuel Grant, April 23, 1792.

		s.	d.	
8 lb. of Cambridge butter	at	0	6	per lb. £
17 lb. of new cheese	at	0	4	
½ Firkin of butter, wt. 28 lb.	at	0	5½	
5 Cheshire cheeses, wt. 127 lb.	at	0	4	
2 Warwickshire do. wt. 15 lb.	at	0	3	
12 lb. of cream cheese	at	0	6	

£. 3 .. 14 .. 7

CORN-CHANDLER'S.

Mr. Abraham Doyley,
            Bought of Isaac Jones, April 29, 1792.

			s.	d.	
Tares,	19 bushels	- at	1 ..	10	per bushel £
Peas,	18 bushels	- at	3 ..	9½	- -
Malt,	7 quarters	at	25 ..	0	per quarter
Hops,	15 lb.	- at	1 ..	5	per lb.
Oats,	6 quarters	at	2 ..	4	per bushel
Beans,	12 bushels	- at	4 ..	8	- -

                                £. 23 .. 7 .. 4

REDUCTION

IS the bringing or reducing numbers of one denomination into other numbers of another denomination, retaining the same value, and is performed by multiplication and division.

First, All great names are brought into small by multiplying with so many of the less as make one of the greater.

Secondly, All small names are brought into great, by dividing with so many of the less as make one of the greater.

A TABLE *of such* COINS *as are current in* England.

	l.	s.	d.
Guinea - -	1 ..	1 ..	0
Half ditto - -	0 ..	10 ..	6
Quarter ditto -	0 ..	5 ..	3
Crown - -	0 ..	5 ..	0
Half ditto - -	0 ..	2 ..	6
Shilling - -	0 ..	1 ..	0

Note, *There are several pieces which speak their own value: such as six-pence, four-pence, three-pence, two-pence, penny, half-penny, farthing.*

REDUCTION Descending.

1. In £.8 how many shillings and pence?

    20
   —
   160 *shillings.*
    12
   —
  1920 *pence.*

2. In £12. how many shillings, pence, and farthings? *Anſ.* 240s. 2880d. 11520 *far.*
3. How many shillings, pence, and farthings, are there in £18? *Anſ.* 360s. 4320d. 17280 *far.*
4. Reduce £7. and a crown into shillings and pence. *Facit.* 145s. 1740d.
5. How many farthings are there in 21 guineas? *Anſ.* 21168.
6. In £17..5..3¼ how many farthings? *Anſ.* 16573.
7. In £25..14..1 how many shillings and pence? *Anſ.* 514s. 6169d.
8. In 15 crowns, how many shillings and sixpences. *Anſ.* 75s. 150 *six-pences.*
9. How many crowns and shillings in £25.? *Anſ.* 100 *crowns,* 500s.
10. In 57 half crowns, how many pence and farthings? *Anſ.* 1710d. 6840 *farthings.*
11. In 52 crowns, as many half crowns, shillings, and pence, how many farthings? *Anſ.* 21424.
12. How many half-crowns, sixpences, and threepences, are there in £75.? *Anſ.* 600 *half-crowns,* 3000 *six-pences,* 6000 *three-pences.*

REDUCTION Ascending.

13. In 1920 pence, how many shillings and pounds? *Anſ.* 160s. £8.

   12)1920
   ——
   2|0)16|0 *shillings.*
   ——
    8 *Pounds.*

14. In

ASSISTANT.   Reduction.   37

14. In 11520 farthings, how many pence, shillings, and Pounds?   *Ans.* 2880*l.* 240s. 12*l.*

15. How many pence, shillings, and pounds, are there in 17280 farthings?   *Ans.* 4320*l.* 360s. 18*l.*

16. Reduce 1740 pence into shillings and pounds.
Facit 145s. 7*l.* 5s.

17. How many guineas in 21168 farthings?
Ans. 21 *Guineas.*

18. In 16573 farthings, how many pounds?
Ans. £17::5::3¼.

19. In 6169 pence, how many shillings and pounds?
Ans. 514s. £25::14::1.

20. In 900 pence, how many shillings and crowns?
Ans. 75s. 15 *crowns.*

21. How many crowns and pounds in 500 shillings?
Ans. 100 *crowns,* £25.

22. In 6840 farthings, how many pence and half crowns?
Ans. 1710d. 57 *half crowns.*

23. In 21424 farthings, how many crowns, half crowns, shillings, and pence, and of each an equal number?
Ans. 52.

24. How many sixpences, half crowns and pounds, in 6000 threepences?
Ans. 3000 *sixpences,* 600 *half crowns,* £75.

    ASCENDING *and* DESCENDING.

25. In 1560 pence, how many crowns and shillings?
Ans. 26 *crowns,* 130s.

          6|0)156|0
          ―――――
             26
              5
          ―――――
            130

26. Reduce 130 shillings into crowns and pence.
Facit 26 *crowns,* 1560*l.*

27. How many shillings, crowns and pounds in 60 guineas?
Ans. 1260s. 252 *crowns,* £63.

28. In £63, how many crowns, shillings, and guineas?
Ans. 252 *crowns,* 1260s. 60 *guineas.*

29. Reduce 76 moidores into shillings and pounds.
Facit 2052s. £102::12.

30. Reduce £102::12 into shillings and moidores.
Facit 2052s. *moidores.*

        E   31. How

31. How many shillings, half crowns, and crowns, are there in £556, and of each an equal number?

Ans 1308 *each, and* 2s. *over.*

32. In 1308 half crowns, as many crowns, and shillings, how many pounds? *Ans.* £555::18.

33. Seven men brought £15::10 each into the mint, to be changed for guineas: How many must they have in all?

Ans. 103 *guineas,* 7s. *over.*

34. If 103 guineas and 7 shillings are to be divided amongst 7 men: How many pounds sterling is that to each?

Ans. £15::10.

35. A certain person had 25 purses, and in each purse 12 guineas, a crown, and a moidore, how many pounds sterling had he in all? *Ans.* £355.

36. A gentleman, in his will, leaves £50 to the poor, and ordered that $\frac{1}{3}$ should be given to ancient men, each to have 5s.—$\frac{1}{4}$ to poor women, each to have 2s. 6d.—$\frac{1}{5}$ to poor boys, each to have 1s.—$\frac{1}{6}$ to poor girls, each to have 9d. and the remainder to the person who distributed it. I demand how many of each sort there were, and what the person that distributed the money had for his pains?

Ans. 66 *men,* 100 *women,* 200 *boys,* 222 *girls,*
£2::13::6 to the person.

TROY WEIGHT.

37. In 27 ounces of gold, how many grains?

Ans. 12960.

38. In 12960 grains of gold, how many ounces?

Ans. 27.

39. In 3 lb. 10 oz. 7 dwts. 5 gr. how many grains?

Ans. 22253.

40. In 8 ingots of silver, each weighing 7 lb. 4 oz. 17 dwt. 15 gr. how many ounces, pennyweights, and grains?

Ans. 711 *oz.* 14221 *dwt.* 341304 *gr.*

41. How many ingots of 7 lb. 4 oz. 17 dwts. 15 gr. each are there in 341304 grains? *Ans.* 8 *ingots.*

42. Bought 7 ingots of silver, each containing 23lb. 5 oz. 7 dwt. how many grains? *Ans.* 945336.

43. A gentleman sent a tankard to his goldsmith, that weighed 50 oz. 8 dwt. and ordered him to make it into spoons, each to weigh 2 oz. 16 dwt. How many had he? *Ans.* 18.

44. A

44. A gentleman delivered to a goldsmith 137 oz. 6 dwt. 9 gr. of silver, and ordered him to make it into tankards of 17 oz. 15 dwt. 10 gr. each, spoons of 21 oz. 11 dwt. 13 gr. per doz. salts of 3 oz. 10 dwt. each, and forks of 21 oz. 11 dwt. 13 gr. per dozen; and, for every tankard, to have one salt, a dozen of spoons, and a dozen of forks: What is the number of each he must have?

Ans. Two of each sort, 8 oz. 9 dwt. 9 gr. over.

AVOIRDUPOISE WEIGHT.

Note, *There are several sorts of fish which are weighed by a great pound of 24 oz. others by the common pound of 16 oz. therefore,*

To bring great pounds into common, multiply by 3, and divide by 2, or add one half.

To bring small pounds into great, multiply by 2, and divide by 3, or subtract one third.

Things bought and sold by the Tale.

Dozens.		Paper and Parchment.
12 Pieces or things make 1 Doz.		24 Sheets make 1 Quire
12 Dozen - - 1 Gross.		20 Quire - 1 Ream
12 Gross or 144 Doz } 1 Great Gross.		2 Reams - 1 Bund.
		1 Doz. of Par. 12 Skins.
		5 Doz. - 1 Roll

45. In 14769 ounces: How many cwt.?

Ans. 8 cwt. 0 qrs. 27 lb. 1 oz.

46. Reduce 8 cwt. 0 qr. 27 lb. 1 oz. into quarters, pounds, and ounces.

Facit 32 qrs. 923 lb. 14769 oz.

47. Bought 32 bags of hops, each 2 cwt. 1 qr. 14 lb. and another of 150 lb. How many cwt. in the whole?

Ans. 77 cwt. 1 qr. 10 lb.

48. In 34 ton, 17 cwt. 1 qr. 19 lb. how many pounds?

Ans. 78111 lb.

49. In 350 great pounds, how many common? *Ans. 525 lb.*

50. In 27 cwt. of rains, how many parcels of 18 lb. each?

Ans. 168.

51. In 9 cwt. 2 qrs. 14 lb. of indigo, ...ds?

52. In 547 great pounds, how many common pounds? *Anf.* 820 common lb. 8 oz.

53. Bought 27 bags of hops, each 2cwt. 1qr. 15lb. and 1 bag of 137lb. How many hundreds in the whole? *Anf.* 65 cwt. 2 qrs. 10 lb.

54. How many pounds in 27 hogsheads of tobacco, each weighing neat 8cwt. ¾? *Anf.* 26460.

55. In 552 common pounds of silk, how many great pounds? *Anf.* 368.

56. How many parcels of sugar of 16 lb. 2 oz. are there in 16 cwt. 1 qr. 15 lb.? *Anf.* 113 par. 12 lb. 14 oz.

The Allowances usually made in this Weight are TARE, TRET *and* CLOFF.

TARE is an allowance made to the buyer for the weight of the box, barrel, bag, &c. which contains the goods bought, and is either

At so much per box, bag, barrel, &c.
At so much per cent. or,
At so much in the grofs weight,

TRET is an allowance of 4lb. in every 104lb. for waste, dust, &c. made by the merchant to the buyer.

CLOFF is an allowance of 2lb to the citizens of London, on every draught above 3cwt. on some sort of goods.

GROSS WEIGHT is the whole weight of any sort of goods, and that which contains it.

SUTTLE is when part of the allowance is deducted from the grofs.

NEAT is the pure weight, when all allowances are deducted.

RULE 1st. When the tare is at so much per bag, barrel, &c. multiply the number of bags, barrels, &c. by the tare, and subtract the produce from the grofs, the remainder is neat.

Note, *To reduce pounds into gallons, multiply by 2, divide by 15.*

57. In 7 frails of raifins, each weighing 5 cwt. 2 qrs. 5lb. grofs, tare at 23lb. per frail, how much neat weight? *Anf.* 37 cwt. 1 qr. 14 lb.

58. In

```
              28          5 .. 2 .. 5          5 .. 2 .. 5
               7              7                       23
            ────)4}       ─────────          ─────────
         28)161(5         38 → 3 .. 7 = grofs.  5 .. 1 .. 10
            140 1 .. 1.   1 .. 1 .. 21 = tare.          7
            ────          ─────────          ─────────
             21           37 .. 1 .. 14 neat.  37 .. 1 .. 14
```

58. In 241 barrels of figs, each 3 qrs. 19 lb. grofs, tare 10 lb. per barrel, how many pounds neat? Anf. 22413.

59. What is the neat weight of 25 hogfheads of tobacco, weighing grofs 163 cwt. 2 qrs. 15 lb. tare 100 lb. per hogfhead? Anf. 141 cwt. 1 qr. 7 lb.

60. In 16 bags of pepper, each 85 lb. 4 oz. grofs, tare per bag, 3 lb. 5 oz. how many pounds neat? Anf. 1311.

RULE 2. When the tare is at fo much in the whole grofs weight, fubtract the given tare from the grofs, the remainder is neat.

61. What is the neat weight of 5 hogfheads of tobacco, weighing grofs 75 cwt. 1 qr. 14 lb. tare in the whole 752 lb.? Anf. 68 cwt. 2 qrs. 18 lb.

62. In 75 barrels of figs, each 2 qrs. 27 lb. grofs, tare in the whole 597 lb. how much neat weight? Anf. 50 cwt. 1 qr.

RULE 3. When the tare is at fo much per cwt. divide the grofs weight by the aliquot parts of an cwt. which fubtract from the grofs, the remainder is neat.

Note, 7 lb. is $\frac{1}{16}$. 8 lb. is $\frac{1}{14}$. 14 lb. is $\frac{1}{8}$. 16 lb. $\frac{1}{7}$.

63. What is the neat weight of 18 butts of currants, each 8 cwt. 2 qrs. 5 lb. tare at 14 lb. per cwt.?

```
              8 .. 2 .. 5
                  9 × 2 = 18
              ─────────
             76 .. 3 .. 17
                  2
              ─────────
         14=⅛)153 .. 3 .. 6
             19 .. 0 .. 25¼
              ─────────
            134 .. 2 .. 8¼
              ─────────
```

64. In

64. In 25 barrels of figs, each 2 cwt. 1 qr. grofs, tare *per cent.* 16 lb. how much neat weight?

Anf. 43 cwt. 0 qr. 24 lb.

65. What is the neat weight of 9 hogfheads of nutmegs, each weighing grofs, 8 cwt. 3 qrs. 14 lb. tare 16 lb. *per cent.?*

Anf. 68 cwt. 1 qr. 24 lb.

66. What is the neat weight of 12 cafks of argol, grofs 84 cwt. 2 qrs. 14 lb. tare *per cent.* 14 lb.

Anf. 74 cwt. 0 qr. 5 lb. ¼.

RULE 4. When tret is allowed with tare, divide the pounds futtle by 26, the quotient is the tret, which fubtract from the futtle, the remainder is neat.

67. In one butt of currants, weighing 12 cwt. 2 qrs. 24 lb. grofs, tare 14 lb. *per cent.* trett 4 lb. *per* 104 lb. how many pounds neat?

$$12 .. 2 .. 24$$
$$4$$
$$\overline{}$$
$$50$$
$$28$$
$$\overline{}$$
$$14 = \tfrac{1}{8}) 1424 \; grofs.$$
$$178 \; tare.$$
$$\overline{}$$
$$26) 1246 \; futtle.$$
$$47 \; tret.$$
$$\overline{}$$
$$1199 \; neat.$$

68. In 7 cwt. 3 qrs. 27 lb. grofs, tare 36 lb. tret 4 lb. *per* 104 lb. how many pounds neat? *Anf.* 826 lb.

69. In 152 cwt. 1 qr. 3 lb. grofs, tare 10 lb. *per cent.* tret 4 lb. *per* 104 lb. how much neat weight?

Anf. 103 cwt. 1 qr. 11 lb.

70. In 15 chefts of fugar, weighing 117 cwt. 0 qr. 21 lb. grofs, tare 173 lb. tret 4 lb. *per* 104 lb. how many cwt. neat? *Anf.* 111 cwt. 0 qr. 22 lb.

RULE 5. When cloff is allowed, multiply the cwt. futtle by 2, divide the product by 3, the quotient will be the pounds cloff, which fubtract from the futtle, the remainder will be neat.

71. What

ASSISTANT.   Reduction.   43

71. What is the neat weight of 3 hogsheads of tobacco, weighing 15 cwt. 3 qrs. 20 lb. grofs, tare 7lb. per cent. tret 4lb. per 104 lb. cloff 2 lb. for 3 cwt. ?

Anf. 14 cwt. 1 qr. 3 lb.

$$7 = \tfrac{1}{16})15 .. 3 .. 20 \quad grofs.$$
$$\phantom{7 = \tfrac{1}{16})15 ..} 3 .. 27\tfrac{1}{2} \quad tare.$$

$$14 .. 3 .. 20\tfrac{1}{2} \quad futtle.$$
$$ 2 .. 8 \quad tret.$$

$$14 .. 1 .. 12\tfrac{1}{2} \quad futtle.$$
$$ 9\tfrac{1}{2} \quad cloff.$$

$$14 .. 1 .. 3 \quad neat$$

72. In 7 hogsheads of tobacco, each weighing grofs 5 cwt. 2 qrs. 7 lb. tare 8 lb. per cent. tret 4 lb. per 104 lb. cloff 2 lb. per 3 cwt. how much neat weight ?

Anf. 34 cwt. 2 qrs. 8 lb.

APOTHECARIES WEIGHT.

73. In 27 lb. 7 ℥. 2 ʒ. 1 ℈. 2 gr. how many grains ?
Anf. 159022.

74. How many lb. ℥. ʒ. ℈. and gr. are there in 159022 grains ?   Anf. 27 lb. 7 ℥. 2 ʒ. 1 ℈. 2 gr.

CLOTH MEASURE.

75. In 27 yards, how many nails ?   Anf. 432.
76. In 75 English ells, how many yards ?
Anf. 93 yards, 3 qrs.
77. In 93¾ yards, how many English ells ?   Anf. 75.
78. In 24 pieces, each containing 32 Flemish ells, how many English ells ?   Anf. 460 ells. 4 qrs.
79. In 17 pieces of cloth, each 27 Flemish ells, how many yards ?   Anf. 344 yards, 1 qr.
80. Bought 27 pieces of English stuffs, each 27 ells, how many yards ?   Anf. 911 yards, 1 qr.
81. In 911¼ yards, how many English ells ? Anf. 729.
82. In 12 bales of cloth, each 25 pieces, each 15 English ells, how many yards ?   Anf. 5625.

LONG

LONG MEASURE.

83. 57 miles, how many furlongs and poles?
Anſ. 456 furlongs, 18240 poles.
84. In 7 miles, how many feet, inches and barley-corns?
Anſ. 36960 feet, 443520 inches, 1330560 barley-corns.
85. In 18240 poles, how many furlongs and miles?
Anſ. 456 furlongs, 57 miles.
86. In 72 leagues, how many yards? Anſ. 380160.
87. In 380160 yards, how many miles and leagues?
Anſ. 216 miles, 72 leagues.
88. If from London to York be accounted 50 leagues, I demand how many miles, yards, feet, inches, and barley-corns? Anſ. 150 miles, 264000 yards, 792000 feet, 9504000 inches, 28512000 barley-corns.
89. How many barley-corns will reach round the world, which is 360 degrees, each degree 69 miles and a half?
Anſ. 4755801600 barley-corns.

LAND MEASURE.

90. In 27 acres, how many roods and perches?
Anſ. 108 roods, 4320 perches.
91. In 4320 perches, how many acres? Anſ. 27.
92. A perſon having a piece of ground, containing 37 acres, 1 pole, has a mind to diſpoſe of 15 acres to A, I deſire to know how many perches he will have left?
Anſ. 3521.
93. There are 4 fields to be divided into ſhares of 75 perches each; the firſt field containing 5 acres; the ſecond 4 acres, 2 poles; the third, 7 acres 3 roods; and the fourth, 2 acres, 1 rood; I deſire to know how many ſhares are contained therein? Anſ. 40 ſhares, 42 perches.

WINE MEASURE.

94. Bought 5 tuns of port wine; how many gallons and pints? Anſ. 1260 gallons, 10080 pints.
95. In 10080 pints, how many tuns? Anſ. 5.
96. In 5896 gallons of Canary, how many pipes and hogſheads, and of each a like number?
An. 21 of each, 37 gallons over.

97. A

97. A gentleman ordered his butler to bottle off ⅔ of a pipe of French wine into quarts, and the rest into pints; I desire to know how many dozen of each he had?
Ans. 28 dozen of each.

ALE and BEER MEASURE.

98. In 46 barrels of beer, how many pints? *Ans.* 13248.
99. In 10 barrels of ale, how many gallons and quarts?
Ans. 320 gals. 1280 qts.
100. In 72 hogsheads of beer, how many barrels?
Ans. 108 barrels.
101. In 108 barrels of beer, how many hogsheads?
Ans. 72.

DRY MEASURE.

102. In 120 quarters of wheat, how many bushels, pecks, gallons, and quarts?
Ans. 960 bushels, 3840 pecks, 7680 gallons, 30720 qts.
103. In 30720 quarts of corn, how many quarters?
Ans. 120.
104. In 20 chaldrons of coals, how many pecks?
Ans. 2880.
105. In 273 lasts of corn, how many pecks?
Ans. 87360.

TIME.

106. In 72015 hours, how many weeks?
Ans. 428 weeks, 4 days, 15 hours.
107. How many days is it since the birth of our Saviour to Christmas 1755? *Ans.* 641013 days, 18 hours.
108. Stowe writes, London was built 1108 years before our Saviour's birth, how many hours is it since to Christmas 1755? *Ans.* 25272378 hours.
109. From November 17, 1738, to September 12, 1739, how many days? *Ans.* 299.
110. From July 18, 1749, to December 27, in the same year, how many days? *Ans.* 162 days.
111. From July 18, 1723, to April 18, 1750, how many years and days?
Ans. 26 years, 9770 days, reckoning 365 days, 6 hours a year.

The SINGLE RULE of THREE DIRECT

TEACHETH, by three numbers given, to find out a fourth, in such proportion to the third, as the second is to the first.

RULE. First state the question, that is, place the numbers in such order, that the first and third be of one kind, and the second the same as the number required: then bring the first and third numbers into one name, and the second into the lowest term mentioned. Multiply the second and third numbers together, and divide the product by the first, the quotient will be the answer to the question in the same denomination you left the second number in.

EXAMPLES.

1. If 1 lb. of sugar cost $4\frac{1}{2}d$. what cost 54 lb.?

$$1 \ .. \ .. \ 4\frac{1}{2} \ .. \ 54$$
$$ 4 \quad\ \ 18$$
$$\overline{ 18 \quad 4)972}$$
$$ 12)243$$
$$ 20s. \ 3d.$$

Ans. 1 .. 0 .. 3.

2. If a gallon of beer cost $3d$. what is that *per* barrel? Ans. 9s.

3. If a pair of shoes cost 4s. 6d. what will 12 dozen come to? Ans. £32..8..0.

4. If 12 dozen pair of stockings cost £32..8..0. what is that *per* pair? Ans. 4s. 6d.

5. If 1 yard of cloth cost 15s. 6d. what will 32 yards cost at the same rate? Ans. 24..16..0.

6. If 32 yards of cloth cost £24..16..0. what is the value of 1 yard? Ans. 15s. 6d.

7. If 1 lb. of sugar cost $10\frac{1}{2}d$. what is the worth of 1 cwt.? Ans. £4..18..0.

8. If I gave £4..18..0. for 1 cwt. of sugar, at what rate did I buy it *per* lb.? Ans. $10\frac{1}{2}d$.

9. If I buy 20 pieces of cloth, each 20 ells, for 12s. 6d. *per* ell, what is the value of the whole? Ans. £250.

10. Bought 20 pieces of Holland, each 20 ells, for £250, what is that *per* ell? Ans. 12s. 6d.

11. What

ASSISTANT. *Single Rule of Three Direct.* 47

11. What will 25 cwt. 3 qrs. 14 lb. of tobacco come to, at $15\frac{1}{2}d$. per lb. *Anf.* £187..3..3.

12. I gave £187..3..3. for 25 cwt. 3 qrs. 14 lb. of tobacco, at what rate did I buy it at per lb.? *Anf.* $15\frac{1}{2}d$.

13. Bought $27\frac{1}{4}$ yds. muslin, at 6s. $9\frac{1}{2}d$. per yard, what does it amount to? *Anf.* £9..5..$0\frac{1}{4}$. 2 rem.

14. Bought 17 cwt. 1 qr. 14 lb. of iron, at $3\frac{1}{4}d$. per lb. what does it come to? *Anf.* £26..7..$0\frac{1}{2}$.

15. If coffee is fold for $5\frac{1}{2}d$. per ounce, what muft be given for 2 cwt.? *Anf.* £82..2..8.

16. How many yards of cloth may be bought for £21..11..$1\frac{1}{2}$, when $3\frac{1}{2}$ yards coft £2..14..3.?
Anf. 27 yds. 3 rs. 1 nail, 84 rem.

17. If $3\frac{1}{2}$ lb. of Cheshire cheese coft 1s. 1d. what coft 1 cwt.? *Anf.* £1..14..8.

18. If 1 cwt. of Cheshire cheese coft £1..14..8. what muft I give for $3\frac{1}{2}$ lb. *Anf.* 1s. 1d.

19. Bought 1 cwt. 24 lb. 8 oz. of old lead, at 9s. per cwt. what does it come to? *Anf.* 10s. $11\frac{1}{2}d$. 112 rem.

20. If 1 cwt. 24 lb. 8 oz. of lead be worth 10s. $11\frac{1}{2}d$. $\frac{112}{224}$ what is that per cwt. *Anf.* 9s.

21. If a gentleman's income is £500 a year, and he spends 19s. 4d. per day, how much does he lay by at the year's end?
Anf. 147..3..4.

22. If I buy 14 yards of cloth for 10 guineas, how many Flemifh ells can I buy for £283..17..6. at the fame rate?
Anf. 504 Fl. ells, 2 qrs.

23. If 283..17..6. will buy 504 Flemifh ells, 2 quarters, what quantity of yards can I have for £10..10..0.?
Anf. 14 yds.

24. If 504 Flemifh ells, 2 quarters, coft £283..17..6. at what rate muft I give for 14 yards? *Anf.* £10..10..0.

25. Gave £1..1..8. for 3 lb. of coffee, what muft be given for 29 lb. 4 oz. *Anf.* £10..11..3.

26. Bought 29 lb. 4 oz. of coffee, for £10..11..3. what is the value of 3 lb. *Anf.* £1..1..8.

27. If $1\frac{1}{2}$ oz. of coffee coft $6\frac{1}{4}d$. what will $3\frac{1}{4}$ oz. coft at the fame rate? *Anf.* 1s. $1\frac{3}{4}d$. 1 rem.

28. If 1 Englifh ell, 2 quarters, coft 4s. 7d. what will $39\frac{1}{2}$ yards coft at the fame rate? *Anf.* 5l. 3s. $5\frac{1}{4}d$.

29. If 1 ounce of gold is worth £5..4..2. what is the worth of 1 grain? *Anf.* $2\frac{1}{2}d$. 20 rem.

30. If

30. If 14 yards of broad cloth cost £9..12..0. what is the purchase of 75 yards?   *Ans.* £51..8..6¼. 6 rem.

31. If 27 yards of Holland cost £51..12..6. how many ells English can I buy for £100?   *Ans.* 384.

32. If 1 cwt. cost £12..12..6. what must I give for 14 cwt. 1 qr. 19 lb.?   *Ans.* £182..0..11¼. 8 rem.

33. Bought 7 yards of cloth for 17s. 8d. what must be given for 5 pieces, each containing 27½ yards?
Ans. 17..7..0¼. 2 rem.

34. If 7 oz. 11 dwt. of gold be worth £85. what is the value of 14 lb. 9 oz. 12 dwt. 16 gr. at the same rate?
Ans. £823..9..3¼. 552 rem.

35. A draper bought 420 yards of broad cloth, at the rate of 14s. 10¼d. per ell English, how much did he pay for the whole?   *Ans.* £250..5..0.

36. A gentleman bought a wedge of gold, which weighed 14 lb. 3 oz. 8 dwt. for the sum of £514..4..0. at what rate did he pay for it *per* ounce?   *Ans.* £3.

37. A grocer bought 4 hogsheads of sugar, each weighing neat 6 cwt. 2 qrs. 14 lb. which cost him £2..8..6. per cwt. what is the value of the 4 hogsheads?   *Ans.* £64..5..3.

38. A draper bought 8 packs of cloth, each containing 4 parcels, each parcel 10 pieces, and each piece 26 yards, and gave after the rate of £4..16..0. for 6 yards, I desire to know what the 8 packs stood him in?   *Ans.* £6656.

39. If 24 lb. of raisins cost 6s. 6d. what will 18 frails cost, each weighing neat 3 qrs. 18 lb.?   *Ans.* £24..17..3.

40. If 1 ounce of silver be worth 5s. what is the price of 14 ingots, each weighing 7 lb. 5 oz. 10 dwt.   £313..5.

41. What is the price of a pack of wool weighing 2 cwt. 1 qr. 19 lb. at 8s. 6d. per stone?   *Ans.* £8..4..6¼. 10 rem.

42. Bought 59 cwt. 2 qrs. 24 lb. of tobacco, at £2..17..4. per cwt. what does it come to?   *Ans.* £171..3..7¼. 80 rem.

43. What is the half year's rent of 547 acres of land, at 15s. 6d. per acre *per annum*?   *Ans.* £211..19..3.

44. Bought 171 ton of lead, at £14 *per* ton; paid carriage and other incident charges, £4..10..0. I require the value of the lead, and what it stands me in *per* lb.?
Ans. £2398..10..0 *value*, 1½d. per lb. 432 rem.

45. If a pair of stockings cost 10 groats, how many dozen may I buy for £43..5..0.?   *Ans.* 21 doz. 7½ pair.

46. Bought

ASSISTANT.   *Rule of Three Inverse.*   49

46. Bought 27 dozen, 5lb. of candles, after the rate of 17d. per 3lb. What did they cost me?
Anf. £7..15..4¼. 1 rem.

47. If an ounce of fine gold is fold for £3..10..0. what comes 7 ingots to, each weighing 3 lb. 7 oz. 14 dwt. 21 gr. at the fame price?   *Anf.* £1071..14..5¼.

48. If my horfe ftands me in 9d½ per day keeping, what will be the charge of 11 horfes for the year?
Anf. £158..18..6½.

49. A factor bought 86 pieces of ftuff, which coft him £517..19..4. at 4s. 10d. per yard, I demand how many yards there were, and how many ells Englifh in a piece?
Anf. 2143 yards ¼, 56 rem. *and* 19 *ells*, 4 *quarters*, 2 *nails*, 64 *rem. in a piece.*

50. A gentleman hath an annuity of £896..17..0. *per annum.* I defire to know how much he may fpend daily, that at the year's end he may lay up 200 guineas, and give to the poor quarterly 10 moidores?   £1..14..8. 44 *rem.*

The RULE *of* THREE INVERSE.

INVERSE PROPORTION is, when more requires lefs, and lefs requires more. More requires lefs, is when the third term is greater than the firft, and requires the fourth term to be lefs than the fecond. And lefs requires more, is when the third term is lefs than the firft, and requires the fourth term to be greater than the fecond.

RULE. Multiply the firft and fecond terms together, and divide the product by the third, the quotient will bear fuch proportion to the fecond as the firft does to the third.

EXAMPLE.

1. If 8 men can do a piece of work in 12 days, how many days can 16 men perform the fame in?   *Anf.* 6 *days.*
$$8 : 12 :: 16 :: 6$$
$$\underline{8}$$
$$16)96(6 \; days.$$

2. If 54 men can build a houfe in 90 days, how many men can do the fame in 50 days?   *Anf.* 97 *men.*

3. If

3. If, when a peck of wheat is fold for 2s. the penny loaf weighs 8 oz. how much will it weigh when the peck is worth but 1s. 6d? *Anſ.* 10 oz. 10 dr. ¼.

4. How many pieces of money of 20s. value are equal to 240 pieces of 12s. each? *Anſ.* 144.

5. How many yards of three quarters wide are equal in meaſure to 30 yards of 5 quarters wide? *Anſ.* 50.

6. If I lend my friend £200 for twelve months, how long ought he to lend me £150. to requite my kindneſs? *Anſ.* 16 months.

7. If for 24s. I have 1200 lb. carried 36 miles, how many pounds can I have carried 24 miles for the ſame money? *Anſ.* 1800 lb.

8. If 108 workmen finiſh a piece of work in 12 days, how many are ſufficient to finiſh it in 3 days? *Anſ.* 432.

9. An army beſieging a town, in which were 1000 ſoldiers, with proviſion for three months, how many ſoldiers departed, when the proviſions laſted them ſix months? *Anſ.* 500.

10. If £20. worth of wine is ſufficient to ſerve an ordinary of 100 men, when the tun is ſold for £30. how many will £20. worth ſuffice, when the tun is ſold but for £24? *Anſ.* 125 men.

11. A courier makes a journey in 24 days, when the day is but 12 hours long, how many days will he be going the ſame journey, when the days are 16 hours long? *Adſ.* 18 days.

12. How much pluſh is ſufficient for a cloak, which has in it 4 yards of 7 quarters wide of ſtuff for the lining, the pluſh being but 3 quarters wide? *Anſ.* 9 yards ⅓.

13. If 14 pioneers make a trench in 18 days, how many days will 34 take to do the ſame?
Anſ. 7 days, 4 hours, 56 minutes, 16 rem.

14. Borrowed of my friend £64. for 8 months, and he hath occaſion another time to borrow of me for 12 months, how much muſt I lend him to requite his former kindneſs to me? *Anſ.* 42..13..4.

15. A regiment of ſoldiers, conſiſting of 1000 men, are to have new coats, each coat to contain 2 yards ½ of cloth, 5 quarters wide, and to be lined with ſhalloon of 3 quarters wide: I demand how many yards of ſhalloon will line them?
Anſ. 4166 yards, 2 quarters, 2 nails, 2 rem.

The DOUBLE RULE of THREE

IS so called, because it is composed of 5 numbers given to find a sixth, which, if the proportion is direct, must bear such proportion to the 4th and 5th, as the 3d bears to the 1st and 2d. But if inverse, the 6th number must bear such proportion to the 4th and 5th, as the 1st bears to the 2d and 3d. The three first terms are a supposition; the two last, a demand.

RULE 1. Let the principal cause of loss or gain, interest or decrease, action or passion, be put in the first place.

2. Let that which betokeneth time, distance of place, and the like, be in the second place, and the remaining one in the third.

3. Place the other two terms under their like, in the supposition.

4. If the blank falls under the third term, multiply the first and second terms for a divisor, and the other three for a dividend. But,

5. If the blank falls under the first or second term, multiply the third and fourth terms for a divisor, and the other three for the dividend, and the quotient will be the answer.

PROOF. By two single rules of three.

EXAMPLES.

1. If 14 horses eat 56 bushels of oats in 16 days, how many bushels will be sufficient for 20 horse for 24 days?

By two single rules.

hor. bu.   hor. bu.
1. As 14 : 56 : : 20 : 80
days. bu.   days. bu.
2. As 16 : 80 : : 24 : 120

or in one stating, worked thus:

hor. days. bu.
14 : 16 : 56
20 : 24 : —

$$\frac{56 \times 20 \times 24}{14 \times 16} = 120$$

2. If 8 men in 14 days can mow 112 acres of grass, how many men must there be to mow 2000 acres in ten days?

acres. days. acres. days.
1. As 112 : 14 : : 2000 : 250
days. men. days. men.
2. As 250 : 8 : : 10 : 200

men. days. acres.
8 : 14 : 112
0 : 10 : 2000

$$\frac{8 \times 14 \times 2000}{112 \times 10} = 200$$

3. If £100. in 12 months gain £6. intereſt, how much will £75. gain in 9 months? Anſ. 3..7..6.

4. If a carrier receives £2..2..0. for the carriage of 3 cwt. 150 miles, how much ought he to receive for the carriage of 7cwt. 3qrs. 14lb. for 50 miles? Anſ. 1..16..9.

5. If a regiment of ſoldiers, conſiſting of 136 men, conſume 351 quarters of wheat in 108 days, how many quarters of wheat will 11232 ſoldiers conſume in 56 days?
Anſ. 15031.

6. If 40 acres of graſs be mowed by 8 men in 7 days, how many acres can be mowed by 24 men in 28 days?
Anſ. 480.

7. If 40s. will pay 8 men for 5 days work, how much will pay 32 men for 24 days work? Anſ. £38..8..0.

8. If £100. in 12 months gain £6. intereſt, what principal will gain £3..7..6. in 9 months? Anſ. £75.

9. If a regiment, conſiſting of 939 ſoldiers, conſume 351 quarters of wheat in 168 days, how many ſoldiers will conſume 1404 quarters in 56 days? Anſ. 11268.

10. In a family, conſiſting of 7 perſons, there are drank out 2 kilderkins of beer in 12 days, how many kilderkins will there be drank out by another family of 14 perſons in 8 days?
Anſ. 2 kil. 12 gal.

11. If the carriage of 60 cwt. 20 miles coſt £14..10..0. what weight can I have carried 30 miles for £5..8..9. at the ſame rate of carriage? Anſ. 15 cwt.

12. If 2 horſes eat 8 buſhels of oats in 16 days, how many horſes will eat up 3000 quarters in 24 days? Anſ. 4000.

13. If £100. in 12 months gain £7. intereſt, what is the intereſt of £571. for 6 years? Anſ. £239..16..4¾.

14. If I pay 10s. for the carriage of 2 tons 6 miles, what muſt I pay for the carriage of 12 tons, 17 cwt. 17 miles?
Anſ. £9..2..0½.

PRACTICE

IS ſo called from the general uſe thereof by all perſons concerned in trade and buſineſs.

All queſtions in this rule are performed by taking aliquot or even parts, by which means many tedious reductions are avoided; the table of which is as follows:

Of

Of a Pound. s. d.		*Of a Shilling.* d.		*Of a Ton.* cwt.		*Of an Hundred.* qrs. lb.	
10 .. - -	is $\frac{1}{2}$	6 is .. - -	$\frac{1}{2}$	10 - is - -	$\frac{1}{2}$	2 or 56 - is	$\frac{1}{2}$
6 .. - 8 - -	$\frac{1}{3}$	4 - .. - -	$\frac{1}{3}$	5 - - - -	$\frac{1}{4}$	1 or 28 - -	$\frac{1}{4}$
5 .. - - - -	$\frac{1}{4}$	3 - .. - -	$\frac{1}{4}$	4 - 8 - -	1	14 - -	$\frac{1}{8}$
4 .. - - - -	$\frac{1}{5}$	2 - .. - -	$\frac{1}{6}$	$2\frac{1}{2}$ - - -	$\frac{1}{8}$	*Of a Quarter.*	
3 .. 4 - -	$\frac{1}{6}$	$1\frac{1}{2}$ .. - -	$\frac{1}{8}$	2 - -	$\frac{1}{10}$	14 - - - -	$\frac{1}{2}$
2 .. 6 - -	$\frac{1}{8}$	1 - .. -	$\frac{1}{12}$			7 - - - -	$\frac{1}{4}$
2 .. - - -	$\frac{1}{10}$					4 - - - -	$\frac{1}{7}$
1 .. 8 -	$\frac{1}{12}$					$3\frac{1}{2}$ - - -	$\frac{1}{8}$

RULE 1. When the price is less than a penny, divide by the aliquot parts that are in a penny; then by 12 and 20, it will be the answer.

$\frac{1}{4}$ is $\frac{1}{4}$ 5704 *lb. at* $\frac{1}{4}$ 12)1426 2|0)11|8..10 £5..18..10	7695 at $\frac{1}{2}$ *Facit* £16 - $7\frac{1}{2}$ 5740 at $\frac{1}{2}$ *Facit* £11..19..2	6547 at $\frac{3}{4}$ *Facit* £20..9..$2\frac{1}{4}$ 4573 at $\frac{3}{4}$ *Facit* £14..5..$9\frac{3}{4}$

RULE 2. When the price is less than a shilling, take the aliquot part or parts that are in a shilling, add them together, and divide by 20, as before.

1 is $\frac{1}{12}$ 7547 at 1*d.* 2|0)62|8..11 £31..8..11	6254 at $1d\frac{3}{4}$ *Facit* £45..12-$\frac{1}{2}$ 2351 at 2*d.* *Facit* £19..11..10	7062 at $3\frac{1}{4}$ *Facit* £95..12..$7\frac{1}{2}$ 2147 at $3d\frac{1}{2}$. *Facit* £31..6..$2\frac{1}{2}$
1 is $\frac{1}{12}$ 3751 at $1d\frac{1}{4}$. $\frac{1}{4}$ is $\frac{1}{4}$) 312..7 78..$1\frac{3}{4}$ 2|0)39|0..$8\frac{3}{4}$ £ 19..10..$8\frac{3}{4}$	7210 at $2d\frac{1}{4}$. *Facit* £67..11..$10\frac{1}{2}$ 2710 at $2d\frac{1}{2}$. *Facit* £28..4..7 3250 at $2d\frac{3}{4}$. *Facit* £37..4..$9\frac{1}{2}$	7000 at $3d\frac{3}{4}$. *Facit* £109..7..6 3257 at 4*d.* *Facit* £54..5..8 2056 at $4d\frac{1}{4}$. *Facit* £36..8..2
54325 at $1d\frac{1}{2}$ *Facit* £339..10..$7\frac{1}{2}$	2715 at 3*d.* *Facit* £33..18..9	3752 at $4d\frac{1}{2}$. *Facit* £70..7..–

2107 at 4*d*¾. *Facit* £41..14..–¼	325¼ at 7*d*¼. *Facit* £98..5..11½	2150 at 9*d*¾. *Facit* £87..6..10½
3210 at 5*d*. *Facit* £66..17..6	2701 at 7*d*½. *Facit* £84..8..1½	6325 at 10*d*. *Facit* £263..10..10
2715 at 5*d*¼. *Facit* £59..7..9¾	3714 at 7*d*¾. *Facit* £119..18..7½	5724 at 10*d*¼. *Facit* £244..9..3
3120 at 5*d*½. *Facit* £71..10..-	2710 at 8*d*. *Facit* £90..6..8	6327 at 10*d*¼. *Facit* £270..4..3¾
7521 at 5*d*¾. *Facit* £180..3..9¾	3514 at 8*d*¼. *Facit* £120..15..10½	3254 at 10*d*½. *Facit* £142..7..3
3271 at 6d. *Facit* £81..15..6	2759 at 8½. *Facit* £97..14..3½	7291 at 10*d*¾. *Facit* £326..11..6¾
7914 at 6*d*¼. *Facit* £206..1..10½	9872 at 8*d*¾. *Facit* 359..18..4	3256 at 11*d*. *Facit* £149..4..8
3250 at 6*d*½ *Facit* £88..–..5	5272 at 9*d*. *Facit* £197..14..–	7254 at 11*d*¼. *Facit* £340..–..7½
2708 at 6*d*¾. *Facit* £76..3..3	6325 at 9¼. *Facit* £243..15..6¼	3754 at 11*d*½. *Facit* £179..17..7
3271 at 7*d*. *Facit* £95..8..1	7924 at 9*d*½. *Facit* £243..13..2	7972 at 11*d*¾. *Facit* £390..5..11

RULE 3. When the price is more than one shilling, and less than two, take the part or parts, with so much of the given price as is more than a shilling, which add to the given quantity, and divide by 20, it will give the answer.

¼ 1/12 2106 at 12*d*¼.	½ 1/24 3715 at 12*d*½.	2712 at 12¾.
43..10½	154..9½	*Facit* £144..1..6
2|0)214|9..10½	2|0)386|9..9½	
£107..9..10½	£193..9..9½	2107 at 1*s*. 1*d*. *Facit* £114..2..7

ASSISTANT.   Practice.   55

3215 at 1s. 1d¼.	3725 at 1s. 5d.	1004 at 1s. 8d¼.
Facit £177..9..10¼	Facit £263..17..1	Facit £86..16..1
2790 at 1s. 1d½.	7250 at 1s. 5d¼.	2104 at 1s. 9d.
Facit £156..18..9	Facit £521..1..10½	Facit £184..2..-
7924 at 1s. 1d¾.	2507 at 1s. 5d½.	2571 at 1s. 9d¼.
Facit £452..16..8	Facit £189..7..3½	Facit £227..12..9¼
3750 at 1s. 2d.	7210 at 1s. 5d¾.	2104 at 1s. 9d½.
Facit £218..15..-	Facit £533..4..9½	Facit 183..9..8
3291 at 1s. 2d¼.	7524 at 1s. 6d.	7506 at 1s. 9d¾.
Facit £195..8..-¼	Facit £564..6..-	Facit £680..4..7½
9254 at 1s. 2d½.	7103 at 1s. 6d¼.	1071 at 10s. 10d.
Facit £559..1..11	Facit £540..2..5¼	Facit £98..3..6
7250 at 1s. 2d¾.	3254 at 1s. 6d½.	5200 at 1s. 10d¼.
Facit £445..11..5½	Facit £250..16..7	Facit £482..1..8
7591 at 1s. 3d.	7925 at 1s. 6d¾.	2117 at 1s. 10d½.
Facit £474..8..9	Facit £619..2..9¼	Facit £198..19..4½
6325 at 1s. 3d¼.	9271 at 1s. 7d.	1007 at 1s. 10d¾.
Facit £401..18..-¼	Facit £733..19..1	Facit £95..9..1¼
5271 at 1s. 3d½.	7210 at 1s. 7d¼.	5000 at 1s. 11d.
Facit £340..8..4½	Facit £578..6..-½	Facit £479..3..4
3254 at 1s. 3d¾.	2310 at 1s. 7d½.	2105 at 1s. 11d¼.
Facit £213.10.10½	Facit £187..13..9	Facit £203..18.5d¼
2915 at 1s. 4d.	2504 at 1s. 7d¾.	1006 at 1s. 11½.
Facit £194..6..8	Facit £206..1..2	Facit £98..10..1
3270 at 1s. 4d¼.	7152 at 1s. 8d.	2705 at 1s. 11d¾.
Facit £221..8..1d½	Facit £596..-	Facit £267..13..7½
7059 at 1s. 4d½.	2905 at 1s. 8d¼.	5000 at 1s. 11½.
Facit £485..6..1½	Facit £245..2..2¼	Facit £489..11..8
2750 at 1s. 4d¾.	7104 at 1s. 8d½.	4000 at 1s. 11d¾.
Facit £191..18..6½	Facit £606..16..-	Facit £395..16..8

56 Practice.   The Tutor's

RULE 4. When the price consists of any even number of shillings under 20, multiply the given quantity by half the price, doubling the first figure of the product for shillings, and the rest of the product will be pounds.

| 2750 at 2s. | 2102 at 10s. | 1075 at 16s. |
| Facit £275..-..- | Facit £1051..-..- | Facit £860..-.. |

| 3254 at 4s. | 2101 at 12s. | 1621 at 18s. |
| Facit £650..16..- | Facit £1260..12..- | Facit £1458..18..- |

| 2710 at 6s. | 5271 at 14s. | |
| Facit £813..-..- | Facit £3689..14..- | Note. When the price is 10s. take half of the quantity, and if any remains, it is 10s. |

| 1572 at 8s. | 3123 at 16s. | |
| Facit £628..16..- | Facit £2498..8..- | |

RULE 5. When the price consists of odd shillings, multiply the given quantity by the price, and divide by 20, the product will be the answer.

| 2703 at 1s. | 2715 at 7s. | 2150 at 15s. |
| Facit £135..-3..- | Facit £950..5..- | Facit £1612..10..- |

| 3270 at 3s. | 3214 at 9s. | 3142 at 17s. |
| 3 | Facit £1446..6..- | Facit £2670..14..- |

| 2|0)981|0 | 2710 at 11s. | 2150 at 19s. |
| | Facit £1490..10..- | Facit £2042..10..- |

490..10..-	3179 at 13s.	7157 at 19s.
3271 at 5s.	Facit £2066..7..-	Facit £6799..3..-
Facit £817..15..-		

Note, When the price is 5s. divide the quantity by 4, and if any remains it is 5s.

RULE 6. When the price is shillings and pence, and they the aliquot part of a pound, divide by the aliquot part, and it will give the answer at once; but if they are not an aliquot part, then multiply the quantity by the shillings, and take parts for the rest, add them together, and divide by 20.

ASSISTANT. Practice. 57

s. d.			
6..8	⅓	2710 at 6s. 8d. Facit £903..6..8	

	3150 at 3s. 4d. Facit £525..0..0
	2715 at 2s. 6d. Facit £339..7..6
	7150 at 1s. 8d. Facit £595..16..8
	3215 at 1s. 4d. Facit £214..6..8
	7211 at 1s. 3d. Facit £450..13..9

d.		
2	⅙	2710 at 3s. 2d.
		3
		8130
		451..8
	2|0	858|1..8
		£429..1..8

7514 at 4s. 7d.
Facit £1721..19..2

2517 at 5s. 3d.
Facit £660..14. 3

2547 at 7s. 3½d.
Facit £928.11.10½

3271 at 5s. 9¼d.
Facit £943.16.4¾

2103 at 15s. 4½d.
Facit £1616.13.7½

7152 at 17s. 6¼d.
Facit £6280..7..0

2510 at 14s. 7¼d.
Facit £1832.16.5½

3715 at 9s. 4½d.
Facit £1741.8.1½

2572 at 13s. 7d½.
Facit £1752..3..6

7251 at 14s. 8¼d.
Facit £5324.19.0¾

3210 at 15s. 7¾d.
Facit £2511.3.1½

2710 at 19s. 2½d.
Facit £2602.14.7

Rule 7. 1*st*, When the price is pounds and shillings, multiply the quantity by the pounds, and proceed with the shillings, if they are even as in the 4th rule; if odd, take the aliquot parts, add them together, the sum will be the answer.

2*dly*, When pounds, shillings and pence, and the shillings and pence the aliquot parts of a pound, multiply the quantity by the pounds, and take parts for the rest.

3*dly*, When the price is pounds, shillings, pence, and farthings, and the shillings and pence not the aliquot parts

of

of a pound, reduce the pounds and ſhillings into ſhillings, multiply the quantity by the ſhillings, take parts for the reſt, add them together, and divide by 20.

Note. *When the given quantity is no more than three figures, proceed as in* Compound Multiplication.

4	$\frac{1}{5}$	7215 at £7..4..0
		7
		50505
		1443
		51948 £.
s. d.		
2..6	$\frac{1}{8}$	2104 at £5..3..0
		5
		10520
6	$\frac{1}{5}$	263
		52.12
		10835. 12
		2107 at £2..8..0
		Facit £5056.16.0
		7156 at £5..6..0
		Facit £37926.16.0
6	$\frac{1}{2}$	2710 at £2..3..7½
		43
		116530
1½	$\frac{1}{4}$	1355
		338..9
	2|0	11822|3..9
		£5911..3..9
		3215 at £1..17..0
		Facit £5947..15..0

2107 at £1..13..0
Facit £3476..11..0

3215 at £4..6..8
Facit £13931.13.4

2154 at £7..1..3
Facit £15212.12.6

2701 at £2..3..4
Facit £5852..3..4

2715 at £1..17..2½
Facit £5051..0..7½

2157 at £3.15.2¼
Facit £8108.19.5½

3210 at £1.18.6¾
Facit £6189.5.7½

2157 at £2..7..4½
Facit £5109.7.10½

142 at £1..15..2¼
Facit £250..2..6½

95 at £15..14..7¼
Facit £1494.7.4¾

37 at £1..19..5¾
Facit £73..0..8¾

2175 at £2.15.4½
Facit £6022.0.7½

2150 at £17.16.1½
Facit £38283..8..9

ASSISTANT.   Practice.   59

RULE 8. When the price and quantity given are of several denominations, multiply the price by the integers, and take part with the parts of the integers for the rest.

1. At £3..17..6. per cwt. what is the value of 25 cwt. 2 qrs. 14 lb. of tobacco?

2	½	£3 .. 17 .. 6	5×5=25
		5	
		19 .. 7 .. 6	
		5	
lb.		96 .. 17 .. 6	
14	¼	1 .. 18 .. 9	
		9 .. 8¼	
		99 .. 5 .. 11¼	

2. At £1..4..9. per cwt. what comes 17 cwt. 1 qr. 17 lb. of cheese to?   Ans. £21..10..8.
3. Sold 85 cwt. 1 qr. 10 lb. of cheese, at £1..7..8. per cwt. what does it come to?   Ans. 118..1..0¼.
4. Hops at £4..5..8. per cwt. what must be given for 72 cwt. 1 qr. 18 lb?   Ans. £310..3..2.
5. At £1..1..4. per cwt. what is the value of 27 cwt. 2 qrs. 15 lb. of Malaga raisins?   Ans. 29..9..6¼.
6. Bought 78 cwt. 3 qrs. 12 lb. of currants, at £2..17..9. per cwt. what did I give for the whole? Ans. £227.14..0.
7. Sold 56 cwt. 1 qr. 17 lb. of sugar, at £2..15..9. the cwt. what does it come to?   Ans. 157..4..4¼.
8. Tobacco at £3..17..10. the cwt. what is the worth of 97 cwt. 15 lb.?   Ans. 378..0..3.
9. At £4..14..6. the cwt. what is the value of 37 cwt. 2 qrs. 13 lb. of double refined sugar?   Ans. £177..14..8¼.
10. Bought sugar at £3..14..6. the cwt. what did I give for 15 cwt. 1 qr. 10 lb.?   Ans. £57..2..9.
11. At £4..15..4. the cwt. the value of 172 cwt. 3 qrs. 12 lb. of tobacco is required?   Ans. 823..19..0¼.
12. Soap at £3..11..6. the cwt. what is the value of 53 cwt. 17 lb.?   Ans. £190..0..4.

INTEREST.

INTEREST.

INTEREST is either SIMPLE or COMPOUND.

SIMPLE INTEREST

IS the Profit allowed in lending or forbearance of any sum of money, for a determined space of time.

The Principal is the money lent, for which interest is to be received.

The Rate per Cent. is a certain sum agreed on between the Borrower and Lender, to be paid for every £100. for the use of the Principal 12 months.

The Amount is the Principal and Interest added together.

Interest is also applied to Commission, Brokage, Purchasing of Stocks, and Insurance.

To find the Interest of any Sum of Money for a Year.

Rule. Multiply the Principal by the Rate per Cent. that product divided by 100, will give the interest required.

For several Years.

Multiply the Interest of one year by the number of Years given in the question, and the product will be the answer.

Examples.

1. What is the interest of £375. for a year, at 5 per cent. per annum?

$$\begin{array}{r} 375 \\ 5 \\ \hline 18|75 \\ 20 \\ \hline 15|00 \end{array}$$ Ans. £18..15..0.

2. What is the interest of £268. for one year, at 4 per cent. per annum? Ans. £10..14..4¾.

3. What is the interest of £945..10..0. for a year, at 4 per cent. per annum? Ans. £37..16..4¾.

4. What is the interest of £547..15..0. at 5 per cent. per annum, for 3 years? Ans. £82..3..3.

5. What

ASSISTANT. *Interest.* 61

5. What is the Interest of £254..17..6. for 5 years, at 4 per cent. per annum? Ans. £50..19.6.

6. What is the interest of £556..13..4. at 5 per cent. per annum, for 5 years? Ans. £139..3..4.

COMMISSION

Is an allowance from merchants to their factors or correspondents, in the buying or selling of goods, and is generally at a certain rate per cent. according to the custom of the country where the factor resides.

RULE. Multiply the principal by the rate per cent. as before; and for ¼, ½, or ¾, take the part or parts from the Principal, which added to the product, and divided by 100, will give the answer.

7. What is the commission of £287..10..—. at 3¼ per cent.?

£ ¼, 287..10
3
———
862..10 = 3
143..15 = ¼
———
10|06..5 = 3¼
20
———
1|25
1|3
———
3|00

Ans. £10..1..3.

8. What must I allow my correspondent for disbursing on my account £529..18..5. at 2¼ per cent.? Ans. £11..18..5¼.

9. My correspondent writes me word, that he has bought goods to the amount of £754..16..—. on my account, what does his commission come to at 2½ per cent.? Ans. £18..17..4¼.

10. If I allow my factor 3¾ per cent. for commission, what may he demand on the laying out £876..5..10? Ans. £32..17..2¼.

PURCHASING of STOCKS.

RULE. Multiply the sum to be purchased by the excess, above 100; divide that product by 100, the produce of which, added to the given sum, is the purchase required.

If under Par, (that is under £100.) multiply by the Rate per Cent. that product, divided by 100, gives the purchase thereof.

11. What is the purchase of £575..10..–. Bank Stock, at 131¾ *per cent.*?

```
        6×5+1=31
        575..10
              6
        -------
        3453
           5
        -------
     17265..–..–=30
   ½ ½   575..10..–= 1
   ½ ½   287..15..–= ½
         143..17..6= ¼
     ---------------------
     182|72.. 2..6=31¾
          20
        -----
         14|42
            12
        -----
          5|10
     575..10..–
     182..14..5
     ------------
   £758.. 4..5 Ans.
```

12. What is the purchase of £254..17..–. Bank Annuities at 97¼ *per cent.*?

```
        12×8+1=97
        254..17
             12
        -------
        3058.. 4
                8
        -------
     24465..12..–=96
     254..17..–= 1
   ¼ ¼  63..14..3= ¼
     ---------------------
     247|84.. 3..3=97¼
          20
        -----
         16|83
            12
        -----
          9|99
             4
        -----
          3|96
   £247..16..9¼ Answer.
```

13. At 110¼ *per cent.* what is the purchase of £2054..16..–. South Sea Stock? *Ans.* £2265..8..4.

14. At 104⅜ *per cent.* South Sea Annuities, what is the purchase of £1797..14..–.? *Ans.* £1876..6..11¼.

15. What is the purchase of £2750..17..–. South Sea Old Annuities, at 102⅝ *per cent.*? *Ans.* £2823..1..2¼.

16. At 96¾ *per cent.* what is the purchase of £577..19..–. Bank Annuities? *Ans.* £559..3..3½.

17. At 124⅝ *per cent.* what is the purchase of £758..17..10. India Stock? *Ans.* £945..15..4½.

BROKAGE

BROKAGE

Is an allowance to brokers, for helping merchants or factors to persons to buy or sell them goods.

RULE. Divide the sum given by 100, and take parts from the quotient with the rate per cent.

18. If I employ a broker to sell goods for me, to the value of £2575..17..6, what is the brokage, at 4s. *per cent.*?

```
2575..17.
      20
    ----
    1517
      12
    ----
    2|10
    ----

4s. 1/5  25..15..2
         ---------
Ans.  £5..3..-¼
```

19. What is the brokage of £796..14..7. at 6s. *per cent.*? *Ans.* £2..7..9½.

20. When a broker sells goods to the amount of £7105..5..10. what may he demand for brokage, if he is allowed 5s. 6d. *per cent.*? *Ans.* £19..10..9¼.

21. If a broker is employed to buy a quantity of goods, to the value of £975..6..4. what is the brokage at 6s. 6d. *per cent.*? *Ans.* £3..3..4½.

When the time is ¼, ½, or ¾ of a year, besides a number of years given.

RULE. Take parts of the interest for one year, which add to the interest of the several years given, and it will give the answer.

22. What is the interest of £554..10..–. for 3 months, at 4 *per cent. per annum*?

```
      554..10
            4
      -------
      22|18..–
         20
      ------
       3|60
         12
      ------
 m.    7|20
 3 ¼   22.. 3..7
      ----------
 Ans.  5..10..10¾
```

23. What is the interest of £336..15..6. for 2 years ½, at 5 *per cent. per annum*?

```
  336..15..6
           5
  ----------
  16|83..17..6
     20
  ----
  16|77
     12
  ----
   9|30
      4
  ----
   1|20

           16..16..9¼
                    2
          -----------
           33..13..6½
 ½  ½       8..8..4½
 ¼  ½       4..4..2¼
          -----------
 Ans.      46..6..1¼
```


24. What

24. What is the interest of £325..7..6. at 6 per cent. per annum, for 3 years and a half? Ans. £68..6..6 .

25. What is the interest of £547..2..4. for 5 years and a half, at 4 per cent. per annum? Ans. £120..7..3¼.

26. What is the interest of £257..5..1. at 4 per cent. for a year and three quarters? Ans. £18..—..1½.

27. What is the interest of £479..5..—. for 5 years ¼ quarter, at 5 per cent. per annum? Ans. £125..16..—¼.

When the rate per cent. is ¼, ½, or ¾, more than the pounds given in the rate, proceed as in commission, and it will give the answer for one year; and, for several, proceed as in the last rule.

28. What is the interest of £175..17..—. for 2 years and 3 quarters, at 4½ per cent. per annum?

```
¼ ½   175..17
        4
      ─────────          ¼ ½   7..18..3
      703.. 8..—                   2
       87..18..6                ─────────
      ─────────                15..16..6
      7|91..6..6        ¼ ½   3..19..1½
         20                   1..19..6¾
      ─────────                ─────────
       18|26                  £ 21..15..2¼ Ans.
         12
      ─────────
         3|18
```

29. What is the interest of £397..9..5, for 2 years and 1 quarter at 3½ per cent. per annum? Ans. £31..6..—.

30. What is the interest of £576..2..7. for 7 years and 1 quarter, at 4½ per cent. per annum? Ans. £187..19..1¼.

31. What is the interest of £279..13..8. at 5¼ per cent. per annum, for 3 years and a half? Ans. £51..7.10.

When the interest is required for any number of weeks.

RULE. As 52 weeks are to the interest of the given sum or a year: so are the weeks given, to the interest required.

32. What is the interest of £379..13..2. for four weeks, at 4 per cent. per annum?

```
    w.   £.  s.  d.  w.              379..13..2
As 52 : 15..3..8¼ :: 4;                    4
          20                         ─────────
        ─────                        15|18..12..8
         303                               20
          12                         ─────────
        ─────                           3|72
         3644                              12
            4                        ─────────
        ─────                           8|72
         14578                              4
             4                       ─────────
        ─────4)                         2|88
    52)58312(1121
       52                  Or thus: multiply by the num-
       ── 12)280¼          ber of weeks, and divide the pro-
       63                  duct by 4 and 13, being
       52  2|0)2|3..4¼     4×13=52  13)15..3..8¼
      ───                              ─────────
       111    1..3..4¼                    1..3..4¼
       104
      ───                  N. B. As it is 4 weeks, I don't
        72                 multiply, but only divide by 13.
        52
      ───
        20
```

33. What is the interest of £259..13..5. for 20 weeks, at 5 per cent. per annum?   Ans. £4..19..10¼.

34. What is the amount of £375..6..1. for 12 weeks, at 4½ per cent. per annum?   Ans. £379..4..0¼.

35. What is the amount of £256..5..3. for 25 weeks, at 2¾ per cent. per annum?   Ans. £259..13..0.

When the interest is for any number of days.

RULE. Multiply the pence of the principal by the days and rate *per cent.* for a dividend, cut off two figures on the right hand, and divide by 365, the quotient will be the answer in pence. Or,

As 365 days are to the interest of the given sum for a year: so are the days given, to the interest required.

36. What

66 Interest.   The TUTOR's

36. What is the interest of £240. for 120 days, at 4 per cent. per annum?

```
         240                    |         Or thus:
         240                    |    240   As 365:9..12::120
        ————                    |      4          20
        57600                   |    ————        ———
          120                   |    9|60        192
       ————                     |     20         120
        6912000                 |    ————        ———
             4                  |    12,00      2|0)
        ————    12)             |           365)23040(6|3
   365)27648000(757             |                2190
       2555                     |               ————  £3:3:1¼
       ————   2|0)6|3..1        |                1140
       2098                     |                1095
       1825   £3..3..1¼         |                ———
       ————                     |                  45
       2730                     |                  12
       2555                     |                ———
       ————                     |               )540(1
        175                     |                365
          4                     |                ———
        ———                     |                175
       )700(1                   |                  4
        365                     |                ———
        ———                     |               )700(1
        335                     |                365
                                |                ———
                                |                335
```

37. What is the interest of £379..5..4. for three years and 75 days, at 5 per cent. per annum?   Ans. £60..15..8.

38. At 5¼ per cent. per annum, what is the interest of £985..2..7. for 5 years, 127 days?   Ans. £289..15..3.

39. What is the interest of £2726..1..4. at 4½ per cent. per annum, for 3 years, 154 days?   Ans. £419..15..6¼.

When the amount, time, and rate per cent. are given, to find the principal.

RULE. As the amount of £100. at the rate and time given : is to £100 :: so is the amount given ; to the principal required.

40. What

40. What principal being put to interest will amount to £402..10..0 in 5 years, at 3 per cent. per annum?

$3 \times 5 + 100 = £115 : 100 :: 402..10$

```
              20           20
             ----         ----
             2300         8050
                           100
                          ----
              23|00)8050|00(£350. Anſ.
```

41. What principal being put to interest for 9 years will amount to £734..8..0 at 4 per cent. per annum? Anſ. £540

42. What principal being put to interest for 7 years, at 5 per cent. per annum, will amount to £334..16..0? Anſ. £248

When the principal, rate per cent. and amount are given, to find the time.

RULE. As the interest of the principal for 1 year : is to 1 year : so is the whole interest to the time required.

43. In what time will £350 amount to £402..10..0 at 3 per cent. per annum?

```
 350           As 10..10.. : 1 :: 52..10 : 5
   3                20           20
 ----               
 10|50              210      21|0)105|0(5 years Anſ. 402..10
   20                             105                 350.. 0
 ----                             ---                ------
 10|00                                                52..10
```

44. In what time will £540. amount to £734..8..0. at 4 per cent. per annum? Anſ. 9 years.

45. In what time will £248. amount to £334..16..0. at 5 per cent. per annum? Anſ. 7 years.

When the principal, amount, and time are given, to find the rate per cent.

RULE. As the principal : is to the interest for the whole time : so is £100 : to the interest for the same time. Divide that interest by the time, and the quotient will be the rate per cent.

46. At

68 *Interest.*   *The* TUTOR's

46. At what rate *per cent.* will £350. amount to £402..10..0. in 5 years time?

```
   350           As 350 : 52..10 :: 100 : £15.
  ─────                  20
  52..10..0           ─────
                        1050
                         100
                       ─────
              35|0)10500|0(300s. £15÷5=3 per cent.
```

47. At what rate *per cent.* will £248. amount to £334..16..0. in 7 years time?   *Ans.* 5 per cent.

48. At what rate *per cent.* will £540. amount to £734..8..0. in 9 years time?   *Ans.* 4 per cent.

Compound INTEREST

IS that which arises both from the principal and interest; that is, when the interest on money becomes due, and not paid, the same interest is allowed on that interest unpaid, as was on the principal before.

RULE 1. Find the first year's interest, which add to the principal: then find the interest of that sum, which add as before, and so on for the number of years.

2. Subtract the given sum from the last amount, and it will give the compound interest required.

EXAMPLES.

1. What is the compound interest of £500. forborne 3 years, at 5 *per cent. per annum?*

```
  500      500         525
    5       25         26..5
 ─────   ─────       ─────
 25|00    525 1st year.  551..5  2d year.
            5               5
          ─────                       551.. 5
          26|25           27|56..5    27..11..3
             20               20      ─────
          ─────           ─────       578..16..3  3d year.
           5|00            11|25       500        Prin. sub.
                              12      ─────
                           ─────      78..16..3 = interest
                            3|00                 for 3 years.
```

2. What is the amount of £400. forborne 3½ years, at 6 *per cent. per annum,* compound interest? *Ans.* £490..13..11¼.

3. What

3. What will £650. amount to in 5 years, at 5 per cent. per annum, compound intereſt? Anſ. £829..11..7½.

4. What is the amount of £550..10..0. for 3 years and 6 months, at 6 per cent. per annum, compound intereſt?
Anſ. £675..6..5.

5. What is the compound intereſt of £764. for 4 years and 9 months, at 6 per cent. per annum? Anſ. £243..18..8.

6. What is the compound intereſt of £75..10..6. for 5 years, 7 months and 15 days, at 5 per cent. per annum?
Anſ. £18..3..8¼.

7. What is the compound intereſt of £259..10..0. for 3 years, 9 months and 10 days, at 4½ per cent. per annum?
Anſ. £46..19..10⅖.

REBATE or DISCOUNT

IS the abating ſo much money on a debt, to be received before it is due, as that money, if put to intereſt, would gain in the ſame time, and at the ſame rate. As £100. preſent money would diſcharge a debt of £105. to be paid a year to come, rebate being made at 5 per cent.

RULE. As £100. with the intereſt for the time given : is to that intereſt : : ſo is the ſum given : to the rebate required.

Subtract the rebate from the given ſum, and the remainder will be the preſent worth.

EXAMPLES.

1. What is the diſcount and preſent worth of £487..12. for 6 months, at 6 per cent. per annum?

```
   6m ½6         As 103 : 3 : : 487..12
                        20           20
      3
    100           2060          9752
                                   3
    103                        ─────
                                £.  s.
                      206|0)2925|6(14..¼ rebate.
   487..12                   206
    14..4                    ───
                             865
Anſ. 473..8..0 preſent worth. 824
                             ───
                             416 = 4s.
```

2. What

70 *Equation of Payments.* The TUTOR's

2. What is the present payment of £357..10..0. which was agreed to be paid 9 months hence, at 5 *per cent. per annum* ? Ans. £344..11..7.

3. What is the discount of £275..10..0. for 7 months, at 5 *per cent. per annum* ? Ans. £7..16..1¼.

4. Bought goods to the value of £109..10..0. to be paid at 9 months, what present money will discharge the same, if I am allowed 6 *per cent. per annum* discount ?
Ans. £104..15..8¼.

5. What is the present worth of £527..9..1. payable 7 months hence, at 4¼ *per cent.* ? Ans. £514..13..10¼.

6. What is the discount of £85..10..0. due September the 8th, this being July the 4th, rebate at 5 *per cent. per annum* ?
Ans. 15s. 3d¼.

7. Sold goods for £875..5..6. to be paid 5 months hence, what is the present worth at 4½ *per cent.* ?
Ans. £859..3..4.

8. What is the present worth of £500. payable in 10 months, at 5 *per cent. per annum* ? Ans. £480.

9. How much ready money can I receive for a note of £75. due 15 months hence, at 5 *per cent.* ?
Ans. £70..11..9¼.

10. What will be the present worth of £150. payable at 3 four months ; *i. e.* one third at 4 months, one third at 8 months, and one third at 12 months, at 5 *per cent.* discount ?
Ans. £145..3..9¼.

11. Sold goods to the value of £575..10..0. to be paid at two 3 months, what must be discounted for present payment, at 5 *per cent.* ? Ans. £10..11..4¼.

12. What is is the present worth of £500. at 4 *per cent.* £100. being to be paid down, and the rest at two 6 months ?
Ans. £488..7..9.

EQUATION of PAYMENTS

IS when several sums are due at different times, to find a mean time for paying the whole debt : to do which, this is the common.

RULE. Multiply each term by its time, and divide the sum of the products by the whole debt, the quotient is accounted the mean time.

EXAMPLES.

Examples.

1. A owes B £200. whereof £40 is to be paid at 3 months, £60 at 5 months, and £100 at 10 months; at what time may the whole debt be paid together, without prejudice to either?

$$
\begin{array}{rcl}
£. & m. & \\
40 \times & 3 = & 120 \\
60 \times & 5 = & 300 \\
100 \times & 10 = & 1000 \\
& 2{\mid}00){\overline{1420}} &
\end{array}
$$

7 months $\frac{11}{16}$.

2. B owes C £800. whereof £200 is to be paid at 3 months, £100 at 4 months, £300 at 5 months, and £200 at 6 months; but they agreeing to make but one payment of the whole, I demand what that time must be? *Anf.* 4 months, 18 days.

3. I bought of K a quantity of goods to the value of £360. which was to have been paid as follows: £120 at 2 months, £200 at 4 months, and the reft at 5 months; but we afterwards agreed to have it paid at one mean time; the time is demanded. *Anf.* 3 months, 13 days.

4. A merchant bought goods to the value of £500. to pay £100 at the end of 4 months, £150 at the end of 6 months, and £250 at the end of 12 months; but afterwards they agreed to difcharge the debt at one payment; at what time was this payment made? *Anf.* 8 months, 12 days.

5. H is indebted to L a certain fum, which is to be paid at 6 different payments, that is $\frac{1}{4}$ at 2 months, $\frac{1}{8}$ at 3 months, $\frac{1}{8}$ at 4 months, $\frac{1}{4}$ at 5 months, $\frac{1}{8}$ at 6 months, and the reft at 7 months; but they agree that the whole fhall be paid at one equated time, what is that time? *Anf.* 4 months, one quarter.

6. A is indebted to B £120. whereof $\frac{1}{3}$ is to be paid at 3 months, $\frac{1}{4}$ at 6 months, and the reft at 9 months, what is the equated time of the whole payments? *Anf.* 5 months, 7 days.

BARTER

BARTER

IS the exchanging one commodity for another, and informs the traders so to proportion their goods, that neither may sustain loss.

RULE 1*st*. Find the value of that commodity whose quantity is given; then find what quantity of the other, at the rate proposed, you may have for the same money.

2*dly*. When one has goods at a certain price, *ready money*, but in Bartering advances it to something more, find what the other ought to rate his goods at, in proportion to that advance, and then proceed as before.

EXAMPLES.

1. What quantity of chocolate, at 4s. per lb. must be delivered in barter for 2 cwt. of tea, at 9s. per lb.?

```
     2 cwt.
      112
      ———
      224
        9
      ———
   4)2016  the value of the tea.
      ———
      504 lb. of chocolate.
```

2. A and B barter; A hath 20 cwt. of prunes, at 4d. per lb. ready money, but in barter will have 5d. per lb. and B hath hops worth 3 2s. per cwt. ready money; what ought B to rate his hops at in barter, and what quantity must be given for the 20 cwt. of prunes?

```
                    112  As 4 : 5 :: 32
         20                          5
   s.    ———                        ———
   40   2240                       4)160
   12      5
   ———   ———            cwt. qr. lb.  40 S.
   48|0)1120|0(23 : 1 : 9 6/48 Ans.
          96
          ———
          160
          144
          ———
           16 = 1 qr. 9 lb. 16/48
```

3. How

3. How much tea, at 9s. per lb. can I have in barter for 4 cwt. 2 qrs. of chocolate, at 4s. per lb.? *Ans.* 2 cwt.

4. Two merchants barter: A hath 20 cwt. of cheese, at 21s. 6d. per cwt. B hath 8 pieces of Irish cloth, at £3..14..0. per piece; I desire to know who must receive the difference, and how much?

Ans. B must receive of A £8..2..0.

5. A and B barter: A hath $8\frac{1}{4}$ lb. of pepper, at $13d\frac{1}{2}$. per lb. B hath ginger, at $15d\frac{1}{4}$. per lb. how much ginger must he deliver in barter for the pepper? *Ans.* 3 lb. 1 oz. $3\frac{5}{7}$.

6. How many dozen of candles, at 5s. 2d. per dozen, must be delivered in barter for 3 cwt. 2 qrs. 16 lb. of tallow, at 37s. 4d. per cwt.? *Ans.* 26 doz. 3 lb.

7. A hath 608 yards of cloth, worth 14s. per yard, for which B giveth him £125..12..0. in ready money, and 85 cwt. 2 qrs. 24 lb. of bees-wax. The question is, what did B reckon his bees-wax at per cwt.? *Ans.* £3..10..0.

8. A and B barter: A hath 320 dozen of candles, at 4s. 6d. per dozen; for which B giveth him £30. in money, and the rest in cotton, at 8d. per lb. I desire to know how much cotton B gave A besides the money.

Ans. 11 cwt. 1 qr.

9. If B hath cotton, at 1s. 2d. per lb. how much must he give A for 114 lb. of tobacco, at 6d. per lb.?

Ans. 48 lb. $\frac{12}{14}$.

10. C hath nutmegs worth 7s. 6d. per lb. ready money, but in barter will have 8s. per lb. and D hath leaf tobacco worth 9d. per lb. ready money, how much must D rate his tobacco at per lb. that his profit may be equivalent with C's?

Ans. $9d\frac{1}{2}. \frac{16}{90}.$

PROFIT AND LOSS

IS a rule that discovers what is got or lost in the buying or selling of goods, and instructs us to rise or fall the price, so as to gain or lose so much *per cent.* or otherwise.

The questions in this rule are performed by the Rule of Three.

Profit and Loſs.

EXAMPLES.

1. If a yard of cloth is bought for 11s. and ſold for 12s. 6d. what is the gain *per cent.*?

```
  As 11 : 1 ..6 :: 100
          12         20
          ──         ──
          18        2000
                      18
  12..6              ────
  11..0         11)36000
  ────
   1..6         12)3272

                2|0)27|2..8
```

Anſ. 13..12..8 $\frac{8}{11}$.

2. If 60 ells of holland coſt £18. what muſt 1 ell be ſold for to gain 8 *per cent.*?

```
  As 100 : 18 :: 108
         108
         ────        12×5=60
  1'00)19'44
          20      12)19.8.9¼
         ───
         8|80      5)1.12.4¼
          12         ──────
         ───         6..5¼
         9,60
           4
         ───
         2|40
```

Anſ. 6s. 5d¼.

3. If 1 lb. of tobacco coſt 16d. and is ſold for 20d. what is the gain *per cent.*? *Anſ.* £25.

4. If a parcel of cloth be ſold for £560. and at £12. *per cent.* gain, what was the prime coſt? *Anſ.* £500.

5. If a yard of cloth is bought for 13s. 4d. and ſold again for 16s. what is the gain *per cent.*? *Anſ.* £20.

6. If 112 lb. of iron coſt 27s. 6d. what muſt 1 cwt. be ſold for to gain 15 *per cent.*? *Anſ.* £1..11..7½.

7. If 375 yards of broad cloth be ſold for £490. and 20 *per cent.* profit, what did it coſt *per* yard? *Anſ.* £1..1..9¼.

8. Sold 1 cwt. of hops for £6..15..0. at the rate of 25 *per cent.* profit, what would have been the gain *per cent.* if I had ſold them for £8. per cwt.? *Anſ.* £48..2..11½.

9. If 90 ells of cambrick coſt £60. how muſt I ſell it *per* yard to gain £18. *per cent.*? *Anſ.* 12s. 7d.

10. A plumber ſold 10 fother of lead for £204..15..0. (the fother being 19 cwt. ½) and gained after the rate of £12..10..0. *per cent.* what did it coſt him *per* cwt.? *Anſ.* 18s. 8d.

11. Bought 436 yards of cloth, at the rate of 8s. 6d. *per* yard, and ſold it for 10s. 4d. per yard, what was the gain of the whole? *Anſ.* £39..19..4.

12. Paid £69. for one ton of ſteel, which is retailed at 6d. *per* lb. what is the profit or loſs by the ſale of 14 tons? *Anſ.* £182. loſs.

13. Bought

13. Bought 124 yards of linen for £32. how should the same be retailed *per* yard to gain £15. *per cent.* ?

Ans. 5s. 11d.$\frac{28}{124}$.

14. Bought 249 yards of cloth, at 3s. 4d. *per* yard, retailed the same at 4s. 2d. *per* yard, what is the profit in the whole, and how much *per cent.* ?

Ans. £10..7..6. *profit, and* 25 *per cent.*

FELLOWSHIP

IS when two or more join their stock and trade together, so to determine each person's particular share of the gain or loss, in proportion to his principal in the joint stock.

By this rule a bankrupt's estate may be divided amongst his creditors; as also legacies may be adjusted when there is a deficiency of assets or effects.

FELLOWSHIP *is either with or without* TIME.

FELLOWSHIP *without* TIME.

RULE. As the whole stock : is to the whole gain or loss : : so is each man's share in stock : to his share of the gain or loss.

PROOF. Add all the shares together, and the sum will be equal to the given gain or loss—but the surest way is, as the whole gain or loss : is to the whole stock : : so is each man's share of the gain or loss : to his share in stock.

EXAMPLES.

1. Two merchants trade together; A put into stock £20. and B £40. they gained £50. what is each person's share thereof?

$$20+40=60$$

As 60 : 50 : : 20   As 60 : 50 : : 40   33..6..8 B's *share*.
          20   40   16..13..4 A's.
       ─────   ─────   ─────────
      6|0)100|0   6|0)200|0   50..0..0.

76 Fellowship.   The TUTOR'S

2. Three merchants trade together, A, B, and C; A put in £20. B £30. and C £40. they gained £180. what is each man's part of the gain?   Anſ. A £40. B £60. C £80.

3. A, B, and C, enter into partnerſhip: A puts in £364. B £482. and C £500. and they gained £867. what is each man's ſhare in proportion to his ſtock?

Anſ. A £234..9..3¼—rem. 70.   B £310..9..5—rem. 248
      C £322..1..3½—rem. 1028.

4. Four merchants, B, C, D, and E, made a ſtock? B put in £227. C £349. D £115. and E £439. in trading they gained £428. I demand each merchant's ſhare of the gain?

Anſ. B £85..19..6¾—690.   C £132..3..9—120.
      D £43..11..1¾—250.   E £166..5..6¼—70.

5. Three perſons, D, E, and F, join in company; D's ſtock was £750. E's £460. and F's £500. and at the end of 12 months they gained £684. what is each man's particular ſhare of the gain?   Anſ. D £300. E £184. and F £200.

6. A merchant is indebted to B £275..14..0. to C £304..7..0. to D £152. and to E £104..6..0. but upon his deceaſe, his eſtate is found to be worth but £673..15..0. how muſt it be divided among his creditors?

Anſ. B's £222..15..2—6584.   C's £245..18..1½—15750.
      D's £122..16..2¼—12227, and E's £84..5..5—15620.

7. Four perſons trading together in a joint ſtock, of which A has ⅓, B ¼, C ⅕, and D ⅙, and at the end of 6 months they gain £100. what is each man's ſhare of the ſaid gain?

Anſ. A £35..1..9—48. B £26..6..3¾—36. C £21..1..0½.
      —120, and D £17..10..10½.—24.

8. Two perſons purchaſed an eſtate of £1700. per annum freehold, for £27200. when money was at 6 per cent. intereſt, and 4s. per pound land-tax, whereof D paid £15000. and E the reſt; ſome time after the intereſt of the money falling to 5 per cent. and 2s. per pound land-tax, they ſell the ſaid eſtate for 24 years purchaſe; I deſire to know each perſon's ſhare?   Anſ. D £22500. E £18300.

9. D, E, and F, join their ſtocks in trade; the amount of their ſtock is £647. and are in proportion as 4, 6 and 8 are to one another, and the amount of this gain is equal to D's ſtock; what is each man's ſtock and gain?

D's ſtock, £143..15..6½ ⅔ gain, £31..19..0.—184036
E's - - -   215..13..4   47..18..6—414080
F's - - - - 287..11..1¾ ⅛   63..18..0—506098

10. D,

10. D, E, and F, join stocks in trade: the amount of their stocks was £100. D's gain £3. E's £5. and F's £8. what was each man's stock?

Anſ. D's ſtock £18..15..0. E's £31..5..0. and F's £50.

FELLOWSHIP with TIME.

RULE. As the ſum of the products of each man's money and time : is to the whole gain or loſs : : ſo is each man's product : to his ſhare of the gain or loſs.

PROOF. As in Fellowſhip without Time.

EXAMPLES.

1. D and E enter into partnerſhip ; D puts in £40. for three months, and E £75. for four months, and they gained £70. What is each man's ſhare of the gain?

Anſ. D. £20. E. £50.

40×3=120   As 420 : 70 : : 120   As 420 : 70 : : 300
75×4=300   120   300
─────
420   42|0)840|0(20   42|0)2100|0(50

2. Three merchants join in company: D puts in ſtock £195..14..0. for 3 months, E £169..18..3. for 5 months, and F £59..14..10. for 11 months, they gained £364..18..0. What is each man's part of the gain?

Anſ. D's £102..6..4.—5008. E's £148..1..1½—48280¼ and F's £114..10..6¼—14707.

3. Three merchants join in company for 18 months: D put in £500. and at five months end took out £200; at 10 months end put in £300. and at the end of 14 months takes out £130. E puts in £400. and at the end of 3 months, £270 more; at 9 months he takes out £140 but puts in £100. at the end of 12 months, and withdraws £99 at the end of 15 months. F puts in £900. and at 6 months took out £200; at the end of 11 months put in £500. but takes out that and £100. more at the end of 13 months. They gained £200. I deſire to know each man's ſhare of the gain?

Anſ. D £50..7..6—21720. E £62..12..5¼—29859. and F £87..0..0¼—14167.

H 3   4. D,

4. D, E, and F, hold a piece of ground in common, for which they are to pay £36..10..6. D puts in 23 oxen 27 days; E 21 oxen 35 days; and F 16 oxen 23 days. What is each man to pay of the said rent?

Anf. D £13..3..1½—624. E £15..11..5—1688. and F £7..15..11—1136.

ALLIGATION.

ALLIGATION is either MEDIAL or ALTERNATE.

ALLIGATION MEDIAL.

IS when the price and quantities of feveral fimples are given to be mixed, to find the mean price of that mixture.

RULE. As the whole compofition : is to its total value :: fo is any part of the compofition : to its mean price.

PROOF. Find the value of the whole mixtue at the mean rate, and if it agrees with the total value of the feveral quantities at their refpective prices, the work is right.

EXAMPLES.

1. A farmer mixed 20 bufhels of wheat, at 5s. per bufhel, and 36 bufhels of rye, at 3s. per bufhel, with 40 bufhels of barley at 2s. per bufhel. I defire to know the worth of a bufhel of this mixture.

20 × 5 = 100
36 × 3 = 108
40 × 2 = 80
――― ―――
96   288

As 96 : 288 :: 1 : 3.

Anf. 3s.

2. A vintner mingles 15 gallons of Canary, at 8s. per gallon, with 20 gallons, at 7s. 4d. per gallon, 10 gallons of fherry at 6s. 8d. per gallon, and 24 gallons of white wine, at 4s. per gallon. What is the worth of a gallon of this mixture? Anf. 6s. 2d¼. 45/69.

3. A grocer mingled 4 cwt. of fugar, at 56s. per cwt. 7 cwt. at 43s. per cwt. and 5 cwt. at 37s. per cwt. I demand the price of 2 cwt. of this mixture? Anf. £4..8..9.

4. A

4. A maltster mingles 30 quarters of brown malt, at 28s. per quarter, with 46 quarters of pale, at 30s. per quarter, and 24 quarters of high-dried ditto, at 25s. per quarter. What is the value of 8 bushels of this mixture?
Ans. £1..8..2¼. $\frac{6}{10}$.

5. If I mix 27 bushels of wheat, at 5s. 6d. per bushel, with the same quantity of rye, at 4s. per bushel, and 14 bushels of barley at 2s. 8d. per bushel, what is the worth of a bushel of this mixture? *Ans.* 4s. 3d¼. $\frac{28}{68}$.

6. A grocer mingled 3 cwt. of sugar, at 56s. per cwt. 6 cwt. at £1..17..4. per cwt. and 3 cwt. at £3..14..8 per cwt. What is 1 cwt. of this mixture worth?
Ans. £2..11..4.

7. A mealman has flour of several sorts, and would mix 3 bushels, at 3s. 5d. per bushel, 4 bushels, at 5s. 6d. per bushel, and 5 bushels at 4s. 8d. per bushel. What is the worth of a bushel of this mixture? *Ans.* 4s. 7d½. $\frac{4}{12}$.

8. A vintner mixes 20 gallons of Port, at 5s. 4d. per gallon, with 12 gallons of white wine, at 5s. per gallon, 30 gallons of Lisbon, at 6s. per gallon, and 20 gallons of mountain, at 4s. 6d. per gallon. What is a gallon of this mixture worth? *Ans.* 5s. 3d¼. $\frac{50}{12}$.

9. A farmer mingled 20 bushels of wheat, at 5s. per bushel, and 36 bushels of rye, at 3s. per bushel, with 40 bushels of barley, at 2s. per bushel. I desire to know the worth of a bushel of this mixture? *Ans.* 3s.

10. A person mixing a quantity of oats, at 2s. 6d. per bushel, with the like quantity of beans, at 4s. 6d. per bushel, would be glad to know the price of one bushel of that mixture? *Ans.* 3s. 6d.

11. A refiner having 12 lb. of silver bullion, of 6 oz. fine, would melt it with 8 lb. of 7 oz. fine, and 10 lb. of 8 oz. fine, required the fineness of 1 lb. of that mixture?
Ans. 6 oz. 18 dwt. 16 gr.

12. If with 40 bushels of corn, at 4s. per bushel, there are mixed 10 bushels, at 6s. per bushel, 30 bushels, at 5s. per bushel, and 20 bushels, at 3s. per bushel, what will 10 bushels of that mixture be worth? *Ans.* £2..3..0.

13. A tobacconist would mix 50 lb. of tobacco, at 11d. per lb. with 30 lb. at 14d. per lb. 25 lb. at 22d. per lb. and 37 lb. at 2s. per lb. What will 1 lb. of this mixture be worth? *Ans.* 16d¼. $\frac{118}{142}$.

ALLIGA-

80   Alligation.   The Tutor's

ALLIGATION ALTERNATE

Is when the price of several things are given, to find such quantities of them to make a mixture, that may bear a price propounded.

In ordering the rates and given price, observe,

1. Place them one under the other, and the propounded price or mean rate at the left hand of them, thus

$$22\begin{cases}18\\20\\34\\28\end{cases}\qquad\begin{matrix}2\\6\\4\\2\end{matrix}$$

2. Link the several rates together, by 2 and 2, always observing to join a greater and a less than the mean.

3. Against each extreme place the difference of the mean and its yoke-fellow.

When the prices of the several simples and the mean rate are given without any quantity, to find how much of each simple is required to compose the mixture.

RULE. Take the difference between each price and the mean rate, and set them alternately, they will be the answer required.

PROOF. By Alligation Medial.

EXAMPLES.

1. A vintner would mix four sorts of wines together, of 18d. 20d. 24d. and 28d. per quart, what quantity of each must he take to sell the mixture at 22d. per quart?

```
       Answer.              Proof.  |        Or thus.          Proof.
    18────┐  2 of 18d. =  36d.  |    18────┐  6 of 18d. =  108d.
 22 20──┐ │  6 of 20d. = 120    | 22 20──┐ │  2 of 20d. =   40
    24──┘ │  4 of 24d. =  96    |    24──┘ │  2 of 24d. =   48
    28────┘  2 of 28d. =  56    |    28────┘  4 of 28d. =  112
             ──                 ────         ──                ────
             14                )308          14               )308
                               ────                           ────
                                22d.                           22d.
```

Note. Questions in this Rule admit of a great variety of answers, according to the manner of linking them.

2. A grocer would mix sugar, at 4d. 6d. and 10d. per lb. so as to sell the compound for 8d. per lb. What quantity of each must he take? *Ans.* 2 lb. at 4d. 2 lb. at 6d. and 6lb. at 10d.

3. I desire

3. I desire to know how much tea, at 16s. 14s. 9s. and 8s. per lb. will compose a mixture worth 10s. per lb.?
     Ans. 1 lb. at 16s. 2 lb. at 14s. 6 lb. at 9s. and 4 lb. at 8s.
4. A farmer would mix as much barley at 3s. 6d. per bushel, rye at 4s. per bushel, and oats at 2s. per bushel, as to make a mixture worth 2s. 6d. per bushel. How much is that of each sort? Ans. 6 of barley, 6 of rye, and 30 of oats.
5. A grocer would mix raisins of the sun at 7d. per lb. with Malaga's, at 6d. and Smyrna's at 4d. per lb. I desire to know what quantity of each sort he must take to sell them at 5d. per lb.? Ans. 1 lb. of raisins of the sun, 1 lb. of Malaga's, and 3 lb. of Smyrna's.
6. A tobacconist would mix tobacco of 2s. 1s. 6d. and 1s. 3d. per lb. so as the compound may bear a price of 1s. 8d. per lb. What quantity of each sort must he take?
     Ans. 7 lb. at 2s. 4 lb. at 1s. 6d. and 4 lb. at 1s. 3d.

ALTERNATION PARTIAL

IS when the prices of all the simples, the quantity of but one of them, and the mean rate, are given, to find the several quantities of the rest in proportion to that given.

RULE. Take the difference between each price, and the mean rate, as before. Then,

  As the difference of that simple, whose quantity is given : is to the rest of the differences severally : : so is the quantity given : to the several quantities required.

EXAMPLES.

1. A tobacconist being determined to mix 20 lb. of tobacco, at 15d. per lb. with others at 16d. per lb. 18d. per lb. and 22d. per lb. how many pounds of each sort must he take to make one pound of that mixture worth 17d.?

```
        Answer.         Proof.
    15 ─────┐  5    20 lb. at 15d.=300d.   As 5 : 1 :: 20 : 4
  16 16 ──┐ │  1     4 lb. at 16d.= 64d.   As 5 : 1 :: 20 : 4
     18 ──┘ │  1     4 lb. at 18d.= 72d.   As 5 : 2 :: 20 : 8
     22 ────┘  1     2 lb. at 22d.=176d.

        Ans. 36 lb.  :   612d. :: 1 lb. : 17d.
```

82   *Alternation Total.*   *The* TUTOR's

2. A farmer would mix 20 bushels of wheat at 60*d.* per bushel, with rye at 36*d.* barley at 24*d.* and oats at 18*d.* per bushel. How much must he take of each sort, to make the composition worth 32*d.* per bushel?

Anf. 20 bushels of wheat, 35 bushels of rye, 70 bushels of barley, and 10 bushels of oats.

3. A person is desirous of mixing wheat at 4*s.* per bushel, rye at 3*s.* per bushel, and barley at 2*s.* per bushel, with 12 bushels of oats, at 18*d.* per bushel. I would be glad to know how many bushels of each sort he must take to make the composition worth 3*s.* 6*d.* per bushel?

Anf. 96 bushels of wheat, 12 bushels of rye, 12 of barley, and 12 of oats.

4. A distiller would mix 40 gallons of French brandy, at 12*s.* per gallon, with English at 7*s.* and spirits at 4*s.* per gallon. What quantity of each sort must he take, to afford it for 8*s.* per gallon?

Anf. 40 gallons French, 32 English, and 32 spirits.

5. A grocer would mix teas of 12*s.* 10*s.* and 6*s.* with 20 lb. at 4*s.* per lb. How much of each sort must he take to make the composition worth 8*s.* per lb.?

Anf. 20 lb. at 4*s.* 10 lb. at 6*s.* 10 lb. at 10*s.* and 20 lb. at 12*s.*

6. A wine merchant is desirous of mixing 18 gallons of Canary, at 6*s.* 9*d.* per gallon, with Malaga at 7*s.* 6*d.* per gallon; sherry at 5*s.* per gallon; and white wine, at 4*s.* 3*d.* per gallon. How much of each sort must he take, that the mixture may be sold for 6*s.* per gallon?

Anf. 18 gallons of Canary, 31⅖ of Malaga, 13⅖ of sherry, and 27 of white wine.

ALTERNATION TOTAL

Is when the price of each simple, the quantity to be compounded, and the mean rate are given, to find how much of each sort will make that quantity.

RULE. Take the difference between each price, and the mean rate, as before; then,

As the sum of the difference : is to each particular difference : : so is the quantity given : to the quantity required.

EXAMPLES.

EXAMPLES.

1. A grocer has four forts of sugar, viz. 12d. 10d. 6d. and 4d. per lb. and would make a composition of 144 lb. worth 8d. per lb. I desire to know what quantity of each he must take?

```
              Answer.        Proof.
       12 ┐  4 - - 48 at 12d. 576    As 12 :   : : 144 : 48
    8  10 ┐│ 2 - - 24 at 10d. 240    As 12 : 2 : : 144 : 24
        6 ┘│ 2 - - 24 at  6d. 144
        4 ┘  4 - - 48 at  4d. 142
              ─          ───
              12          144       (1152(8d.
```

2. A druggist having four forts of tea, of 5s. 6s. 8s. and 9s. per lb. would have a composition of 87 lb. worth 7s. per lb. What quantity must there be of each?
Anf. 14½ lb. of 5s. 29 lb. 6s. 29 lb. of 8s. and 14½ of 9s.

3. A vintner had four forts of wine, viz. white wine, at 4s. per gallon; Flemish, at 6s. per gallon; Malaga, at 8s. per gallon; and Canary, at 10s. per gallon: would make a mixture of 60 gallons, to be worth 5s. per gallon. What quantity of each must he take?
Anf. 45 gallons of white wine, 5 gallons of Flemish, 5 gallons of Malaga, and 5 gallons of Canary.

4. A grocer having four forts of currants, of 11d. 9d. 6d. and 4d. per lb. is desirous of making a composition of 240 lb. worth 8d. per lb. How much of each must he take?
Anf. 96 lb. at 11d. 48 lb. at 9d. 24 lb. at 6d. and 72 lb. at 4d.

5. A silversmith hath four forts of gold, viz. of 24 carats fine, of 22, 20, and 15 carats fine; would mix as much of each fort together, so as to have 42 oz. of 17 carats fine. How much must he take of each?
Anf. 4 of 24, 4 of 22, 4 of 20, and 30 of 15 carats fine.

6. A druggist having some drugs of 8s. 5s. and 4s. per lb. made them into two parcels; one of 28 lb. at 6s. per lb. the other of 42 lb. at 7s. per lb. How much of every fort did he take for each parcel?

Anf. 12 lb. of 8s.   Anf. 30 lb. of 8s.
     8 lb. of 5s.   6 lb. of 5s.
     8 lb. of 4s.   6 lb. of 4s.
    ──   ──
    28 lb. at 6s. per lb.   42 lb. at 7s. per lb.

POSITION,

POSITION, or the RULE OF FALSE,

IS a rule that, by false or supposed numbers, taken at pleasure, discovers the true one required. It is divided into two parts; SINGLE and DOUBLE.

SINGLE POSITION

Is, by using one supposed number, and working with it as the true one, you find the real number required, by the following

RULE. As the total of the errors : to the true total : : so is the supposed number : to the true one required.

PROOF. Add the several parts of the sum together, and, if it agrees with the sum, it is right.

EXAMPLES.

1. A schoolmaster being asked how many scholars he had, said, if I had as many, half as many, and one quarter as many more, I should have 88. How many had he? *Ans.* 32.

Suppose he had - 40	As 110 : 88 : : 40	32
as many - - 40	40	32
half as many 20	———	16
¼ as many - 10	110)3520(32	8
———		———
110		88 *proof.*

2. A person having about him a certain number of Portugal pieces, said, if the third, fourth, and sixth of them were added together, they would make 54. I desire to know how many he had? *Ans.* 72.

3. A gentleman bought a chaise, horse and harness, for £60. the horse came to twice the price of the harness, and the chaise to twice the price of the horse and harness. What did he give for each?
Ans. Horse £13..6..8. Harness £6..13..4. Chaise £40.

4. A, B and C being determined to buy a quantity of goods, which would cost them £120. agreed amongst themselves that B should have a third part more than A, and C a fourth part more than B. I desire to know what each man must pay? *Ans.* A £30. B £40. C £50.

5. A man

ASSISTANT.   *Position, or the Rule of False.*   85

5. A man overtaking a maid driving a flock of geese, said to her, How do you do, sweetheart? where are you going with these 30 geese? No, Sir, said she, I have not 30; but if I had as many more, half as many more, and 5 geese besides, I should have 30. How many had she?
Ans. 10.

6. A person delivered to another a sum of money, unknown, to receive interest for the same, at 6 *per cent. per annum*, simple interest, and at the end of ten years received for principal and interest £300. What was the sum lent?
Ans. £187..10..0.

DOUBLE POSITION

Is by making use of two supposed numbers, and if both prove false, (as it generally happens) they are with their errors to be thus ordered.

RULE 1. Place each error against its respective position.
2. Multiply them cross-ways.
3. If the errors are alike, *i. e.* both greater, or both less than the given number, take their difference for a divisor, and the difference of their products for a dividend. But if unlike, take their sum for a divisor, and the sum of their products for a dividend, the quotient will be the answer.

EXAMPLES.

1. A, B, and C, would divide £200. between them, so that B may have £6. more than A, and C £8. more than B. How much must each have?

```
Suppose A had 40        Then suppose A had 50
  then   B had 46         then   B must have 56
  and    C  -- 54         and    C  - - - - 64
         ---                            ---
         140 too little by 60.         170 too little by 30.
    sup. errors.
       40 X 60
       50   30                    60           60 A
       ---                        30           66 B
       3000 1200                  ---          74 C
            1200                  30 divisor.  ---
       3|0)180|0                               200 proof.
          60 Ans. for A.
```

2. A man had 2 silver cups, of unequal weight, having one cover to both, of 5 oz. now if the cover is put on the lesser cup, it will double the weight of the greater cup; and set on the greater cup, it will be thrice as heavy as the lesser cup. What is the weight of each cup?

Ans. 3 ounces lesser; 4 greater.

3. A, B, and C, playing at hazard together, the money staked was 196 guineas; but disagreeing, each seized as many as he could: A got a certain quantity; B as many as A, and 16 more; and C the 6th part of both their sums. How many had each? *Ans. A 76, B 92, and C 28.*

4. A gentleman bought a house with a garden, and a horse in the stable, for £500. now he paid 4 times the price of the horse for the garden, and 5 times the price of the garden for the house. What was the value of the house, garden, and horse, separately?

Ans. horse £20. garden 80, house 400.

5. Three persons discoursed concerning their ages; says H, I am 30 years of age; says K, I am as old as H; and $\frac{1}{4}$ of L; and says L, I am as old as you both.. What was the age of each person?

Ans. H 30; K 50; and L 80.

6. D, E, and F, playing at cards, staked 324 crowns; but disputing about the tricks, each man took as many as he could: D got a certain number; E as many as D, and 15 more; and F got a 5th part of both their sums added together. How many did each get?

Ans. D $127\frac{1}{2}$; E $142\frac{1}{2}$; and F 54.

7. A, stealing apples was taken by B, and to appease him gave him half of what he had, and B gives him back 10; going farther he meets C, who took from him half of what he had left, and gives him back 4: after that, meeting with D, he gives him half of what he had, and he returns him back 1; at last getting safe away, he finds he had 13 left. How many had he at first? *Ans. 60.*

8. A gentleman going into a garden, meets with some ladies, and says to them, Good morning to you 10 fair maids. Sir, you mistake, answered one of them, we are not 10; but if we were twice as many more as we are, we should be as many above 10 as we are now under. How many were they? *Ans. 5.*

EXCHANGE

EXCHANGE

IS the receiving money in one country for the same value paid in another.

The Par of Exchange is always fixed and certain, it being the intrinsic value of foreign money, compared with sterling; but the Course of Exchange rises and falls, upon various occasions.

I. FRANCE.

They keep their accounts at Paris, Lyons, and Rouen, in livres, sols, and deniers, and exchange by the crown, = 4s. 6d. at par.

NOTE. 12 *deniers make* 1 *sol.*
20 *sols* - - - 1 *Livre.*
3 *livres* - - - 1 *crown.*

To change French into Sterling.

RULE. As 1 crown : is to the given rate : : so is the French sum : to the sterling required.

To change Sterling into French.

RULE. As the rate of exchange : is to 1 crown : : so is the sterling sum : to the French required.

EXAMPLES.

1. How many crowns must be paid at Paris, to receive in London £180. exchange, at 4s. 6d. per crown?

```
    d.   c.   £.
As 54 : 1 :: 180 :
              240
              ————crowns.
        54)43200(800
           432
           ———
           ...
```

2. A merchant at Paris remits to his correspondent in London 800 crowns, at 4s. 6d. each; what is the value in sterling?

```
   cr.  d.   cr.
    1 : 54 :: 800 :
               54
              ————
           12)43200
              ————
            2|0)360|0
              ————
              £180.
```

3. How much sterling must be paid in London, to receive in Paris 758 crowns, exchange at 56d. per crown?

Ans. £176..17..4.

4. A

4. A merchant in London remits £176..17..4. to his correspondent at Paris ? what is the value of French crowns, at 56d. per crown ? *Anf.* 758.

5. Change 725 crowns, 17 fols, 7 deniers, at 54d. ½ per crown, into sterling, what is the sum ? *Anf.* £164..14..0¼.

6. Change £164..14..0¼. sterling into French crowns, exchange at 54d. ½ per crown ?
Anf. 725 crowns, 17 fols, 7 deniers.

II. SPAIN.

They keep their accounts at Madrid, Cadiz, and Seville, in dollars, rials, and maravedies, and exchange by the piece of eight = 4s. 6d. at par.

NOTE. 34 maravedies make 1 rial.
        8 rials - - - - - 1 piaftre, or piece of eight.
       10 rials - - - - - 1 dollar.
RULE. As with France

EXAMPLES.

7. A merchant at Cadiz remits to London 2547 pieces of eight, at 56d. per piece, how much sterling is the sum ?
Anf. £594..6..0.

8. How many pieces of eight, at 56d. each, will answer a bill of £594..6..0. sterling ? *Anf.* 2547.

9. If I pay a bill here of £2500. what Spanish money may I draw my bill for at Madrid, exchange at 57d. ½ per piece of eight ? *Anf.* 10434 pieces of eight, 6 rials, 8 mar.

III. ITALY.

They keep their accounts at Genoa and Leghorn, in livres, fols, and deniers, and exchange by the piece of eight, or dollars = 4s. 6d. at par.

NOTE. 12 deniers make 1 fol.
      20 fols - - - - 1 livre.
      5 livres - - - - 1 piece of eight at Genoa.
      6 livres - - - - 1 piece of eight at Leghorn.

N. B. The exchange at Florence is by ducatoons; the exchange at Venice by ducats.

NOTE. 6 folidi make 1 grofs.
      24 grofs - - 1 ducat.
RULE. The fame as before.

10. How

10. How much sterling money may a person receive in London, if he pays in Genoa 976 dollars, at 53*d*. per dollar? *Ans.* £215..10.8.

11. A merchant remitted £215..10..8. sterling to Leghorn, how many dollars will he receive there, the exchange being at 53*d*. per dollar? *Ans.* 976.

12. A factor hath sold goods at Florence, for 250 ducatoons, at 54*d*. each, what is the value in pounds sterling? *Ans.* £56..5..—.

13. A bill of £56..5..—. is remitted to Florence to be paid in ducatoons, at 54*d*. each, how many will be received? *Ans.* 250.

14. If 275 ducats, at 4*s*. 5*d*. each, be remitted from Venice to London, what is the value in pounds sterling? *Ans.* £60..14..7.

15. A gentleman travelling, would exchange £60..14..7. sterling for Venice ducats, at 4*s*. 5*d*. each, how many must he receive? *Ans.* 275.

IV. PORTUGAL.

They keep their accounts at Oporto and Lisbon, in *reas*, and exchange on the *milrea* = 6*s*. 8*d*. ½ at par.

NOTE. 1000 *reas* make 1 *milrea*.

RULE. The same as with France.

EXAMPLES.

16. A gentleman being desirous to remit to his correspondent in London 2750 milreas, exchange at 6*s*. 5*d*. per milrea, how much sterling will he be creditor for in London? *Ans.* £882..5..10.

17. If a bill be drawn from London of £882..5..10. sterling, how many milreas, at 6*s*. 5*d*. each, is equal in value to the said sum? *Ans.* 2750.

18. A merchant at Oporto remits to London 4366 milreas, and 183 reas, at 5*s*. 5*d*. ⅝ exchange per milrea, how much sterling must be paid in London for this remittance? *Ans.* £1193..17..6¼.

19. If I pay a bill at London of £1193..17..6¼. what must I draw for on my correspondent at Lisbon, exchange at 5*s*. 5*d*. ⅝ per milrea? *Ans.* 4366 milreas, 183 reas.

V. HOLLAND,

V. HOLLAND, FLANDERS, and GERMANY.

They keep their accounts at Antwerp, Amsterdam, Brussels, Rotterdam, and Hamburgh; some in pounds, shillings, and pence, as in England: others in guilders, stivers, and pennings; and exchange with us in our pound, at 33s. 4d. Flemish, at par.

NOTE. 8 *pennings* - make 1 *groat*.
2 *groats* or 16 *pennings* 1 *stiver*.
20 *stivers* - - - - - 1 *guilder or florin*.

ALSO

12 *groats* or 6 *stivers* - make 1 *schelling*.
20 *schellings* or 6 *guilders* - 1 *pound*.

To change Flemish into Sterling.

RULE. As the given rate : is to 1 pound :: so is the Flemish sum : to the sterling required.

To change Sterling into Flemish.

RULE. As £1 sterling : is to the given rate :: so is the sterling given : to the Flemish sought.

EXAMPLES.

20. Remitted from London to Amsterdam a bill of £754..10..—. sterling, how many pounds Flemish is the sum, the exchange at 33s. 6d. Flemish *per* pound sterling?
Ans. £1263..15..9. *Flemish*

21. A merchant at Rotterdam remits £1263..15..9. Flemish to be paid in London, how much sterling money must he draw for, the exchange being at 33s. 6d. Flemish *per* pound sterling? Ans. £754..10..—.

22. If I pay in London £852..12..6. sterling, how many guilders must I draw for at Amsterdam, exchange at 34 schel. 4½ groats Flemish *per* pound sterling?
Ans. 8792 guild. 13 stiv. 14½ *pennings*.

23. What must I draw for at London, if I pay at Amsterdam 8792 guild. 13 stiv. 14½ pennings; exchange at 34 schel. 4½ groats *per* pound sterling? Ans. £852..12..6.

To

To convert Bank Money into current, and the contrary.

NOTE. *The* Bank *money is worth more than the* Current. *The difference between the one and the other is called* agio, *and is generally from* 3 *to* 6 *per cent. in favour of the* Bank.

To change Bank *into* Current *money.*

RULE. As 100 guilders Bank : is to 100 with the agio added : : so is the Bank given : to the Current required.

To change Current *money into* Bank.

RULE. As 100 with the agio added : is to 100 Bank : : so is the Current money given : to the Bank required.

24. Change 794 guilders, 15 stivers, current money, into Bank florins, agio 4¾ *per cent.*
Ans. 751 *guilders,* 8 *stivers,* 11 *pennings.*

25. Change 761 guilders, 9 stivers Bank, into Current money, agio 4¾ *per cent.*
Ans. 794 *guilders,* 15 *stivers,* 4 *pennings.*

VI. IRELAND.

26. A gentleman remits to Ireland £575..15..—. sterling, what will he receive there, the exchange being at 10 *per cent.*? *Ans.* £633..6..6.

27. What must be paid in London for a remittance of £633..6..6. Irish, exchange at 10 *per cent.*?
Ans. £575..15..—.

COMPARISON *of* WEIGHTS *and* MEASURES.

EXAMPLES.

1. If 50 Dutch pence be worth 65 French pence, how many Dutch pence are equal to 350 French pence ? *Ans.* 269 3/13.

2. If 12 yards at London make 8 ells at Paris, how many ells at Paris will make 64 yards at London? *Ans.* 42 8/12.

3. If 30 lb. at London make 28 lb. at Amsterdam, how many lb. at London will be equal to 350 lb. at Amsterdam?
Ans. 375.

4. If 95 lb. Flemish make 100 lb. English, how many lb. English are equal to 275 lb. Flemish? *Ans.* 289 45/95.

CONJOINED

CONJOINED PROPORTION

IS when the coin, weight, or measures of several countries are compared in the same question; or it is linking together a variety of proportions.

When it is required to find how many of the first sort of coin, weight, or measure, mentioned in the question, are equal to a given quantity of the last.

RULE. Place the numbers alternately, beginning at the left-hand, and let the last number stand on the left-hand; then multiply the first row continually for a dividend, and the second for a divisor.

PROOF. By as many single Rules of Three as the question requires.

EXAMPLES.

1. If 20 lb. at London make 23 lb. at Antwerp, and 155 lb. at Antwerp, make 180 lb. at Leghorn, how many lb. at London are equal to 72 lb. at Leghorn?

Left.   Right.
20   23 $20 \times 155 \times 72$ 223200
155   180 $23 \times 180 = 4140$) 223200 ($53 \frac{372}{414}$.
72

2. If 12 lb. at London make 10 lb. at Amsterdam, 100 lb. at Amsterdam 120 lb. at Thoulouse, how many lb. at London is equal to 40 lb. at Thoulouse?   *Anf.* 40.

3. If 140 braces at Venice are equal to 156 braces at Leghorn, and 7 braces at Leghorn equal to 4 ells English, how many braces at Venice are equal to 16 ells English?

Anf. $25 \frac{80}{224}$.

4. If 40 lb. at London make 36 lb. at Amsterdam, and 90 lb. at Amsterdam make 116 lb. at Dantzick, how many lb. at London are equal to 130 lb. at Dantzick?

Anf. $112 \frac{288}{4176}$.

When it is required to find how many of the last sort of coin, weight, or measure, mentioned in the question, is equal to a quantity of the first.

RULE. Place the numbers alternately, beginning at the left-hand, and let the last number stand on the right-hand; then multiply the first row for a divisor, and the second for a dividend.

EXAMPLES.

EXAMPLES.

5. If 12 lb. at London make 10 lb. at Amsterdam, 100 lb. at Amsterdam 120 lb. at Thoulouse, how many lb. at Thoulouse are equal to 40 lb. at London ?   *Ans.* 40 lb.

6. If 40 lb. at London make 36 lb. at Amsterdam, and 90 lb. at Amsterdam 116 lb. at Dantzick, how many lb. at Dantzick are equal to 122 lb. at London ? *Ans.* $141\frac{1872}{3100}$.

PROGRESSION

Consists of Two Parts,

ARITHMETICAL AND GEOMETRICAL.

ARITHMETICAL PROGRESSION

IS when the rank of numbers increase or decrease regularly by the continual adding or subtracting of the equal numbers: As 1, 2, 3, 4, 5, 6, are in Arithmetical Progression by the continual increasing or adding of one; 11, 9, 7, 5, 3, 1, by the continual decreasing or subtracting of two.

NOTE. *When any even number of terms differ by Arithmetical Progression, the sum of the two extremes will be equal to the two middle numbers, or any two means equally distant from the extremes:* as 2, 4, 6, 8, 10, 12, where $6 + 8$, the two middle numbers, are $= 12 + 2$, the two extremes, and $= 10, + 4$, the two means, $= 14$.

When the number of terms are odd, *the double of* the middle term *will be equal to the two extremes, or if any two means equally distant from the* middle term; as 1, 2, 3, 4, 5, *where* the double of $3 = 5 + 1 = 2 + 4 = 6$.

In Arithmetical Progression five things are to be observed, viz.

1. The first term ; *better expressed thus,* F.
2. The last term -   -   -   -   L.
3. The number of terms -   -   N.
4. The equal difference -   -   D.
5. The sum of all the terms -   -   S.

Any three of which being given, the other two may be found.

The

The first, second, and third terms given to find the fifth.

RULE. Multiply the sum of the two extremes by half the number of terms, or multiply half the sum of the two extremes by the whole number of terms, the product is the total of all the terms: *or thus,*

I. F. L. N. are given to find S.

$$F + L \times \frac{N}{2} = S.$$

EXAMPLES.

1. How many strokes does the hammer of a clock strike in 12 hours? *Ans.* 78.

$$12 + 1 = 13, \text{ then } 13 \times 6 = 78.$$

2. A man buys 17 yards of cloth, and gave for the first yard 2s. and for the last 10s. what did the 17 yards amount to? *Ans.* £5..2..—.

3. If 100 eggs were placed in a right line, exactly a yard asunder from one another, and the first a yard from a basket, what length of ground does that man go who gathers up these 100 eggs singly, returning with every egg to the basket to put it in? *Ans.* 5 *miles,* 1300 *yards.*

The first, second, and third terms given to find the fourth.

RULE. From the second subtract the first, the remainder divided by the third less one, gives the fourth: *or thus,*

II. F. L. N. are given to find D.

$$\frac{L. - F.}{N. - 1} = D.$$

EXAMPLES.

4. A man had eight sons, the youngest was 4 years old, and the eldest 32, they increase in Arithmetical Progression, what was the common difference of their ages? *Ans.* 4.

$$32 - 4 = 28, \text{ then } 28 \div 8 - 1 = 4 \text{ common difference.}$$

5. A man is to travel from London to a certain place in 12 days, and to go but 3 miles the first day, increasing every day by an equal excess, so that the last day's journey may be 58 miles, what is the daily increase, and how many miles distant is that place from London? *Ans.* 5 *daily increase.*

Therefore, as three miles is the first day's journey,

$3 + 5 = 8$ the second day.
$8 + 5 = 13$ the third day, &c.

The whole distance is 366 miles.

Or thus, $58 + 3 = 61$ then $61 \times 6 = 366$.

The first, second, and fourth terms given, to find the third.

RULE. From the second subtract the first, the remainder divide by the fourth, and to the quotient add 1, gives the third : *or thus,*

III. F. L. D. are given to find N.

$$\frac{L-F}{D}+1=N.$$

EXAMPLES.

6. A person travelling into the country, went 3 miles the first day, and increased every day by 5 miles, till at last he went 58 miles in one day, how many days did he travel?
Anf. 12.

58—3=55, then 55÷5=11+1=12 *the number of days.*

7. A man being asked how many sons he had, said, that the youngest was 4 years old, and the oldest 32, and that he increased one in his family every 4 years, how many had he?
Anf. 8.

The second, third, and fourth terms given, to find the first.

RULE. Multiply the fourth by the third made less by 1, the product subtracted from the second gives the first : *or thus,*

IV. L. N. D. are given to find F.

$$L-\overline{D\times N-1}=F.$$

EXAMPLES.

8. A man in 10 days went from London to a certain town in the country, every day's journey increasing the former by 4, and the last he went was 46 miles, what was the first?
Anf. 10 *miles.*

4×10—1=36, then 46—36=10, *the first day's journey.*

9. A man takes out of his pocket at 8 several times, so many different numbers of shillings, every one exceeding the former by 6, the last 46, what was the first? *Anf.* 4.

The fourth, third, and fifth given, to find the first.

RULE. Divide, the fifth by the third, and from the quotient subtract half the product of the fourth multiplied by the third less 1 gives the first : *or thus,*

V. N. D. S. are given to find F.

$$\frac{S}{N}-\frac{D\times N-1}{2}=F$$

EXAMPLES.

Examples.

10. A man is to receive £360. at 12 several payments, each to exceed the former by £4. and is willing to bestow the first payment on any one that can tell him what it is. What will that person have for his pains? Ans. £8.

$$360 \div 12 = 30, \text{ then } 30 - \frac{4 \times 12 - 1}{2} = 8 \text{ the first payment.}$$

The first, third, and fourth given to find the second.

RULE. Subtract the fourth from the product of the third, multiplied by the fourth, that remainder added to the first gives the second: *or thus*,

VI. F. N. D. are given to find L.
$$ND - D + F = L.$$

Examples.

11. What is the last number of an Arithmetical Progression, beginning at 6, and continuing by the increase of 8 to 20 places? Ans. 158.

$$20 \times 8 - 8 = 152, \text{ then } 152 + 6 = 158 \text{ the last number.}$$

GEOMETRICAL PROGRESSION

IS the increasing or decreasing of any rank of numbers by some common ratio; that is, by the continual multiplication or division of some equal number: as 2, 4, 8, 16, increase by the multiplier 2, and 16, 8, 4, 2, decrease by the divisor 2.

NOTE. When any number of terms in continued, in geometrical progression, the product of the two extremes will be equal to any two means, *equally distant from the* extremes: as 2, 4, 8, 16, 32, 64, *where* 64×2 *are* $= 4 \times 32$, *and* $8 \times 16 = 128$.

When the number of terms are odd, the middle term *multiplied into itself will be equal to the two extremes, or any two means, equally distant from the mean*: as 2, 4, 8, 16, 32, where $2 \times 32 = 4 \times 16 = 8 \times 8 = 64$.

In Geometrical Progression the same five things are to be observed as in Arithmetical, viz.

1. The first term.
2. The last term.
3. The number of terms.
4. The equal difference or ratio.
5. The sum of all the terms.

NOTE. *As the last term in a long series of numbers is very tedious to come at, by continual multiplication; therefore, for the readier finding it out, there is a series of numbers made use of in* Arithmetical Proportion, *called* indices, *beginning with an* unit, *whose common difference is one; whatever number of indices you make use of, set as many numbers (in such* geometrical proportion *as is given in the question) under them.*

As 1, 2, 3, 4, 5, 6.   Indices.
    2, 4, 8, 16, 32, 64. Numbers in geometrical proportion.

But if *the* first term *in* geometrical proportion *be different from the* ratio, *the* indices *must begin with a* cypher.

As 0, 1, 2, 3, 4, 5, 6. Indices.
    1, 2, 4, 8, 16, 32, 64. Numbers in geometrical proportion.

When the indices *begin with a cypher, the sum of the* indices *made choice of must always be one less than the number of terms given in the question; for* 1 *in the* indices *is over the second term, and two over the third,* &c.

Add any two of the indices together, and that sum will agree with the product of their respective terms:
As in the first table of indices $2 + 5 = 7$
Geometrical proportion $4 \times 32 = 128$

Then the second $2 + 4 = 6$
                                   $4 \times 16 = 64$

In any geometrical progression proceeding from unity, the ratio being known, to find any remote term, without producing all the intermediate terms.

RULE. Find what figures of the indices added together would give the exponent of the term wanted: then multiply the numbers standing under such exponent into each other, and it will give the term required.

NOTE, *When the* exponent 1 *stands over the* second term, *the number of* exponents *must be* 1 *less than the number of terms.*

EXAMPLES.

1. A man agrees for 12 peaches, to pay only the price of the last, reckoning a farthing for the first, a halfpenny for the second, &c. doubling the price to the last, what must he give for them? Anf. £2..2..8.

```
 0, 1, 2, 3, 4,   Exponents.         16=  4
 1, 2, 4, 8, 16,  No. of terms.      16=  4
                                     ─────────
                                     256=  8
                                       8=  3
For 4+4+3=11, No. of terms less 1.   ─────────
                                     4)2048=11 No. of far.
                                       ─────────
                                     12)512
                                       ─────────
                                     2|0)4|2..8
                                       ─────────
                                           2..2..8
```

2. A country gentleman going to a fair to buy some oxen, meets with a person who had 23; he demanded the price of them, was answered £16. a piece: the gentleman bids him £15. a piece and he would buy all: the other tells him it could not be taken; but if he would give what the last ox would come to, at a farthing for the first, and doubling it to the last, he should have all. what was the price of the oxen? Anf. £4369..1..4.

In any geometrical progression, not proceeding from unity, the ratio being given, to find any remote term, without producing all the intermediate terms.

RULE. Proceed as in the last, only observe, that every product must be divided by the first term.

EXAMPLES.

EXAMPLES.

3. A sum of money is to be divided among 8 persons, the first to have £20. the second £60. and so on in triple proportion; what will the last have? *Ans.* 43740.

0, 1, 2, 3, $\dfrac{540 \times 540}{20} = 14580$, then $\dfrac{14580 \times 60}{20} = 43740$
20, 60, 180, 540,

$3+3+1=7$, *one less than the number of terms.*

4. A gentleman dying left nine sons, to whom and to his executors he bequeathed his estate in manner following: To his executors £50. his youngest son was to have as much more as the executors, and each son to exceed the next younger by as much more; what was the eldest son's portion?
Ans. £25600.

The first term, ratio, and number of terms given, to find the sum of all the terms.

RULE. Find the last term as before, then subtract the first from it, and divide the remainder by the ratio, less one; to the quotient of which add the greater, gives the sum required.

EXAMPLES.

5. A servant skilled in numbers agreed with a gentleman to serve him twelve months, provided he would give him a farthing for his first month's service, a penny for the second and 4*d.* for the third, &c. what did his wages amount to?
Ans. £5825..8..5¼.

$256 \times 256 = 65536$ then $65536 \times 64 = 4194304$

0, 1, 2, 3, 4, $4194304 - 1$
1, 4, 16, 64, 256, $\dfrac{}{} = 1398101$, then
$4+4+3=11$, *No. of terms less* 1. $4-1$.

$1398101 + 4194304 = 5592405$ farthings.

6. A man bought a horse, and by agreement was to give a farthing for the first nail, three for the second, &c. there were four shoes, and in each shoe 8 nails; what was the worth of the horse? *Ans.* £965114681693..13..4.

7. A certain person married his daughter on New-year's day, and gave her husband 1*s.* towards her portion, promising to double it on the first day of every month for one year; what was her portion? *Ans.* £204..15..—.

8. A laceman, well versed in numbers, agreed with a gentleman to sell him 22 yards of rich gold brocade lace, for 2 pins the first yard, 6 pins the second, &c. in triple proportion; I desire to know what he sold the lace for, if the pins were valued at 100 for a farthing; also what the laceman got or lost by the sale thereof, supposing the lace stood him in £7. per yard?

Ans. The lace sold for £326886..–..9.
Gain £326732..–..9.

PERMUTATION

Is the changing or varying the order of things.

RULE. Multiply all the given terms one into another, and the last product will be the number of changes required.

EXAMPLES.

1. How many changes may be rung upon 12 bells; and how long would they be ringing but once over, supposing 10 changes might be rung in 1 minute, and the year to contain 365 days, 6 hours?

Answer.

$1 \times 2 \times 3 \times 4 \times 5 \times 6 \times 7 \times 8 \times 9 \times 10 \times 11 \times 12 = 479001600$ changes, which ÷ 10 = 47900160 *minutes*; and, if reduced, is = 91 *years*, 3 *weeks*, 5 *days*, 6 *hours*.

2. A young scholar coming into town for the convenience of a good library, demands of a gentleman with whom he lodged, what his diet would cost for a year, who told him £10. but the scholar not being certain what time he should stay, asked him what he must give him for so long as he should place his family, consisting of 6 persons besides himself, in different positions, every day at dinner: the gentleman thinking it would not be long, tells him £5. to which the scholar agrees. What time did the scholar stay with the gentleman? *Ans.* 5040 *days.*

THE
TUTOR's ASSISTANT.

PART II.

VULGAR FRACTIONS.

A FRACTION is a part or parts of an unit, and written with two figures, with a line between them, as ¼, ⅝, ⅜, &c.

The figure above the line is called the numerator, and the under one the denominator; which shews how many parts the unit is divided into; and the numerator shews how many of those parts are meant by the fraction.

There are four sorts of vulgar fractions; *proper, improper, compound,* and *mixed, viz.*

1. A PROPER FRACTION is when the numerator is less than the denominator, as $\frac{2}{4}$, $\frac{3}{6}$, $\frac{7}{8}$, $\frac{9}{11}$, $\frac{101}{715}$, &c.

2. An IMPROPER FRACTION is when the numerator is equal to, or greater than the denominator, as $\frac{4}{3}$, $\frac{8}{4}$, $\frac{12}{2}$, $\frac{207}{2}$, &c.

3. A COMPOUND FRACTION is the fraction of a fraction, and known by the word *of*, as ½ of ⅔ of $\frac{7}{9}$, of $\frac{8}{17}$, of $\frac{9}{12}$, &c.

4. A MIXED NUMBER or FRACTION is composed of a whole number and fraction, as 8 $\frac{3}{7}$, 17 ½, 8 $\frac{34}{97}$, &c.

K 3   REDUCTION

REDUCTION of VULGAR FRACTIONS.

1. *To reduce fractions to a common denominator.*

Rule 1. Multiply each numerator into all the denominators, except its own, for a new numerator; and all the denominators for a common denominator. Or,

2. Multiply the common denominator by the several given numerators separately, and divide the product by their several denominators, The quotient will be the new numerators.

EXAMPLES.

1. Reduce $\frac{2}{4}$ and $\frac{4}{7}$ to a common denominator.

$$\text{Facit } \frac{14}{28}, \text{ and } \frac{16}{28}.$$

1st num.   2d num.

$2\times 7=14$ $4\times 4=16$, then $4\times 7=28$ den. $=\frac{14}{28}$, and $\frac{16}{28}$.

2. Reduce $\frac{1}{2}$, $\frac{3}{4}$, and $\frac{5}{8}$ to a common denominator.

$$\text{Facit } \frac{32}{64}, \frac{48}{64}, \frac{40}{64}.$$

3. Reduce $\frac{7}{8}$, $\frac{4}{5}$, $\frac{6}{10}$, and $\frac{5}{7}$ to a common denominator.

$$\text{Facit } \frac{2940}{3360}, \frac{2240}{3360}, \frac{2016}{3360}, \frac{2880}{3360}.$$

4. Reduce $\frac{6}{10}$, $\frac{2}{4}$, $\frac{1}{7}$, $\frac{3}{6}$ to a common denominator.

$$\text{Facit } \frac{1008}{1680}, \frac{840}{1680}, \frac{240}{1680}, \frac{840}{1680}.$$

5. Reduce $\frac{4}{5}$, $\frac{2}{3}$, $\frac{3}{7}$, and $\frac{1}{8}$ to a common denominator.

$$\text{Facit } \frac{672}{840}, \frac{560}{840}, \frac{360}{840}, \frac{105}{840}.$$

6. Reduce $\frac{2}{6}$, $\frac{5}{3}$, $\frac{2}{8}$, and $\frac{3}{5}$ to a common denominator.

$$\text{Facit } \frac{720}{2160}, \frac{1200}{2160}, \frac{540}{2160}, \frac{1296}{2160}.$$

2. *To reduce a vulgar fraction to its lowest terms.*

Rule. Find a common measure by dividing the lower term by the upper, and that divisor by the remainder following, till nothing remain; the last divisor is the common measure; then divide both parts of the fraction by the common measure, and the quotient will give the fraction required.

Note. If the common measure happen to be one, the fraction is already in its lowest term; and when a fraction hath cyphers at the right hand, it may be abreviated by cutting them off; as $\frac{20}{10}$.

EXAMPLE.

7. Reduce $\frac{24}{32}$ to its lowest terms.

24)32(1
   24

Common measure 8)24(3
       24

then 8)$\frac{24}{32}$($=\frac{3}{4}$ *Facit.*

8. Reduce

ASSISTANT. *Reduction of Vulgar Fractions.* 103

8. Reduce $\frac{30}{125}$ to its lowest terms.   *Facit* $\frac{6}{25}$.
9. Reduce $\frac{208}{684}$ to its lowest terms.   *Facit* $\frac{52}{171}$.
10. Reduce $\frac{192}{576}$ to its lowest terms.   *Facit* $\frac{1}{3}$.
11. Reduce $\frac{825}{960}$ to its lowest terms.   *Facit* $\frac{55}{64}$.
12. Reduce $\frac{5184}{6912}$ to its lowest terms.   *Facit* $\frac{3}{4}$.

3. *To reduce a mixed number to an improper fraction.*

RULE. Multiply the whole number by the denominator of the fraction, and to the product add the numerator for a new numerator, which place over the denominator.

Note, *To express a whole number fraction-ways, set* 1 *for the denominator given.*

EXAMPLES.

13. Reduce $83\frac{3}{7}$ to an improper fraction.   *Facit* $\frac{129}{7}$.
$$18 \times 7 + 3 = 129 \text{ new numerator, } \frac{129}{7}.$$
14. Reduce $56\frac{13}{22}$ to an improper fraction.   *Facit* $\frac{1245}{22}$.
15. Reduce $183\frac{5}{21}$ to an improper fraction.   *Facit* $\frac{3848}{21}$.
16. Reduce $13\frac{4}{5}$ to an improper fraction.   *Facit* $\frac{69}{5}$.
17. Reduce $27\frac{2}{9}$ to an improper fraction.   *Facit* $\frac{245}{9}$.
18. Reduce $514\frac{5}{16}$ to an improper fraction.   *Facit* $\frac{8229}{16}$.

4. *To reduce an improper fraction to its proper terms.*

RULE. Divide the upper term by the lower.

EXAMPLES.

19. Reduce $\frac{129}{7}$ to its proper terms.   *Facit* $18\frac{3}{7}$.
$$129 \div 7 = 18\frac{3}{7}.$$
20. Reduce $\frac{1245}{22}$ to its proper terms.   *Facit* $56\frac{13}{22}$.
21. Reduce $\frac{3848}{21}$ to its proper terms.   *Facit* $183\frac{5}{21}$.
22. Reduce $\frac{69}{5}$ to its proper terms.   *Facit* $13\frac{4}{5}$.
23. Reduce $\frac{245}{9}$ to its proper terms.   *Facit* $27\frac{2}{9}$.
24. Reduce $\frac{8229}{16}$ to its proper terms.   *Facit* $514\frac{5}{16}$.

5. *To reduce a compound fraction to a single one.*

RULE. Multiply all the numerators for a new numerator, and all the denominators for a new denominator.
Reduce the new fraction to its lowest terms, by RULE 2.

EXAMPLES,

104   Reduction of Vulgar Fractions. The Tutor's

Examples.

25. Reduce $\frac{2}{3}$ of $\frac{3}{5}$ of $\frac{5}{8}$ to a single fraction.

$$\text{Facit } \frac{2\times3\times5}{3\times5\times8}=\frac{30}{120} \text{ reduced to the lowest term}=\frac{1}{4}$$

26. Reduce $\frac{3}{5}$ of $\frac{4}{7}$ of $\frac{1}{2}\frac{1}{2}$ to a single fraction.

$$\text{Facit } \frac{30}{756}=\frac{15}{189}$$

27. Reduce $\frac{1}{1}\frac{1}{2}$ of $\frac{1}{5}\frac{1}{2}$ of $\frac{2}{2}\frac{1}{5}$ to a single fraction.

$$\text{Facit } \frac{3003}{4872}=\frac{143}{232}.$$

28. Reduce $\frac{1}{4}$ of $\frac{1}{6}$ of $\frac{9}{10}$ to a single fraction.

$$\text{Facit } \frac{9}{240}=\frac{3}{80}.$$

29. Reduce $\frac{4}{5}$ of $\frac{1}{8}$ of $\frac{7}{9}$ to a single fraction.

$$\text{Facit } \frac{168}{360}=\frac{7}{15}.$$

30. Reduce $\frac{1}{2}$ of $\frac{5}{9}$ of $\frac{8}{10}$ to a single fraction.

$$\text{Facit } \frac{80}{130}=\frac{8}{13}.$$

6. To reduce fractions of one denomination to the fraction of another, but greater, retaining the same value.

Rule. Reduce the given fraction to a compound one, by comparing it with all the denominations between it, and that denomination which you would reduce it to; then reduce that compound fraction to a single one.

Examples.

31. Reduce $\frac{7}{8}$ of a penny to the fraction of a pound.

$$\text{Facit } \tfrac{7}{8} \text{ of } \tfrac{1}{12} \text{ of } \tfrac{1}{20}=\tfrac{7}{1920}$$

32. Reduce $\frac{1}{4}$ of a penny to the fraction of a pound.

$$\text{Facit } \tfrac{1}{960}.$$

33. Reduce $\frac{4}{5}$ of a dwt. to the fraction of a lb. troy.

$$\text{Facit } \tfrac{4}{1200}.$$

34. Reduce $\frac{4}{7}$ of a lb. avoirdupoise to the fraction of an cwt.

$$\text{Facit } \tfrac{4}{784}.$$

7. To reduce fractions of one denomination to the fraction of another, but less, retaining the same value.

Rule. Multiply the numerator by the parts contained in the several denominations between it, and that you would reduce it to, for a new numerator, and place it over the given denominator.

Reduce the new fraction to its lowest terms.

Examples.

ASSISTANT. *Reduction of Vulgar Fractions.* 105

EXAMPLES.

35. Reduce $\frac{7}{1920}$ of a pound to the fraction of a penny.
Facit $\frac{1}{8}$.

$7 \times 20 \times 12 = 1680$ $\frac{1680}{1920}$ *reduced to its lowest term* $= \frac{7}{8}$.

36. Reduce $\frac{1}{960}$ of a pound to the fraction of a penny.
Facit $\frac{1}{4}$.

37. Reduce $\frac{4}{1200}$ of a pound troy to the fraction of a penny-weight.
Facit $\frac{4}{5}$.

38. Reduce $\frac{4}{184}$ of an cwt. to the fraction of a lb.
Facit $\frac{4}{7}$.

8. *To reduce fractions of one denomination to another of the same value, having the numerator given of the required fraction.*

RULE. As the numerator of the given fraction : is to its denominator : : so is the numerator of its intended fraction : to its denominator.

EXAMPLES.

39. Reduce $\frac{2}{3}$ to a fraction of the fame value, whofe numerator fhall be 12. *As* 2 : 3 :: 12 : 18. Facit $\frac{12}{18}$.

40. Reduce $\frac{5}{7}$ to a fraction of the fame value, whofe numerator fhall be 25. Facit $\frac{25}{35}$.

41. Reduce $\frac{5}{7}$ to a fraction of the fame value, whofe numerator fhall be 47.
Facit $\frac{47}{65\frac{4}{5}}$.

9. *To reduce fractions of one denomination to another of the same value, having the denominator given, of the fraction required.*

RULE. As the denominator of the given fraction : is to its numerator : : so is the denominator of the intended fraction : to its numerator.

EXAMPLES.

42. Reduce $\frac{2}{3}$ to a fraction of the fame value, whofe denominator fhall be 18. *As* 3 : 2 :: 18 : 12. Facit $\frac{12}{18}$.

43. Reduce $\frac{5}{7}$ to a fraction of the fame value, whofe denominator fhall be 35. Facit $\frac{25}{35}$.

44. Reduce $\frac{5}{7}$ to a fraction of the fame value, whofe denominator fhall be $65\frac{4}{5}$.
Facit $\frac{47}{65\frac{4}{5}}$.

10. *To*

10. *To reduce a mixed fraction to a single one.*

RULE. When the numerator is the integral part, multiply it by the denominator of the fractional part, adding in the numerator of the fractional part for a new numerator; then multiply the denominator of the fraction by the denominator of the fractional part for a new denominator.

EXAMPLES.

45. Reduce $\dfrac{36\frac{2}{3}}{48}$ to a simple fraction. *Facit* $\dfrac{110}{144}=\dfrac{55}{72}$.

$36 \times 3 + 2 = 110$ *numerator.*
$48 \times 3 = 144$ *denominator.*

46. Reduce $\dfrac{23\frac{5}{7}}{38}$ to a simple fraction. *Facit* $\dfrac{166}{266}=\dfrac{83}{133}$.

When the denominator is the integral part, multiply it by the denominator of the fractional part, adding in the numerator of the fractional part for a new denominator; then multiply the numerator of the fraction by the denominator of the fractional part for a new numerator.

EXAMPLES.

47. Reduce $\dfrac{47}{65\frac{4}{3}}$ to a simple fraction. *Facit* $\dfrac{235}{329}=\dfrac{5}{7}$.

48. Reduce $\dfrac{19}{4\frac{1}{3}}$ to a simple fraction. *Facit* $\dfrac{57}{133}=\dfrac{3}{7}$.

11. *To find the proper quantity of a fraction in the known parts of an integer.*

RULE. Multiply the numerator by the common parts of the integer, and divide by the denominator.

EXAMPLES.

49. Reduce $\frac{3}{4}$ of a pound sterling to its proper quantity.
$3 \times 20 = 60 \div 4 = 15s.$ *Facit* 15s.

50. Reduce $\frac{2}{3}$ of a shilling to its proper quantity.
Facit 4d. 3 qrs. $\frac{1}{3}$.

51. Reduce $\frac{4}{7}$ of a lb. avoirdupoise to its proper quantity.
Facit 9 oz. 2 dr. $\frac{2}{7}$.

52. Reduce $\frac{7}{9}$ of an cwt. to its proper quantity.
Facit 3 qrs. 3 lb. 1 oz. 12 dr. $\frac{4}{9}$.

53. Reduce

53. Reduce $\frac{3}{5}$ of a pound to troy its proper quantity.
Facit 7 oz. 4 dwt.

54. Reduce $\frac{5}{9}$ of an ell English to its proper quantity.
Facit 2 qrs. 3 nalls $\frac{1}{9}$.

55. Reduce $\frac{4}{5}$ of a mile to its proper quantity.
Facit 6 furl. 16 poles.

56. Reduce $\frac{5}{8}$ of an acre to its proper quantity.
Facit 2 roods, 20 poles.

57. Reduce $\frac{6}{7}$ of an hogshead of wine to its proper quantity.
Facit 54 gallons.

58. Reduce $\frac{1}{3}$ of a barrel of beer to its proper quantity.
Facit 12 gallons.

59. Reduce $\frac{5}{12}$ of a chaldron of coals to its proper quantity.
Facit 15 bushels.

60. Reduce $\frac{1}{7}$ of a month to its proper time.
Facit 2 weeks, 2 days, 19 hours, 12 minutes.

12. *To reduce any given quantity to the fraction of any greater denomination, retaining the same value.*

RULE. Reduce the given quantity to the lowest term mentioned for a numerator, under which set the integral part (reduce to the same term) for a denominator, and it will give the fraction required.

EXAMPLES.

61. Reduce 15*s.* to the fraction of a pound sterling.
Facit $\frac{15}{20}=\frac{3}{4}$£.

62. Reduce 4*d.* 3 *qrs.* $\frac{1}{5}$ to the fraction of a shilling.
Facit $\frac{2}{5}$.

63. Reduce 9 oz. 2 dr. $\frac{2}{7}$ to the fraction of a lb. avoirdupoise.
Facit $\frac{4}{7}$.

64. Reduce 3 qrs. 3 lb. 1 oz. 12 dr. $\frac{4}{9}$ to the fraction of an cwt.
Facit $\frac{7}{9}$.

65. Reduce 7 oz. 4 dwts. to the fraction of a lb. troy.
Facit $\frac{3}{5}$.

66. Reduce 2 qrs. 3 nails, $\frac{1}{9}$ to the fraction of an English ell.
Facit $\frac{5}{9}$.

67. Reduce 6 furl. 16 poles to the fraction of a mile.
Facit $\frac{4}{5}$.

68. Reduce 2 roods 20 poles to the fraction of an acre.
Facit $\frac{5}{8}$.

69 Reduce 54 gallons to the fraction of a hogshead of wine.
Facit $\frac{6}{7}$.

70. Reduce

70. Reduce 12 gallons to the fraction of a barrel of beer.
Facit $\frac{1}{3}$.
71. Reduce 15 bushels to the fraction of a chaldron of coals.
Facit $\frac{5}{12}$.
72. Reduce 2 weeks, 2 days, 19 hours, 12 minutes, to the fraction of a month.
Facit $\frac{3}{4}$.

ADDITION of VULGAR FRACTIONS.

RULE.

REDUCE the given fractions to a common denominator, then add all the numerators together, under which place the common denominator.

EXAMPLES.

1. Add $\frac{2}{3}$ and $\frac{4}{7}$ together. Facit $\frac{14}{21} + \frac{15}{21} = \frac{29}{21} = 1\frac{8}{21}$.
2. Add $\frac{1}{4}$, $\frac{2}{7}$ and $\frac{1}{6}$ together. Facit $1\frac{148}{168}$.
3. Add $\frac{1}{3}$, $4\frac{1}{3}$ and $\frac{2}{5}$ together. Facit $4\frac{70}{75}$.
4. Add $7\frac{2}{3}$, and $\frac{2}{5}$ together. Facit $8\frac{1}{15}$.
5. Add $\frac{3}{7}$, and $\frac{2}{3}$ of $\frac{1}{4}$ together. Facit $\frac{11}{14}$.
6. Add 5$\frac{2}{3}$, 6$\frac{7}{8}$, and 4$\frac{1}{2}$ together. Facit $17\frac{1}{24}$.

2. When the fractions are of several denominations, reduce them to their proper quantities, and add as before.

7. Add $\frac{3}{4}$ of a pound to $\frac{5}{6}$ of a shilling. Facit 15s. 10d.
8. Add $\frac{1}{2}$ of a penny to $\frac{2}{3}$ of a pound. Facit 13s. 4½d.
9. Add $\frac{3}{4}$ of a pound troy to $\frac{5}{6}$ of an ounce.
Facit 9 oz. 3 dwts. 8 gr.
10. Add $\frac{4}{5}$ of a ton to $\frac{5}{6}$ of a lb.
Facit 16 cwt. 0 yr. 0 lb. 13 oz. 5 dr. $\frac{1}{3}$.
11. Add $\frac{2}{3}$ of a chaldron to $\frac{1}{4}$ of a bushel.
Facit 24 bushels, 3 pecks.
12. Add $\frac{1}{6}$ of a yard to $\frac{2}{3}$ of an inch.
Facit 6 inch. 2 bar. 0.

SUBTRACTION of VULGAR FRACTIONS.

RULE.

REDUCE the given fractions to a common denominator, then subtract the less numerator from the greater, and place the remainder over the common denominator.

2. When

ASSISTANT. *Multiplication of Vulgar Fractions.* 109

2. When the lower fraction is greater than the upper, subtract the numerator of the lower fraction from the denominator, and to that difference add the upper numerator, carrying one to the unit's place of the lower whole number.

EXAMPLES.

1. From $\frac{1}{4}$ take $\frac{5}{7}$. $3\times7=21$. $5\times4=20$. $21-20=1$ num. $4\times7=28$ den.   Facit $\frac{1}{28}$
2. From $\frac{5}{8}$ take $\frac{2}{3}$ of $\frac{6}{7}$ - - Facit $\frac{11}{24}$
3. From $5\frac{2}{3}$ take $\frac{9}{10}$.   - - Facit $4\frac{23}{30}$.
4. From $\frac{38}{47}$ take $\frac{1}{5}$ - - Facit $\frac{49}{235}$.
5. From $\frac{13}{20}$ take $\frac{1}{7}$ of $\frac{2}{3}$ - - Facit $\frac{359}{420}$.
6. From $64\frac{1}{4}$ take $\frac{2}{3}$ of $\frac{3}{4}$. - - Facit $64\frac{1}{4}$.

3. When the fractions are of several denominaitons, reduce them to their proper quantities, and subtract as before.

7. From $\frac{3}{4}$ of a pound take $\frac{1}{4}$ of a shilling. *Facit* 14s. 3d.
8. From $\frac{2}{3}$ of a shilling take $\frac{1}{3}$ of a penny. *Facit* $7\frac{1}{2}d$.
9. From $\frac{3}{4}$ of a lb. troy take $\frac{1}{5}$ of an ounce.
        Facit 8 oz. 16 dwts. 16 grs.
10. From $\frac{4}{5}$ of a ton take $\frac{2}{5}$ of a lb.
   Facit 15 cwt. 3 qrs. 27 lb. 2 oz. 10 dr. $\frac{2}{5}$.
11. From $\frac{2}{3}$ of a chaldron take $\frac{3}{4}$ of a bushel.
      Facit 23 bushel 1 peck.
12. From $\frac{1}{6}$ of a yard take $\frac{2}{3}$ of an inch. *Facit* 5 in. 1 b.c.

MULTIPLICATION of VULGAR FRACTIONS.

RULE.

PREPARE the given numbers (if they require it) by the rules of Reduction: then multiply the numerators together for a new numerator, and the denominators for a new denominator.

NOTE. *When any number, either whole or mixed, is multiplied by a fraction, the product will be always less than the multiplicand, in the same proportion as the multiplying fraction is less than an unit.*

EXAMPLES.

1. Multiply $\frac{3}{4}$ by $\frac{3}{5}$ *Fa.* $3\times3=9$ num. $4\times5=20$ den. $\frac{9}{20}$
2. Multiply $\frac{7}{9}$ by $\frac{2}{3}$ - - *Facit* $\frac{14}{27}$
3. Multiply $48\frac{3}{4}$ by $13\frac{5}{6}$ - - *Facit* $672\frac{9}{35}$.

                              4. Multiply

110 *Division of Vulgar Fractions.* The Tutor's

4. Multiply $430 \frac{6}{10}$ by $18 \frac{4}{7}$. — Facit $7935 \frac{24}{70}$.
5. Multiply $\frac{16}{27}$ by $\frac{1}{4}$ of $\frac{5}{7}$ of $\frac{4}{5}$. — Facit $\frac{16}{294} = \frac{1}{40}$.
6. Multiply $\frac{7}{10}$ by $\frac{2}{3}$ of $\frac{1}{4}$ of $\frac{3}{5}$. — Facit $\frac{3}{5}$.
7. Multiply $\frac{1}{4}$ of $\frac{2}{3}$ by $\frac{2}{3}$ of $\frac{1}{3}$. — Facit $\frac{1}{27}$.
8. Multiply $\frac{1}{4}$ of $\frac{3}{8}$ by $\frac{5}{7}$. — Facit $\frac{15}{224}$.
9. Multiply $5 \frac{6}{7}$ by $\frac{5}{6}$. — Facit $4 \frac{17}{42}$.
10. Multiply 24 by $\frac{2}{3}$. — Facit 16.
11. Multiply $\frac{1}{4}$ of 9 by $\frac{7}{8}$. — Facit $5 \frac{22}{38}$.
12. Multiply $9 \frac{1}{2}$ by $\frac{5}{7}$. — Facit $3 \frac{1}{4}$.

DIVISION of VULGAR FRACTIONS.

RULE.

PREPARE the given numbers (if they require it) by the rules of Reduction, then multiply the denominator of the divisor into the numerator of the dividend for a new numerator, and the numerator of the divisor into the denominator of the dividend for a new denominator.

Note. When any whole number is divided by a fraction less than unity, the quotient will be greater than the dividend; but if any fraction be divided by a whole number greater than unity, the quotient will be less than the dividend.

EXAMPLES.

1. Divide $\frac{9}{20}$ by $\frac{3}{5}$. $5 \times 9 = 45$ num. $3 \times 20 = 60$ den. $\frac{45}{60} = \frac{3}{4}$.
2. Divide $\frac{14}{27}$ by $\frac{2}{3}$. — Facit $\frac{7}{9}$.
3. Divide $672 \frac{9}{30}$ by $13 \frac{1}{5}$. — Facit $48 \frac{1}{2}$.
4. Divide $7935 \frac{24}{70}$ by $18 \frac{4}{7}$. — Facit $430 \frac{6}{10}$.
5. Divide $\frac{1}{8}$ by $\frac{2}{3}$ of $\frac{1}{4}$ of $\frac{6}{7}$. — Facit $\frac{7}{10}$.
6. Divide $\frac{2}{3}$ of 16 by $\frac{4}{9}$ of $\frac{3}{5}$. — Facit $19 \frac{41}{45}$.
7. Divide $\frac{1}{4}$ of $\frac{2}{5}$ by $\frac{3}{7}$ of $\frac{1}{4}$. — Facit $\frac{56}{35} = \frac{3}{4}$.
8. Divide $9 \frac{2}{12}$ by $\frac{1}{2}$ of 7. — Facit $2 \frac{4}{21}$.
9. Divide $\frac{9}{15}$ by $4 \frac{1}{2}$. — Facit $\frac{1}{8}$.
10. Divide 16 by 24. — Facit $\frac{2}{3}$.
11. Divide $5205 \frac{1}{10}$ by $\frac{4}{5}$ of 91. — Facit $71 \frac{1}{2}$.
12. Divide $3 \frac{1}{8}$ by $9 \frac{1}{3}$. — Facit $\frac{1}{3}$.

The

ASSISTANT.   *The Single Rule of Three.*   111

The SINGLE RULE *of* THREE DIRECT,
in VULGAR FRACTIONS.

RULE.

REDUCE the numbers as before directed in Reduction, so that the third and first may be of the same name: multiply the numerator of the first fraction by the denominator of the second and third, for a new denominator; then multiply the denominator of the first fraction by the numerator of the second and third for a new numerator; that fraction will be the answer to the question, which reduce to its proper quantity. Or, when the three terms are properly reduced, proceed as in the Rule of Three of whole numbers.

EXAMPLES.

1. If $\frac{1}{4}$ of a yard cost $\frac{5}{8}$ of a £. what will $\frac{9}{10}$ of a yard come to at that rate?   Ans. $\frac{18}{24}$ = 15s.

$\frac{1}{4}$ yd. : $\frac{5}{8}$ £. - : : $\frac{9}{10}$ yd. : $\frac{18}{24}$ £.

for $4 \times 5 \times 9 = 180$ num.   or $\frac{5}{8} \times \frac{9}{10} = \frac{45}{80} \div \frac{1}{4}) \frac{45}{80} (\frac{18}{24}|\frac{9}{6}$
and $3 \times 8 \times 10 = 240$ den.

2. If $\frac{1}{6}$ of a yard cost $\frac{2}{3}$ £. what will $\frac{11}{4}$ of a yard cost?   Ans. 14s. 8d.

3. If $\frac{1}{4}$ of a yard of lawn cost 7s. 3d. what will 10 yards $\frac{1}{5}$ cost?   Ans. £4..19..10$\frac{2}{3}$.

4. If $\frac{7}{8}$ lb. cost $\frac{1}{4}$ s. how many pounds will $\frac{3}{4}$ of 1s. buy?   Ans. 1 lb. $\frac{8}{216}$.

5. If $\frac{1}{3}$ ell of Holland cost $\frac{1}{5}$ £. what will 12 ells $\frac{2}{3}$ cost at that rate?   Ans. £.7..--..8$\frac{3}{4}$ $\frac{1}{27}$.

6. If 12 $\frac{1}{2}$ yards of cloth cost 25s. 9d. what will 48 $\frac{1}{4}$ cost at the same rate?   Ans. £.3..9..-$\frac{1}{4}$ $\frac{1}{100}$.

7. If $\frac{1}{10}$ of an cwt. cost 284s. what will 7 cwt. $\frac{1}{4}$ cost at the same rate?   Ans. £118..6..8.

8. If 3 yards of broad cloth cost £2. $\frac{1}{4}$. what will 10 yards $\frac{2}{7}$ cost?   Ans. £9..12..-.

9. If $\frac{1}{4}$ of a yard cost $\frac{3}{4}$ of a £. what will $\frac{1}{2}$ of an ell English come to at the same rate?   Ans. £2.

10. If 1 lb. of cochineal cost £1..5..-. what will 36 lb. $\frac{7}{10}$ come to?   Ans. £45..17..6.

11. If 1 yard of broad cloth cost 25s. $\frac{5}{8}$. what will 4 pieces cost, each containing 27 yards $\frac{3}{4}$.?   Ans. £84..14..3$\frac{1}{4}$. $\frac{40}{24}$.

12. Bought 3 pieces $\frac{3}{4}$ of silk, each containing 24 ells $\frac{3}{5}$, at 6s.-..$\frac{3}{4}$ per ell, I desire to know what the whole quantity cost?   Ans. £25..17..2$\frac{1}{4}$ $\frac{15}{16}$.

L 2   The

The SINGLE RULE of THREE INVERSE, in VULGAR FRACTIONS.

EXAMPLES.

1. IF 48 men can build a wall in 24 days $\frac{1}{2}$, how many men can do the same in 192 days? Ans. 6 men $\frac{48}{768}$.

2. If 25s. $\frac{2}{7}$ will pay for the carriage of cwt. 145 miles $\frac{3}{4}$, how far may 6 cwt. $\frac{1}{3}$ be carried for the same money? Ans. 22 miles $\frac{9}{20}$.

3. If $3\frac{1}{4}$ yards of cloth, that is $1\frac{1}{3}$ yard wide, be sufficient to make a cloak, how much must I have of that sort which is $\frac{4}{5}$ yard wide, to make another of the same bigness? Ans. $4\frac{7}{8}$ yards.

4. If three men can do a piece of work in 4 hours $\frac{1}{2}$, in how many hours will 10 men do the same work? Ans. 1 hour $\frac{7}{20}$.

5. If a penny white loaf weigh 7 oz. when a bushel of wheat cost 5s. 6d. what is the bushel worth when the penny white loaf weighs but 2 oz. $\frac{1}{2}$? Ans. 15s. 4d. $\frac{4}{5}$.

6. What quantity of shalloon that is $\frac{3}{4}$ yard wide will line $7\frac{1}{2}$ yards of cloth that is $1\frac{1}{4}$ yard wide? Ans. 15 yards.

DOUBLE RULE of THREE, in VULGAR FRACTIONS.

EXAMPLES.

1. IF a carrier receives £2. $\frac{1}{10}$. for the carriage of 3 cwt. 150 miles, how much ought he to receive for the carriage of 7 cwt. 3 qrs. $\frac{1}{2}$ 50 miles? Ans. £1..16..9.

2. If £100. in 12 months gain £6. interest, what principal will gain £3. $\frac{3}{4}$. in 9 months? Ans. £75.

3. If 9 students spend £10. $\frac{7}{9}$ in 18 days, how much will 20 students spend in 30 days? Ans. £39..18..4. $\frac{360}{1458}$.

4. A man and his wife having laboured one day, earned 4s. $\frac{3}{8}$, how much must they have for 10 days $\frac{1}{2}$, when their two sons helped them? Ans. £4..17..1. $\frac{1}{2}$.

5. If £50 in 5 months gain £2. $\frac{37}{144}$, what time will £13. $\frac{1}{4}$ require to gain £1. $\frac{1}{12}$? Ans. 9 months.

6. If the carriage of 60 cwt. 20 miles cost £14. $\frac{1}{4}$, what weight can I have carried 30 miles for £5. $\frac{7}{16}$? Ans. 15 cwt.

THE

THE TUTOR's ASSISTANT.

PART III.

DECIMAL FRACTIONS.

IN Decimal Fractions the integer or whole thing, as one pound, one yard, one gallon, &c. is supposed to be divided into ten equal parts, and those parts into tenths, and so on without end.

So that the denominator of a decimal being always known to consist of an unit with as many cyphers as the numerator has places, therefore is never set down; the parts being only distinguished from the whole numbers by a comma prefixed; thus, ,5 which stands for $\frac{5}{10}$, ,25 for $\frac{25}{100}$, ,123 for $\frac{123}{1000}$.

But the different value of figures appear plainer by the following table.

Whole numbers.							Decimal parts.						
7	6	5	4	3	2	1	2	3	4	5	6	7
Millions.	C Thousands.	X Thousands.	Thousands.	Hundreds.	Tens.	Units.	Parts of Tens.	Parts of Hundreds.	Parts of Thousands.	Parts of X Thousands.	Parts of C Thousands.	Parts of Millions.

From which it plainly appears, that, as whole numbers increase in a ten-fold proportion to the left-hand, decimal parts decrease in a ten-fold proportion to the right-hand:

so that cyphers placed before decimal parts decrease their value, by removing them farther from the comma, or units place; thus, ,5 is 5 parts of 10, or $\frac{5}{10}$; ,05 is 5 parts of 100, or $\frac{5}{100}$; ,005 is 5 parts of 1000, or $\frac{5}{1000}$; ,0005 is 5 parts of 10000, or $\frac{5}{10000}$. But cyphers after decimal parts do not alter their value. For ,5 ,50, ,500, &c. are each but $\frac{5}{10}$ of the unit.

A FINITE DECIMAL is that which ends at a certain number of places; but an INFINITE is that which no where ends.

A RECURRING DECIMAL is that wherein one or more figures are continually repeated, as 2,75222.

And 52,275275275 is called a COMPOUND RECURRING DECIMAL.

Note. *A finite decimal may be considered as infinite, by making cyphers to recur; for they do not alter the value of the decimal.*

In all operations, if the result consists of several nines, reject them, and make the next superior place an unit more; thus for 26,25999 write 26,26.

In all circulating numbers, dash the first figure that begins to circulate thus, as in 86,54666.

ADDITION of DECIMALS.

RULE.

IN setting down the proposed numbers to be added, great care must be taken in placing every figure directly underneath those of the same value, whether they be mixed numbers, or pure decimal parts; and to perform which there must be a due regard had to the commas or separating points, which ought always to stand in a direct line, one under another, and to the right-hand of them carefully place the decimal parts, according to their respective values; then add them as in whole numbers.

EXAMPLES.

1. Add 72,5 + 32,071 + 2,1574 + 371,4 + 2,75.
   Facit 480,8784.
2. Add 30,07 + 2,007 + 59,4 + 3207,1.
3. Add 3,5 + 47,25 + 927,01 + 2,0073 + 1,5.
4. Add 52,75 + 47,21 + 724 + 31,452 + ,3075.
5. Add 3275 + 27,514 + 1,005 + 725 + 7,32.
6. Add 27,5 + 52 + 3,2075 + ,5741 + 2720.

SUBTRACTION of DECIMALS.

Rule.

SUBTRACTION of Decimals differs but little from whole numbers, only in placing the numbers, which must be carefully observed, as in addition.

Examples.

1. From ,2754 take ,2371
2. From 2,37 take 1,76
3. From 272 take 215,7
4. From 270,2 take 75,4075
5. From 57 take 54,72
6. From 625 take 76,91
7. From 23,415 take ,3742
8. From ,107 take ,0007

MULTIPLICATION of DECIMALS.

Rule.

PLACE the factors, and multiply them, as in whole numbers, and from the product towards the right-hand cut off as many places for decimals as there are in both factors together; but if there should not be so many places in the product, supply the defect with cyphers to the left-hand.

Examples.

1. Multiply ,2365 by ,2335. Facit ,05522275.
2. Multiply 2,071 by 2,27
3. Multiply 27,15 by 25,3
4. Multiply 72347 by 23,15
5. Multiply 17105 by ,3257
6. Multiply 17105 by ,0237
7. Multiply 27,35 by 7,70071
8. Multiply 57,21 by ,0075
9. Multiply ,007 by ,007
10. Multiply 20,15 by ,2705
11. Multiply ,907 by ,0025

When any number of decimals is to be multiplied by 10, 100, 1000, &c. it is only removing the separating point in the multiplicand so many places towards the right-hand as there are cyphers in the multiplier: thus, ,578 × 10 = 5,78. ,578 × 100 = 57,8. ,578 × 1000 = 578. 578 × 1000 = 5780.

Contracted

Contracted MULTIPLICATION of DECIMALS.
RULE.

PUT the unit's place of the multiplier under that place of the multiplicand that is intended to be kept in the product; then invert the order of all the other figures, *i.e.* write them all the contrary way: then in multiplying, begin at the figure in the multiplicand, which stands over the figure you are then multiplying with, and set down the first figure of each particular product directly one under the other, and have a due regard to the increase arising from the figures on the right-hand of that figure you begin to multiply at in the multiplicand.

Note, *That in multiplying the figure left out every time next the right-hand in the multiplicand, if the product be 5, or upwards, to 15, carry 1; if 15, or upwards, to 25, carry 2; and if 25, or upwards, to 35, carry 3, &c.*

EXAMPLES.

12. Multiply 384,672158 by 36,8345, and let there be only four places of decimals in the product.

Facit 14169,2065.

Contracted Way.	Common Way.
384,672158	384,672158
5438,63	36,8345
115401647	1923360790
23080329	153898632
3077377	1154016474
115402	3077377264
15387	2308032948
1923	1154016474
14169,2065	14169,2066038510

13. Multiply 3,141592 by 52,7438, and leave only 4 places of decimals. *Facit* 165,6994.

14. Multiply 2,38645 by 8,2175, and leave only 4 places of decimals. *Facit* 19,6107.

15. Multiply 375,13758 by 16,7324, and let there be only 1 place of decimals. *Facit* 6276,9.

16. Multiply 375,13758 by 16,7324, and leave only 4 places of decimals. *Facit* 6276,9520.

17. Multiply 395,3756 by ,75642, and let there be only 4 places of decimals. *Facit* 299,0699.

DIVISION of DECIMALS.

THIS Rule is also worked as in whole numbers: the only difficulty is in valuing the quotient, which is done by any of the following Rules:

RULE 1. The first figure in the quotient is always of the same value with that figure of the dividend, which answers or stands over the place of units in the divisor.

2. The quotient must have always so many decimal places, as the dividend has more than the divisor.

Note 1. *If the divisor and dividend have both the same number of decimal parts, the quotient will be a whole number.*

2. *If the dividend hath not so many places of decimals as are in the divisor, then so many cyphers must be annexed to the dividend as will make them equal, and the quotient will then be a whole number.*

3. *But if, when the division is done, the quotient has not so many figures as it should have places of decimals, then so many cyphers must be prefixed as there are places wanting.*

EXAMPLES.

1. Divide 85643,825 by 6,321. *Facit* 13549.
2. Divide 48 by 144.
3. Divide 217,75 by 65.
4. Divide 125 by ,045.
5. Divide 709 by 2,574.
6. Divide 5,714 by 8275.
7. Divide 7382,54 by 6,4252.
8. Divide ,0851648 by 423.
9. Divide 267,15975 by 13,25.
10. Divide 72,1564 by 1347.
11. Divide 715 by ,3075.

When numbers are to be divided by 10, 100, 1000, 10000, &c. it is performed by placing the separating point in the dividend, so many places towards the left hand, as there are cyphers in the divisor.

Thus, 5784 ÷ 10 = 578,4   5784 ÷ 1000 = 5,784.
5784 ÷ 100 = 57,84   5784 ÷ 10000 = ,5784.

Contracted

Contracted DIVISION of DECIMALS.

RULE.

BY the first rule find what is the value of the first figure in the quotient; then by knowing the first figure's denomination, the decimal places may be reduced to any number, by taking as many of the left-hand figures of the dividend as will answer them; and in dividing omit one figure of the divisor at each following operation.

Note, *That in multiplying every figure left out in the divisor, you must carry* 1; *if it be* 5, *or upwards, to* 15; *if* 15 *or upwards, to* 25, *carry* 2; *if* 25, *or upwards, to* 35, *carry* 3, &c.

EXAMPLES.

12. Divide 721,17562 by 2,257432, and let there be only three places of decimals in the quotient.

```
      Contracted.                    Common way.
2,257432)  721,17562  (319.467   2,257432) 721,17562 (319.67
......     6772296                         6772296
           ───────                         ───────
            4394600  .                      4394600|2
            2257430  .                      2257432|2
            ───────                         ───────
             213717  .                       213717|00
             203169  .                       203168|88
             ──────                          ──────
              10548  . . .                    10548|120
               9030  . . .                     9029|728
              ─────                           ─────
               1518  . . . .                   1518|3920
               1354  . . . .                   1354|4592
              ─────                           ─────
                164  . . . . .                  163|9328 0
                158  . . . . .                  158|02024
                ───                            ─────
                  6                            5|91256
```

13. Divide 8,758615 by 5,2714167.
14. Divide 51717591 by 8,7586.
15. Divide 25,1367 by 217,35.
16. Divide 51,47549 by ,123415.
17. Divide 70,23 by 7,9863.
18. Divide 27,184 by 3,712.

REDUCTION

REDUCTION of DECIMALS.

To reduce a Vulgar Fraction to a Decimal.

RULE.

ADD cyphers to the numerator, and divide by the denominator, the quotient is the decimal fraction required.

EXAMPLES.

1. Reduce ¼ - - - - to a decimal.   4)1,00(,25 *Facit.*
2. Reduce ½ - - - - to a decimal.   *Facit* ,5.
3. Reduce ¾ - - - - to a decimal.   *Facit* ,75.
4. Reduce ⅜ - - - - to a decimal.   *Facit* ,375.
5. Reduce 5/26 - - - to a decimal.   *Facit* ,1923076+.
6. Reduce 1⅓ of 1⅖ to a decimal.   *Facit* ,6043956+.

Note, *If the given parts are of several denominations, they may be reduced either by so many distinct operations, as there are different parts, or by first reducing them into their lowest denomination, and then divide as before; or,*

2dly, *Bring the lowest into decimals of the next superior denomination, and on the left hand of the decimal found, place the parts given of the next superior denomination: so proceeding till you bring out the decimal parts of the highest integer required, by still dividing the product by the next superior denominator; or,*

3dly, *To reduce shillings, pence, and farthings. If the number of shillings be even, take half for the first place of decimals, and let the second and third places be filled up with the farthings contained in the remaining pence and farthings, always remembering to add 1, when it is or exceeds 25. But if the number of shillings be odd, the second place of decimals must be increased by 5.*

7. Reduce 5s. to the decimal of a £.   *Facit* ,25.
8. Reduce 9s. to the decimal of a £.   *Facit* ,45.
9. Reduce 16s. to the decimal of a £.   *Facit* ,8.

Reduction of Decimals.

10. Reduce 8s. 4d. to the decimal of a £.   *Facit* ,4166.
11. Reduce 16s. 7¼d. to the decimal of a £.
                                       Facit ,8322916.

first.	*second.*	*third.*
16s. 7¼d.	4)3,00	2)16 7¼
12	———	4
———	12)7,75	,832 —
199	———	32
4	2'0)16,64583	

960)799(,8322916   ,8322916

12. Reduce 19s. 5½d. to the decimal of a £.
                                       Facit ,972916.
13. Reduce 12 grains to the decimal of a lb. troy.
                                       Facit ,002083.
14. Reduce 12 drams to the decimal of a lb. avoirdupoise.
                                       Facit ,046875.
15. Reduce 2 qrs. 14 lb. to the decimal of an cwt.
                                       Facit ,625.
16. Reduce two furlongs to the decimal of a league.
                                       Facit ,0833.
17. Reduce 2 quarts, 1 pint, to the decimal of a gallon.
                                       Facit ,625.
18. Reduce 4 gallons, 2 quarts of wine, to the decimal of an hogshead.   *Facit* ,071428+.
19. Reduce 2 gallons, 1 quart of beer, to the decimal of a barrel.   *Facit* ,0625.
20. Reduce 52 days to the decimal of a year.
                                       Facit ,142465+.

ASSISTANT.   *Reduction of Decimals.*   121

To find the value of any Decimal Fraction, *in the known parts of an* Integer.

RULE. Multiply the decimal given, by the number of parts of the next inferior denomination, cutting off the decimals from the product; then multiply the remainder by the next inferior denomination; thus proceeding, till you have brought in the least known parts of the integer.

EXAMPLES.

21. What is the value of ,8322916 of £. Ans. 16s. 7½d+.

$$\begin{array}{r} ,8322916 \\ 20 \\ \hline 16,6458320 \\ 12 \\ \hline 7,7499840 \\ 4 \\ \hline \tfrac{1}{2},9999360 \end{array}$$

22. What is the value of ,002084 of a lb. troy?
Ans. 12,00384 qrs.
23. What is the value of ,046875 of a lb. Avoirdupoife?
Ans. 12 drams.
24. What is the value of ,625 of an cwt.?
Ans. 2 qrs. 14 lb.
25. What is the value of ,625 of a gallon?
Ans. 2 quarts, 1 pint.
26. What is the value of ,071428 of a hogshead of wine?
4 gallons 1 quart, ,999856.
27. What is the value of ,0625 of a barrel of beer?
Ans. 2 gallons 1 quart.
28. What is the value of ,142465 of a year?
Ans. 51,999725 days.

M   Decimal

Decimal TABLES of COIN, WEIGHT, and MEASURE.

TABLE I.
ENGLISH COIN.
1£. the Integer.

Sh.	dec.	Sh.	dec.
19	,95	9	,45
18	,9	8	,4
17	,85	7	,35
16	,8	6	,3
15	,75	5	,25
14	,7	4	,2
13	,65	3	,15
12	,6	2	,1
11	,55	1	,05
10	,5		

Pence	Decimals.
6	,025
5	,020833
4	,016666
3	,0125
2	,00833
1	,00416

Farth.	Decimals.
3	,003125
2	,0020833
1	,0010416

TABLE II.
ENG. COIN. 1 Sh.
Long Meaſ. 1 Foot the Integer.

Pence & Inches.	Decimals.
6	,5
5	,416666
4	,333333
3	,25
2	,166666
1	,083333

Farthings.	Decimals.
3	,0625
2	,041666
1	,020833

TABLE III.
TROY WEIGHT.
1lb. the Integer.
Ounces the same as Pence in the laſt Table.

Penny weight.	Decimals.
10	,041666
9	,0375
8	,033333
7	,029166
6	,025
5	,020833
4	,016666
3	,0125
2	,008333
1	,004166

Grains	Decimals.
12	,002083
11	,001910
10	,001736
9	,001562
8	,001389
7	,001215
6	,001042
5	,000868
4	,000694
3	,000521
2	,000347
1	,000173

1 Oz. the Integer.
Penny-weights the same as Shillings in the 1ſt. Table.

Grains.	Decimals.
12	,025
11	,022916
10	,020833
9	,01875
8	,016666
7	,014583
6	,0125
5	,010416
4	,008333
3	,00625
2	,004166
1	,002083

TABLE IV.
AVOIRDUP. WT.
112 lb. the Integ.

Qrs.	Decimals.
1	,75
2	,5
3	,25

Pounds	Decimals.
14	,125
13	,116071
12	,107143
11	,098214
10	,089286
9	,080357
8	,071428
7	,0625
6	,053571
5	,044643
4	,035714
3	,026786
2	,017857
1	,008928

Ounces	Decimals.
8	,004464
7	,003906

Decimal TABLES of COIN, WEIGHT, and MEASURE.

,6	,003348
5	,002790
4	,002232
3	,001674
2	,001116
1	,000558

¼ Oz.	Decimals.
3	,000418
2	,000279
1	,000139

TABLE V.
AVOIR. WEIGHT.
1 lb. the Integer.

Ounces.	Decimals.
8	,5
7	,4375
6	,375
5	,3125
4	,25
3	,1875
2	,125
1	,0625

Drams.	Decimals.
8	,03125
7	,027343
6	,023437
5	,019531
4	,015625
3	,011718
2	,007812
1	,003906

TABLE VI.
LIQUID MEASURE
1 Tun the Integer.

Gallons.	Decimals.
100	,396825
90	,357141
80	,317460
70	,27
60	,238095
50	,198412
40	,158730
30	,119047
20	,079365
10	,039682
9	,035714
8	,031746
7	,027
6	,023809
5	,019841
4	,015873
3	,011904
2	,007936
1	,003968

Pints.	Decimals.
4	,001984
3	,001488
2	,000992
1	,000496

A Hogshead the Integer.

Gallons.	Decimals.
30	,476190
20	,317460
10	,158730
9	,142857
8	,126984
7	,111111
6	,095238
5	,079365
4	,063492
3	,047619
2	,031746
1	,015873

Pints.	Decimals.
3	,005952
2	,003968
1	,001984

TABLE VII.
MEASURE.
Liquid.   Dry.
1 Gallon. 1 Quarter.
Integer.

Pints	Decim.	Bush.
4	,5	4
3	,875	3
2	,25	2
1	,125	1

Q.p.	Decim.	Peck.
3	,09375	3
2	,0625	2
1	,03125	1

Decimals.	Q. Pk.
,0234375	3
,015625	2
,0078125	1

Decimals.	Pints.
,005859	3
,003906	2
,001953	1

TABLE VIII.
LONG MEASURE.
1 Mile the Integer.

Yards.	Decimals.
1000	,568182
900	,511364
800	,454545
700	,397727
600	,340909

Decimal TABLES of COIN, WEIGHT, and MEASURE.

500	,284091	70	,191781	**TABLE X.**	
400	,227272	60	,164383	**CLOTH MEASURE.**	
300	,170454	50	,136986	1 Yard the Integer.	
200	,113636	40	,109589	Qrs. the same as	
100	,056818	30	,082192	Table 4.	
90	,051136	20	,054794		
80	,045454	10	,027397	Nails.	Decimals.
70	,039773	9	,024657	2	,125
60	,034091	8	,021918	1	,0625
50	,028409	7	,019178		
40	,022727	6	,016438	**TABLE XI.**	
30	,017045	5	,013698	**LEAD WEIGHT.**	
20	,011364	4	,010959	1 Foth. the Integ.	
10	,005682	3	,008219		
9	,005114	2	,005479	Hund.	Decimals.
8	,004745	1	,002732	10	,512820
7	,003977	1 Day the Integer.		9	,461538
6	,003409	Hours.	Decimals.	8	,410256
5	,002841	12	,5	7	,358974
4	,002273	11	,458333	6	,307692
3	,001704	10	,416666	5	,256410
2	,001136	9	,375	4	,205128
1	,000568	8	,333333	3	,153846
Feet.	Decimals.	7	,291666	2	,102564
2	,0003787	6	,25	1	,051282
1	,0001894	5	,208333	Qrs.	Decimals.
Inch.	Decimals.	4	,166666	2	,025641
6	,0000947	3	,125	1	,012820
3	,0000474	2	,083333	Pound	Decimals.
1	,0000158	1	,041666	14	,0064102
TABLE IX.		Minutes.	Decimals.	13	,0059523
TIME.		30	,020833	12	,0054945
1 Year the Integer.		20	,013888	11	,0050366
Months the same as		10	,006944	10	,0045787
Pence in the se-		9	,00625	9	,0041208
cond Table.		8	,005555	8	,0036630
Days.	Decimals.	7	,004861	7	,0032051
365	1,000000	6	,004166	6	,0027472
300	,821918	5	,003472	5	,0022893
200	,547945	4	,002777	4	,0018315
100	,273973	3	,002083	3	,0013736
90	,246575	2	,001388	2	,0009157
80	,219178	1	,000694	1	,0004578

The RULE of THREE in DECIMALS.

EXAMPLES.

1. IF 26 ½ yards cost £3..16..3. what will 32 ¼ yards come to? *Anf.* £4..12..9½.

```
    Yds.        £.          Yds
    26,5   :  3,8125   ::  32,25 :
                            32,25
    ─────────────────────────────
    26,5)122,953125(4,63974 = £4..12..9½.
```

2. What will the pay of 540 men come to at £1..5..6. per man? *Anf.* £688..10..—.

3. If 7 ¼ yards of cloth cost £2..12..9. what will 140 ½ yards of the same cost? *Anf.* £47..16..3..2,4 qrs.

4. If a chest of sugar, weighing 7 cwt. 2 qrs. 14 lb. cost £36..12..9. what will 2 cwt. 1 qr. 21 lb. of the same cost? *Anf.* £11..14..2..3,5 qrs.

5. A grocer buys 24 ton, 12 cwt. 2 qrs. 14 lb. 12 oz. of tobacco for £3678..6..4. what will 1 oz. come to? *Anf.* 1d.

6. What will 326 lb. 1 qr. of tobacco come to, when 1½ lb. is sold for 3s. 6d.? *Anf.* £38..1..3.

7. What is the worth of 19 oz. 3 dwt. 5 gr. of gold, at £2..19..—. per oz.? *Anf.* £56..10..5..2,99 qrs.

8. What is the worth of 827 ¼ yards of painting, at 10¼d. per yard? *Anf.* £36..4..3..1,5 qrs.

9. If I lent my friend £34. for ⅝ of a year, how much ought he to lend me 5/12 of a year to requite my kindness? *Anf.* £51.

10. If ¼ of a yard of cloth, that is 2 yards ¼ broad, make a garment, how much that is ⅘ of a yard wide will make the same? *Anf.* 2,109375 yards.

11. If one ounce of silver cost 5s. 6d. what is the price of a tankard that weighs 1 lb. 10 oz. 10 dwt. 4 gr.? *Anf.* £6..3..9..2,2 qrs.

12. If 1 lb. of tobacco cost 15d. what cost 3 hogsheads, weighing together 15 cwt. 1 qr. 19 lb.? *Anf.* £107..18..9.

13. If 1 cwt. of currants coſt £2..9..6. what will 45 cwt. 3 qrs. 14 lb. coſt at the ſame rate? *Anſ.* £113..10..9..3 *qrs.*

14. Bought 6 cheſts of ſugar, each 6 cwt. 3 qrs. at £2..16..–. *per* cwt. what do they come to? *Anſ.* £113..8..–.

15. Bought a tankard for £10..12..–. at the rate of 5s. 4d. *per* ounce, what was the weight?   *Anſ.* 39 oz. 15 dwt.

16. Gave £187..3..3. for 25 cwt. 3 qrs. 14 lb. of tobacco, at what rate did I buy it at *per* lb.?   *Anſ.* 15d. 2 *qrs.*

17. Bought 29 lb. 4 oz. of coffee for £10..11..3. what is the value of 3 lb.?   *Anſ.* £1..1..8.

18. If I gave 1s. 1d. for 3 lb. ½ of cheeſe, what will be the value of 1 cwt.?   *Anſ.* £1..14..8.

EXTRACTION *of the* SQUARE ROOT.

EXTRACTING the Square Root is to find out ſuch a number as being multiplied into itſelf, the product will be equal to the given number.

RULE. *Firſt*, Point the given number, beginning at the unit's place, then to the hundreds, and ſo upon every ſecond figure throughout.

Secondly, Seek the greateſt ſquare number in the firſt point towards the left-hand, placing the ſquare number under the firſt point, and the root thereof in the quotient ; ſubtract the ſquare number from the firſt point, and to the remainder bring down the next point, and call that the reſolvend.

Thirdly, Double the quotient, and place it for a diviſor on the left-hand of the reſolvend ; ſeek how often the diviſor is contained in the reſolvend (preſerving always the unit's place,) and put the anſwer in the quotient, and alſo on the right-hand ſide of the diviſor ; then multiply by the figure laſt put in the quotient, and ſubtract the product from the reſolvend ; bring down the next point to the remainder, (if there be any more) and proceed as before.

ROOTS,	1.	2.	3.	4.	5.	6.	7.	8.	9.
SQUARES,	1.	4.	9.	16.	25.	36.	49.	64.	81.

EXAMPLES.

ASSISTANT. *Extraction of the Square Root.*   127

EXAMPLES.

1. What is the square root of 119025?   *Ans.* 345.

```
119025(345
  9
  ─────
64)290
   256
   ─────
  685)3425
       3425
```

2. What is the square root of 106929?   *Ans.* 327.
3. What is the square root of 2268741? *Ans.* 1506,23+.
4. What is the square root of 7596796? *Ans.* 2756,228+.
5. What is the square root of 36372961? *Ans.* 6031.
6. What is the square root of 22071204? *Ans.* 4698.

When the given number consists of a whole number, and decimals together, make the number of decimals even, by adding cyphers to them; so that there may be a point fall on the unit's place of the whole number.

7. What is the square root of 3271,4207? *Ans.* 57,19+.
8. What is the square root of 4795,25731? *Ans.* 69,247+.
9. What is the square root of 4,372594?   *Ans.* 2,091+.
10. What is the square root of 2,2710957? *Ans.* 1,50701+.
11. What is the square root of ,00032754? *Ans.* ,01809+.
12. What is the square root of 1,270054? *Ans.* 1,1269+.

To extract the SQUARE ROOT *of a* VULGAR FRACTION.

RULE. Reduce the fraction to its lowest terms: then extract the square root of the numerator for a new numerator, and the square root of the denominator for a new denominator.

If the fraction be a surd, (i. e.) *a number where a root can never be exactly found, reduce it to a decimal, and extract the root from it.*

EXAMPLES.

13. What is the square root of $\frac{2304}{5184}$? *Ans.* $\frac{2}{3}$.
14. What is the square root of $\frac{2704}{4225}$? *Ans.* $\frac{4}{5}$.
15. What is the square root of $\frac{9216}{12544}$? *Ans.* $\frac{6}{7}$.

SURDS.

Surds.

16. What is the square root of $\frac{273}{41}$? Anf. ,89802+.
17. What is the square root of $\frac{3}{4}\frac{7}{6}$? Anf. ,86602+.
18. What is the square root of $\frac{478}{549}$? Anf. ,93308+.

To extract the Square Root of a Mixed Number.

Rule 1. Reduce the fractional part of the mixed number to its lowest term, and then the mixed number to an improper fraction.

2. Extract the roots of the numerator and denominator for a new numerator and denominator.

If the mixed number given be a surd, reduce the fractional part to a decimal, annex it to the whole number, and extract the square root therefrom.

Examples.

19. What is the square root of $51\frac{21}{25}$? Anf. $7\frac{1}{5}$.
20. What is the square root of $27\frac{9}{16}$? Anf. $5\frac{1}{4}$.
21. What is the square root of $9\frac{43}{49}$? Anf. $3\frac{1}{7}$?

Surds.

22. What is the square root of $85\frac{14}{15}$? Anf. 9,27 +.
23. What is the square root of $8\frac{5}{7}$? Anf. 2,9519+.
24. What is the square root of $6\frac{2}{3}$? Anf. 2,5819+.

Application.

25. There is an army consisting of a certain number of men, who are placed rank and file (that is, in the form of a square, each side having 576 men) I desire to know how many the whole square contains? Anf. 331776.

26. A certain pavement is made exactly square, each side of which contains 97 feet. I demand how many square feet are contained therein? Anf. 9409.

To find a mean proportional between any two given numbers.

Rule. The square root of the product of the given numbers is the mean proportional sought.

Examples.

ASSISTANT. *Extraction of the Square Root.* 129

EXAMPLES.

27. What is the mean proportional between 3 and 12?
Anf. 3×12=36 then √36=6 the mean proportional.
28. What is the mean proportional between 4276 and 842? Anf. 1897,4+.

To find the side of a square equal in area to any given superfices.

RULE. The square root of the content of any given superfices, is equal to the side of the square sought.

EXAMPLES.

29. If the content of a given circle be 160, what is the side of the square? Anf. 12,64911.
30. If the area of a circle is 750, what is the side of the square equal? Anf. 27,38612.

The area of a circle given, to find the diameter.

RULE. As 355 : 452, or, as 1 : 1,273239 :: so is the area : to the square of the diameter :—or, multiply the square root of the area, by 1,12837, and the product will be the diameter.

EXAMPLES.

31. What length of cord will be fit to tie to a cow's tail, the other end fixed in the ground, to let her have liberty of eating an acre of grafs, and no more, fuppofing the cow and tail to be 5½ yards? Anf. 6,136 perches.

The area of a circle given, to find the periphery, or circumference.

RULE. As 113 : 1420, or, as 1 : 12,56637 :: the area to the square of the periphery :—or, multiply the square root of the area by 3,5449, and the product is the circumference.

EXAMPLES.

32. When the area is 12, what is the circumference?
Anf. 12,2798.
33. When the are is 160, what is the periphery?
Anf. 44,830.

Any two sides of a right angled triangle given; to find the third side.

1. The

1. *The base and perpendicular given, to find the hypothenuse.*

RULE. The square root of the sum of the squares of the base and perpendicular is the length of the hypothenuse.

EXAMPLES.

34. The top of a castle from the ground is 45 yards high, and surrounded with a ditch 60 yards broad; what length must a ladder be to reach from the outside of the ditch to the top of the castle? *Ans.* 75 *yards.*

Ditch.
Base 60 yards.
45 yards.
Height of the castle.
Perpendicular.

35. The wall of a town is 25 feet high, which is surrounded by a moat of 30 feet in breadth: I desire to know the length of a ladder that will reach from the outside of the moat to the top of the wall? *Ans.* 39,05 *feet.*

2. *The hypothenuse and perpendicular given, to find the base.*

RULE. The square root of the difference of the squares of the hypothenuse and perpendicular is the length of the base.

3. *The base and hypothenuse given, to find the perpendicular.*

RULE. The square root of the difference of the squares of the hypothenuse and base is the height of the perpendicular.

N. B. *The two last questions may be varied for examples to the two last propositions.*

Any number of men being given, to form them into a square battle, or to find the number of ranks and files.

RULE. The square root of the number of men given, is the number of men either in rank or file.

36. An army consisting of 331776 men, I desire to know how many rank and file? *Ans.* 576.

37. A certain square pavement contains 48841 square stones, all of the same size, I demand how many are contained in one of the sides? *Ans.* 221.

EXTRACTION

EXTRACTION of the CUBE ROOT.

To extract the Cube Root is to find out a number, which being multiplied into itself, and then into that product, produceth the given number.

Rule 1. Point every third figure of the cube given, beginning at the unit's place; seek the greatest cube to the first point, and subtract it therefrom; put the root in the quotient, and bring down the figures in the next point to the remainder for a Resolvend.

2. Find a Divisor by multiplying the square of the quotient by 3. See how often it is contained in the resolvend, rejecting the units and tens, and put the answer in the quotient.

3. To find the Subtrahend. 1. Cube the last figure in the quotient. 2. Multiply all the figures in the quotient by 3, except the last, and that product by the square of the last. 3. Multiply the divisor by the last figure. Add these products together, gives the subtrahend, which subtract from the resolvend; to the remainder bring down the next point, and proceed as before.

Roots. 1. 2. 3. 4. 5. 6. 7. 8. 9.
Cubes. 1. 8. 27. 64. 125. 216. 343. 512. 729.

Examples.

1. What is the cube root of 99252847?

$$99252847.(463$$
$$64 = \text{cube of } 4$$

Divisor.
Square of $4 \times 3 = 48) 35252$ resolvend.

$$216 = \text{cube of } 6.$$
$$432 = 4 \times 3 \times \text{ by square of } 6.$$
$$288 = \text{divisor} \times \text{ by } 6.$$

$$33336 \text{ subtrahend.}$$

Divisor.
Square of $46 \times 3 = 6348) 1916847$ resolvend.

$$27 = \text{cube of } 3.$$
$$1242 = 46 \times 3 \times \text{by square of } 3.$$
$$19044 = \text{divisor} \times \text{ by } 3.$$

$$1916847 \text{ subtrahend.}$$

Another

Another New *and more* Concise Method *of extracting the*
CUBE ROOT.

RULE 1. Point every third figure of the cube given, beginning at the unit's place, then find the highest cube to the first point, and subtract it therefrom, put the root in the quotient, bring down the figures in the next point to the remainder for a resolvend.

2. Square the quotient and triple the square for a divisor, As 4×4×3=48. Find how often it is contained in the resolvend, rejecting units and tens, and put the answer in the quotient.

Square the last figure in the quotient, and put it on the right hand of the divisor.
As 6×6=36 put to the divisor 48=4836.

4. Triple the last figure in the quotient, and multiply by the former, put it under the other, units under the tens, add them together, and multiply the sum by the last figure in the quotient, subtract that product from the resolvend, bring down the next point, and proceed as before.

EXAMPLES.

1. What is the cube root of 99252847?
Square of 4×3=48 *divisor*   99252847(463
Square of 6 *put to* 48=4836   64
6×3×4 = 72
                                 35252
                                 33336
         5556×6
Square of 46=2116×3=6348 *divisor.*
Square of 3=9 *put to* 6348=*634809   1916847
         8×3×46=414

                                 638949×3=1916847.
2. What is the cube root of 389017?   *Ans.* 73.
3. What is the cube root of 5735339?   *Ans.* 179.
4. What is the cube root of 32461759? *Ans.* 319.
5. What is the cube root of 84604519? *Ans.* 439.
6. What is the cube root of 259694072? *Ans.* 638.
7. What is the cube root of 48228544? *Ans.* 364.
* *When the quotient is 2 or 3, there must be a cypher put to supply the place of tens.*
8. What

Assistant. *Extraction of the Cube Root.*

8. What is the cube root of 27054036008 ? *Anf.* 3002.
9. What is the cube root of 22069810125 ? *Anf.* 2805.
10. What is the cube root of 122615327232 ? *Anf.* 4968.
11. What is the cube root of 219365327791 ? *Anf.* 6031.
12. What is the cube root of 673373097125 ? *Anf.* 8765.

When the given number confifts of a whole number and decimal together, make the number of decimals to confift of 3, 6, 9, &c. places by adding cyphers thereto, fo that there may be a point fall on the unit's place of the whole number.

13. What is the cube root of 12,977875 ? *Anf.* 2,35.
14. What is the cube root of 36155,027576 ? *Anf.* 33,06+.
15. What is the cube root of ,001906624 ? *Anf.* ,124.
16. What is the cube root of 33,230979637 ? *Anf.* 3,215+.
17. What is the cube root of 15926,972504 ? *Anf.* 25,16+.
18. What is the cube root of ,053157376 ? *Anf.* ,376.

To extract the cube root of a vulgar fraction.

RULE. Reduce the fraction to its loweft terms, then extract the cube root of its numerator and denominator, for a new numerator and denominator; but if the fraction be a furd, reduce it to a decimal, and then extract the root from it.

EXAEPLES.

19. What is the cube root of $\frac{230}{686}$? *Anf.* $\frac{5}{7}$.
20. What is the cube root of $\frac{324}{1500}$? *Anf.* $\frac{2}{5}$.
21. What is the cube root of $\frac{1520}{3130}$? *Anf.* $\frac{2}{3}$.

SURDS.

22. What is the cube root of $\frac{4}{7}$? *Anf.* ,829+.
23. What is the cube root of $\frac{1}{2}$? *Anf.* ,822+.
24. What is the cube root of $\frac{2}{3}$? *Anf.* ,873+.

To extract the cube of a mixed number.

RULE. Reduce the fractional part to its loweft terms, and then the mixed number to an improper fraction, extract the cube roots of the numerator and denominator for a new numerator and denominator; but if the mixed number given be a furd, reduce the fractional part to a decimal, annex it to the whole number, and extract the root therefrom.

EXAMPLES.

25. What is the cube root of $12\frac{19}{27}$?   Anſ. $2\frac{1}{3}$.
26. What is the cube root of $31\frac{17}{47}$?   Anſ. $3\frac{1}{7}$.
27. What is the cube root of $405\frac{28}{125}$?   Anſ. $7\frac{2}{5}$.

SURDS.

28. What is the cube root of $7\frac{1}{5}$?   Anſ. 1,93+.
29. What is the cube root of $9\frac{1}{6}$?   Anſ. 2,092+.
30. What is the cube root of $8\frac{5}{7}$?   Anſ. 2,057+.

The APPLICATION.

1. If a cubical piece of timber be 47 inches long, 47 inches broad, and 47 inches deep, how many cubical inches doth it contain?   Anſ. 103823.

2. There is a cellar dug, that is 12 feet every way, in length, breadth, and depth, how many ſolid feet of earth were taken out of it?   Anſ. 1728.

3. There is a ſtone of a cubic form, which contains 389017 ſolid feet, what is the ſuperficial content of one of its ſides?   Anſ. 5329.

Between two numbers given, to find two mean proportionals.

RULE. Divide the greater extreme by the leſs, and the cube root of the quotient multiplied by the leſs extreme gives the leſs mean; multiply the ſaid cube root by the leſs mean, and the product will be the greater mean proportional.

EXAMPLES.

4. What are the two mean proportionals between 6 and 162?   Anſ. 18 and 54.
5. What are the two mean proportionals between 4 and 108?   Anſ. 12 and 36.

To find the ſide of a cube that ſhall be equal in ſolidity to any given ſolid, as a globe, cylinder, priſm, cone, &c.

RULE. The cube root of the ſolid content of any ſolid body given, is the ſide of the cube of equal ſolidity.

EXAMPLES.

6. If the ſolid content of a globe is 10648, what is the ſide of a cube of equal ſolidity?   Anſ. 22.

The side of the cube being given, to find the side of the cube that shall be double, treble, &c. in quantity to the cube given.

RULE. Cube the side given, and multiply it by 2, 3, &c. the cube root of the product is the side sought.

EXAMPLES.

7. There is a cubical vessel, whose side is 12 inches, and it is required to find the side of another vessel, that is to contain 3 times as much? *Ans.* 17,306.

EXTRACTING of the BIQUADRATE ROOT.

TO extract the Biquadrate Root is to find out a number, which being involved four times into itself, will produce the given number.

RULE. First extract the square root of the given number, and then extract the square root of that square root, and it will give the Biquadrate required.

EXAMPLES.

1. What is the biquadrate of 27? *Ans.* 531441.
2. What is the biquadrate of 76? *Ans.* 33362176.
3. What is the biquadrate of 275? *Ans.* 5719140625.
4. What is the biquadrate root of 531441? *Ans.* 27.
5. What is the biquadrate root of 33362176? *Ans.* 76.
6. What is the biquadrate root of 5719140625? *Ans.* 275.

A general Rule for Extracting the ROOTS of all POWERS.

1. PREPARE the number given for extraction, by pointing off from the unit's place as the root required directs.

2. Find the first figure in the root by the table of powers, which subtract from the given number.

3. Bring down the first figure in the next point to the remainder, and call it the Dividend.

4. Involve the root into the next inferior power to that which is given, multiply it by the given power, and call it the Divisor.

5. Find

136 *Extracting the Roots of Powers.* The Tutor's

5. Find a quotient figure by common Division, and annex it to the root; then involve the whole root into the given power, and call that the Subtrahend.

6. Subtract that number from as many points of the given power as is brought down, beginning at the lowest place, and to the remainder bring down the first figure of the next point for a new dividend.

7. Find a new divisor, and proceed in all respects as before.

Examples.

1. What is the square root of 141376?

141376(376
9
———
6)51 *dividend.*

1369 *subtrahend.*
———

74) 447 *dividend.*

141376 *subtrahend.*
———

3 × 2 = 6 *divisor.*
37 × 37 = 1369 *subtrahend.*
37 × 2 = 74 *divisor.*
376 × 376 = 141376 *subtrahend.*

2. What is the cube root of 53157376?

53157376(376
27
———
27)261 *dividend.*

50653 *subtrahend.*

4107)25043 *dividend.*

53157376 *subtrahend.*
———

3 × 3 × 3 = 27 *divisor.*
37 × 37 × 37 = 50653 *subtrahend.*
37 × 37 × 3 = 4107 *divisor.*
376 × 376 × 376 = 53157376 *subtrahend.*

3. What

3. What is the biquadrate of 19987173376?

19987173376(376
81

108)1188 *dividend.*

1874161 *subtrahend.*

202612)1245563 *dividend.*

19987173376 *subtrahend.*

3 × 3 × 3 × 4 = 108 *divisor.*
37 × 37 × 37 × 37 = 1874161 *subtrahend.*
37 × 37 × 37 × 4 = 202612 *divisor.*
376 × 376 × 376 × 376 = 19987173376 *subtrahend.*

SIMPLE INTEREST.

THERE are five letters to be observed in Simple Interest, viz.

    P. the Principal.
    T. the Time.
    R. the Ratio, or rate *per cent.*
    I, the Interest.
    A. the Amount.

A TABLE of RATIOS.

3	,03	5½	,055	8	,08
3½	,035	6	,06	8½	,085
4	,04	6½	,065	9	,09
4½	,045	7	,07	9½	,095
5	,05	7½	,075	10	,1

N. The Ratio is the Simple Interest of £1. for one year, at the Rate per Cent. proposed, and is found thus:

£. £. £.
As 100 : 3 : : 1 : ,03.   As 100 : 3,5 : : 1 : ,035.

Simple Interest.

When the principal, time, and rate per cent. are given, to find the interest.

RULE. Multiply the principal, time and rate together, and it will give the interest required.

NOTE. The proposition and rule are better expressed thus:

I. When P, T, R, are given, to find I.
RULE. $ptr = I$.

NOTE. When two or more letters are put together like a word, they are to be multiplied one into another.

EXAMPLES.

1. What is the interest of £945..10..-. for three years, at 5 per cent. per annum?
Ans. £945,5 × ,05 × 3 = 141,825 or £141..16..6.

2. What is the interest of £547..14..-. at 4 per cent. per annum, for 6 years? Ans. £131..8..11. 2 qr. ,08.

3. What is the interest of £796..15..-. at 4½ per cent. per annum, for 5 years? Ans. £179..5..4. 2 qr.

4. What is the interest of £397..9..5. for two years and ⅘, at 3½ per cent. per annum? Ans. £34..15..6. 3,5499 qr.

5. What is the interest of £554..17..6. for 3 years, 8 months, at 4½ per cent. per annum? Ans. £91..11..1.—20.

6. What is the interest of £236..18..8. for 3 years 8 months, at 5½ per cent. per annum? Ans. £47..15..7. 1,4528 qr.

When the interest is for any number of days only.

RULE. Multiply the interest of £1. for 1 day, at the given rate, by the principal and number of days, it will give the answer.

INTEREST OF £1. FOR ONE DAY.

per cent.	Decimals.	per cent.	Decimals.
3	,00008219178	6½	,00017808219
3½	,00009580041	7	,00019178082
4	,00010958904	7½	,00020547945
4½	,00012328767	8	,00021917808
5	,00013698630	8½	,00023287671
5½	,00015068493	9	,00024657534
6	,00016438356	9½	,00026027397

NOTE. *The above Table is thus found:*

As 365 : ,03 : : 1 : ,00008219178. And as 365 : ,035 : : 1 : ,00009589041, &c.

EXAMPLES.

Examples.

7. What is the interest of £240. for 120 days, at 4 per cent. per annum? *Anſ.* .00010958904×240×120=£3.-3..1¼.

8. What is the intereſt of £563. at 6 per cent per annum, for 126 days? *Anſ.* £11..13..2½.

9. What is the intereſt of £560. for 60 days, at 5 per cent. per annum? *Anſ.* £4..12..-½.

10. What is the interest of £364..18..-. for 154 days, at 5 per cent. per annum? *Anſ.* £7..13..11¼.

11. What is the interest of £725..15..-. for 74 days, at 4 per cent. per annum? *Anſ.* £5..17..8½.

12. What is the interest of £100. from the 1ſt of June, 1775, to the 9th of March following, at 5 per cent. per annum? *Anſ.* £3..16..11¼.

II. When P, R, T, are given to find A.

Rule. $prt + p = A$.

Examples.

13. What will £279..12..-. amount to in 7 years, at 4½ per cent. per annum? *Anſ.* £367..13..5. 3,04 qrs.
$$279,6 \times ,045 + 279,6 = 367,674.$$

14. What will £320..17..-. amount to in 5 years, at 3½ per cent. per annum? *Anſ.* £376..19..11. 2,8 qrs.

15. What will £679..13..-. amount to in 6 years, at 5 per cent. per annum? *Anſ.* £883..10..10. 3,2 qrs.

When there is any odd time given with the whole years, reduce the odd time into days, and work with the decimal parts of a year which are equal to thoſe days.

16. What will £926..12..-. amount to in 5 years ½, at 4 per cent. per annum? *Anſ.* £1130..9..-. 1,92 qrs.

17. What will £368..16..-. amount to in 7 years ¼, at 6½ per cent. per annum? *Anſ.* £554..11..7. 3,68 qrs.

18. What will £273..18..-. amount to in 4 years, 175 days, at 3 per cent. per annum?
   Anſ. £310..14..1. 3,35080064 qrs.

III. When A, R, T, are given to find P.

Rule. $\dfrac{a}{rt+1} = P$.

Examples.

Examples.

19. What principal, being put to interest, will amount to £367..13..5. 3,04 qrs. in 7 years, at 4½ per cent. per annum? *Anſ.* ,045×7+1=1,315, then 367,674÷1,315 =£279..12..–.

20. What principal being put to interest, will amount to £376..19..11. 2,8. in 5 years, at 3½ per cent. per annum? *Anſ.* £320..17..–.

21. What principal, being put to interest, will amount to £883..10..10. 3,2 qrs. in 6 years, at 5 per cent. per annum? *Anſ.* £679..13..–.

22. What principal, being put to interest, will amount to £1130..9..–. 1,92 qrs. in 5 years and ¼, at 4 per cent. per annum? *Anſ.* £926..12. –.

23. What principal will amount to £554..11..7. 3,68 qrs. in 7 years ½, at 6½ per cent. per annum? *Anſ.* £368..16–.

24. What principal will amount to £310..14..1. 3,35080064 qrs. in 4 years, 175 days, at 3 per cent. per annum? *Anſ.* £273..18..–.

IV. *When* A, P, T, *are given to find* R.

RULE. $\dfrac{a-p}{pt} = $ R.

Examples.

25. At what rate per cent. will £279..12..–. amount to £367..13..5. 3,04 qrs. in 7 years?
Anſ. 367,674–279,6=88,074. 279,6×7=1957,2, then 88,074÷1957,2=,045 at 4½ *per cent.*

26. At what rate per cent. will £320..17..–. amount to £376..19..11. 2,8 qrs. in 5 years? *Anſ.* 3½ *per cent.*

27. At what rate per cent. will £679..13..–. amount to £883..10..10. 3,2 qrs. in 6 years? *Anſ.* 5 *per cent.*

28. At what rate per cent. will £926..12..–. amount to £1130..9..–. 1,92 qrs. in 5 years ¼? *Anſ.* 4 *per cent.*

29. At what rate per cent. will £368..16..–. amount to £554..18..7. 3,68 qrs. in 7 years ½? *Anſ.* 6½ *per cent.*

30. At what rate per cent. will £273..18..–. amount to £310..14..1. 3,35080064 qrs. in 4 years, 175 days? *Anſ.* 3 *per cent.*

V. *When* A, P, R, *are given to find* T.

RULE. $\dfrac{a-p}{pr} = $ T.

EXAMPLES.

ASSISTANT. *Simple Interest.* 141

EXAMPLES.

31. In what time will £279..12..-. amount to £367..13..5. 3,04 qrs. at 4½ per cent.? *Anſ.* 367,674—279,6=88,074, 279,6×,045=12,5820 then 88,074÷12,5820=7 years.

32. In what time will £320..17..-. amount to £376..19..11. 2,8 qrs. at 3½ per cent.? *Anſ.* 5 years.

33. In what time will £679..13..-. amount to £883..10..10. 3,2 qrs. at 5 per cent.? *Anſ.* 6 years.

34. In what time will £926..12--. amount to £1130..9..--. 1',92 qrs. at 4½ per cent.? *Anſ.* 5 years ½.

35. In what time will £368..16..-.amount to £554..11..7. 3,68 qrs. at 6½ per cent.? *Anſ.* 7 years ¼.

36. In what time will £273..18..-. amount to £310..14..1. 3,35080064 qrs. at 3 per cent.? *Anſ.* 4 years 175 days.

Annuities *or* Pensions, *&c. in* Arrears.

Annuities or Pensions, &c. are said to be in arrears when they are payable or due, either yearly, half-yearly, or quarterly, and are unpaid for any number of payments.

NOTE. U *represents the* annuity, pension, *or* yearly rent. T, R, A, *as before.*

I, U, R, T, *are given to find* A.

RULE. $\dfrac{ttu-tu}{2} \times r : + tu = A.$

EXAMPLES.

37. If a salary of £150. be forborne 5 years, at 5 per cent. what would it amount to? *Anſ.* £825.

$$5\times5\times150-5\times150=3000 \text{ then } \dfrac{3000}{2}\times,05+5\times150=£825$$

38. If £250. yearly pension be forborne 7 years, what will it amount to in that time, at 6 per cent.? *Anſ.* 2065.

39. There is a house let upon a lease for 5 years ½, at £60. per annum, what will be the amount of the whole time, at 4½ per cent.? *Anſ.* £363..8..3.

40. Suppose an annual pension of £28. remain unpaid for 8 years, what would it amount at 5 per cent.? *Anſ.* £263..4..--.

Note

NOTE. *When the annuities, &c. are to be paid half-yearly, or quarterly, then*

For half-yearly payments *take half of the ratio, half of the annuity, &c. and twice the number of years,—and,*

For quarterly payments, *take a fourth part of the ratio, a fourth part of the annuity, &c. and four times the number of years, and work as before.*

EXAMPLES.

41. If a salary of £150. payable every half year, remains unpaid for 5 years, what would it amount to in that time at 5 per cent.? *Ans.* £834..7..6.

42. If a salary o £150. payable every quarter, was left unpaid for 5 years, what would it amount to in that time at 5 per cent.? *Ans.* £839..1..3.

NOTE. *It may be observed, by comparing these last examples, the amount of the half-yearly payments are more advantageous than the yearly, and the quarterly more than the half-yearly.*

II. When A, R, T, *are given, to find* U.

RULE. $\dfrac{2a}{ttr - tr + 2t} = U$

EXAMPLES.

43. If a salary amounted to £825. in 5 years at 5 per cent. what was the salary? *Ans.* £150.

$825 \times 2 = 1650$. $5 \times 5 \times .05 - 5 \times .05 + 5 \times 2 = 11$ then $1650 \div 11 = £.150$.

44. If a house is to be let upon a lease for 5 years ½, and the amount for that time be £363..8..3. at 4½ per cent. what is the yearly rent? *Ans.* £60.

45. If a pension amounted to £2065. in 7 years, at 6 per cent. what is the pension? *Ans.* £250.

46. Suppose the amount of a pension be £263..4..—. in 8 years, at 5 per cent. what is the pension? *Ans.* £28.

NOTE. *When the payments are half-yearly, then take 4 a and half of the ratio, and twice the number of years: and if quarterly, then take 8 a, one fourth of the ratio, and four times the number of years, and proceed as before.*

47. If the amount of a salary, payable half-yearly, for 5 years, and at 5 per cent. be £834..7..6. what is the salary? *Ans.* £150.

48. If

48. If the amount of an annuity payable quarterly, be £839..1..3. for 5 years, at 5 per cent. what is the annuity?
Ans. £150.

III. *When* U, A, T, *are given, to find* R.

Rule. $\dfrac{2a - 2ut}{utt - ut} = R.$

EXAMPLES.

49. If a salary of £150. per annum, amount to £825. in 5 years, what is the rate per cent.? *Ans.* 5 per cent.

$825 \times 2 - 150 \times 5 \times 2 = 150$ then $\dfrac{150}{150 \times 5 \times 5 - 150 \times 5} = ,05$

50. If a house be let upon lease for 5½ years, at £60. per annum, and the amount for that time be £363..8..3. what is the rate per cent.? *Ans.* 4½ per cent.

51. If a pension of £250. per annum amounts to £2065. in 7 years, what is the rate per cent.? *Ans.* 6 per cent.

52. Suppose the amount of an yearly pension of £28. be £263..4. 0. in 8 years, what is the rate per cent.? *Ans.* 5 per cent.

NOTE. *When the payments are half-yearly, take* 4 a—4 ut *for a dividend, and work with half the annuity, and double the number of years for a divisor; if quarterly, take* 8 a—8 ut, *and work with a fourth of the annuity, and four times the number of years.*

53. If a salary of £150. per annum, payable half-yearly, amounts to £834..7..6. in 5 years, what is the rate per cent.? *Ans.* 5 per cent.

54. If an annuity of £150. per annum, payable quarterly, amounts to £839..1..3. in 5 years, what is the rate per cent.? *Ans.* 5 per cent.

IV. *When* U, A, R, *are given, to find* T.

Rule. *First,* $\dfrac{2}{r} - 1 = x:$ *then* $\sqrt{\dfrac{2a}{ur} + \dfrac{xx}{4}} - \dfrac{x}{2} = T.$

EXAMPLES.

55. In what time will a salary of £150. per annum amount to £825. at 5 per cent.? *Ans.* 5 years.

56. If

144   Simple Interest.   *The* Tutor's

$$\frac{2}{,05} - 1 \times 39 \frac{825 \times 2}{150 \times ,05} = 220 \frac{39 \times 39}{4} = 580,25$$

$$\sqrt{220 + 380,25} = 24,5 - \frac{39}{2} = 5 \text{ years.}$$

56. If a house is let upon a lease for a certain time for £60. per annum, and the amount be £363..8..3. at 4½ per cent. what time was it let for?   Ans. 5½ years.

57. If a pension of £250. per annum, being forborne a certain time, amounts to £2065. at 6 per cent. what was the time of forbearance?   -   Ans. 7 years.

58. In what time will a yearly pension of £28. amount to £263..4..0. at 5 per cent.?   Ans. 8 years.

Note. *If the payments are half-yealy, take half the ratio and half the annuity; if quarterly, one fourth of the ratio, and one fourth of the annuity; and* T *will be equal to those half-yearly or quarterly payments.*

59. If an annuity of £150. per annum, payable half-yearly, amounts to £834..7..6. at 5 per cent. what time was the payment forborne?   Ans. 5 years.

60. If a yearly pension of £150. payable quarterly, amounts to £839..1..3. at 5 per cent. what was the time of forbearance?   Ans. 5 years.

Present Worth of ANNUITIES.

Note. P *represents the present worth;* U, T, R, *as before.*

I. *When* U, T, R, *are given to find* P.

Rule. $\dfrac{ttr - tr + 2t}{2tr + 2} \times u = P.$

EXAMPLES.

61. What is the present worth of £150. per annum, to continue 5 years at 5 per cent.?   Ans. £660.

$5 \times 5 \times ,05 - 5 \times ,05 + 5 \times 2 = 11.$ $5 \times ,05 \times 2 + 2 = 2,5.$
Then $11 \div 2,5 \times 150 = £660.$

62. What is the yearly rent of a house of £60. to continue 5½ years, worth in ready money, at 4½ per cent.?
Ans. £291..6..3.

63. What is the present worth of £250. per annum, to continue 7 years, at 6 per cent.?   Ans. £1454..4..6.

64. What is a pension of £28. per annum worth in ready money, at 5 per cent. for 8 years?   Ans. £188.
Note.

Assistant.   Simple Interest.   145

Note. *The same thing is to be observed as in the first rule of annuities in arrears, concerning half-yearly and quarterly payments.*

65. What is the present worth of £150. payable half-yearly, for 5 years, at 5 per cent.?   Ans. £667..10..-.

66. What is the present worth of £150. payable quarterly for 5 years, at 5 per cent.?   Ans. £671..5..-.

Note. *By comparing the last examples it will be found, that the present worth of half-yearly payments is more advantageous than yearly; and quarterly than half-yearly.*

II. When P, T, R, are given to find U,

Rule. $\dfrac{tr+1}{ttr-tr+2t} \times 2p = U.$

EXAMPLES.

67. If the present worth of a salary be £660. to continue 5 years, at 5 per cent. what was the salary? Ans. £150.

$$.5 \times ,05 + 1 = 1,25. \quad 5 \times 5 \times ,05 - 5 \times ,05 + 10 = 11.$$
$$\text{then } \dfrac{1,25}{11} = 660 \times 2 = 150.$$

68. There is a house let upon lease, for 5½ years to come, I desire to know the yearly rent, when the present worth, at 4½ per cent. is £291..6..3?   Ans. £60.

69. What annuity is that which for 7 years continuance, at 6 per cent. produces £1454..4..6. present worth?
Ans. £250.

70. What annuity is that which for 8 years continuance, produces £188. for the present worth, at 5 per cent.?
Ans. £28.

Note. *When the payments are half-yearly, take half the ratio, twice the number of years, and multiply by 4 p; and when quarterly, take one fourth of the ratio, four times the number of years, and multiply by 8 p.*

71. There is an annuity payable half-yearly, for 5 years to come, what is the yearly rent, when the present worth, at 5 per cent. is £667..10..-.?   Ans. £150.

72. There is an annuity payable quarterly, for 5 years to come, I desire to know the yearly income, when the present worth, at 5 per cent. is £671..5..-.?   Ans. £150.

III. When U, P, T, are given, to find R.

Rule. $\dfrac{ut - p \times 2}{2pt + ut - utt} = R$

O   EXAMPLES.

EXAMPLES.

73. At what rate per cent. will an annuity of £150. per annum, to continue 5 years, produce the present worth of £660.? *Anſ.* 5 per cent.

$$150 \times 5 - 660 \times 2 = 180. \ 2 \times 660 \times 5 + 150 \times 5 - 150 \times 5 \times 5$$
$$= 3600 \text{ then } 180 \div 3600 = ,05 = 5 \text{ per cent.}$$

74. If a yearly rent of £60. per annum, to continue 5¼ years produce £291..6..3. for the present worth, what is the rate per cent.? *Anſ.* 4½ per cent.

75. If an annuity of £250. per annum, to continue 7 years, produce £1454..4..6. for the present worth, what is the rate per cent.? *Anſ.* 6 per cent.

76. If a pension of £28. per annum, to continue 8 years, produces £188. for the present worth, what is the rate per cent.? *Anſ.* 5 per cent.

Note. *When the annuities or rents, &c. are to be paid half-yearly, or quarterly, then*

For half-yearly payments, *take half of the annuity, &c. and twice the number of years, the quotient will be the ratio of half the rate per cent.—and,*

For quarterly payments, *take a fourth part of the annuity, &c. and four times the number of years, the quotient will be the ratio of the fourth part of the rate per cent.*

77. If an annuity of £150. per annum, payable half-yearly, having 5 years to come, is sold for £667..10..-. what is the rate per cent.? *Anſ.* 5 per cent.

78. If an annuity of £150. per annum, payable quarterly, having 5 years to come, is sold for £671..5..---. what is the rate per cent.? *Anſ.* 5 per cent.

IV. *When U, P, R, are given, to find* T.

$$\text{Rule.} \quad \frac{2}{r} - \frac{2p}{u} - 1 = x \text{ then } \sqrt{\frac{2p}{ur} + \frac{xx}{4}} - \frac{x}{2} = T.$$

EXAMPLES.

79. If an annuity of £150. per annum produce £660. for the present worth, at 5 per cent. what is the time of its continuance? *Anſ.* 5 years.

ASSISTANT.   Simple Interest.   147

$$\frac{2}{,05} \quad \frac{660 \times 2}{150} - 1 = 30,2 \quad \frac{660 \times 2}{150 \times ,05} = 176$$

$$\frac{30,2 \times 30,2}{4} = 228,01 \text{ or then } \sqrt{228,01 + 176} = 20,1$$

$$20,1 - \frac{30,2}{2} = 5 \text{ years.}$$

80. For what time may a salary of £60. be purchased for £291..6..3. at 4½ per cent.?   Ans. 5½ years.

81. For how long a time may £250. per annum be purchased for £1454..4..6. at 6 per cent.?   Ans. 7 years.

82. What time may a pension of £28. per annum be purchased for £188. at 5 per cent.?   Ans. 8 years.

NOTE. When the payments are half-yearly, then U will be equal to the half annuity, &c. R half the ratio, and T the number of payments; and

When the payments are quarterly, U will be equal to a fourth part of the annuity, &c. R the fourth of the ratio, and T the number of payments.

83. If an annuity of £150. per annum, payable half-yearly, is sold for £667..10..—. at 5 per cent. I desire to know the number of payments, and the time to come?

Ans. 10 payments, 5 years.

84. An annuity of £150. per annum, payable quarterly, is sold for £671..5..—. at 5 per cent. what is the number of payments and time to come?   Ans. 20 payments, 5 years.

ANNUITIES, &c. taken in REVERSION.

1. To find the present worth of an annuity, &c. taken in reversion.

RULE. Find the present worth of the yearly sum at the given rate, and for the time of its continuance, thus,
$$\frac{ttr - tr + 2t}{2tr + 2} \times n = P.$$

2. Change P. into A. and find what principal being put to interest will amount to A. at the same rate, and for the time to come before the annuity, &c. commences, thus,
$$\frac{a}{tr + 1} = P.$$

EXAMPLES.

Examples.

85. What is the present worth of an annuity of £150. per annum, to continue 5 years, but not to commence till the end of 4 years, allowing 5 per cent. to the purchaser?
Ans. £550.

$$\frac{5\times 5\times ,05 - 5\times ,05 + 2\times 5 = 4,4\times 150}{5\times ,05\times 2 + 2} = \frac{160}{4\times ,05 + 1} = 550.$$

86. What is the present worth of a lease of £60. per annum, to continue 4 years, but is not to commence till the end of 5 years, allowing 4 per cent. to the purchaser?
Ans. £152..5..11. 3 qrs.

87. A person having the promise of a pension of £20. per annum, for 8 years, but not to commence till the end of 4 years, is willing to dispose of the same, at 5 per cent. what will be the present worth? *Ans.* £111..18. 1. 14+.

88. A legacy of £40. being left for 6 years to a person of 15 years of age, but is not to commence till he is 21 : he wanting money, is desirous of selling the same at 4 per cent. what is the present worth? *Ans.* £171..14..–.

2. *To find the yearly income of an annuity, &c. in reversion.*

RULE. 1. Find the amount of the present worth at the given rate, and $ptr + p = A.$
for the time before the reversion, *thus,*

2. Change A. into P. and find what annuity being sold will produce P. at the same rate, and for the time of its continuance, *thus,* $\dfrac{tr+1}{ttr - tr + 2t} \times 2p = U.$

Examples.

89. A person having an annuity left him for 5 years, which does not commence till the end of 4 years, disposed of it for £550. allowing 5 per cent. to the purchaser, what was the yearly income? *Ans.* 150.

$$\overline{550\times 4\times ,05 + 550 = 660}$$
$$=;113636\times 660\times 2 = £150.$$

$$\frac{5\times ,05 + 1,}{5\times 5\times ,05 - 5\times ,05 + 5\times 2}$$

90. There

90. There is a leafe of a houfe taken for 4 years, but not to commence till the end of 5 years, the leffee would fell the fame for £152..6-. prefent payment, allowing 4 per cent. to the purchafer, what is the yearly rent?   *Anf.* £50.

91. A perfon having the promife of a penfion for 8 years, which does not commence till the end of 4 years, has difpofed of the fame for £111..18..1. ¼ prefent money, allowing 5 per cent. to the purchafer, what was the penfion?
Anf. £20.

92. There is a certain legacy left to a perfon of 15 years of age, which is to be continued for 6 years, but not to commence till he arrives at the age of 21; he wanting a fum of money, fells it for £171..14..—. allowing 4 per cent. to the buyer, what was the annuity left him?   *Anf.* £40.

REBATE or DISCOUNT.

NOTE. S reprefents the fum to be difcounted.
P the prefent worth.
T the Time.
R the Ratio.

I. *When* S, T, R, *are given, to find* P.

RULE. $\dfrac{S}{tr+1} = P.$

EXAMPLES.

1. What is the prefent worth of £357..10..—. to be paid 9 months hence, at 5 per cent.? *Anf.* £334..11..6. 3,168 qrs.

$$\frac{357.5}{.75 \times .05 + 1} = 344,5783.$$

2. What is the prefent worth of £275..10-. due 7 month hence, at 5 per cent.?   *Anf.* £267..13..10. ,164d.

3. What is the prefent worth of £875..5..6. due 5 months hence, at 4½ per cent.? *Anf.* £859..3..3. 3,2544 qrs. +

4. How much ready money can I receive for a note of £75. due 15 months hence, at 5 per cent.?
Anf. £70..11..9. ,1764d.

II. *When*

Rebate or Discount.

II. When R, P, T, are given, to find S.
RULE. $ptr + p = S$.

EXAMPLES.

5. If the present worth of a sum of money due 9 months hence, allowing 5 per cent. be £344..11..6. 3,168 qrs. what was the sum first due? *Ans.* £357..10..–.

$$344.5783 \times .75 \times .05 + 344.5783 = £357..10..-.$$

6. A person owing a certain sum, payable 7 months hence, agrees with the creditor to pay him down £267..13..10,164d. allowing 5 per cent. for present payment, what is the debt? *Ans.* £275..10..–.

7. A person receives £859..3..3. 3,254 qrs. for a sum of money due 5 months hence, allowing the debtor 4½ per cent. for present payment, what was the sum due? *Ans.* £875..5..6.

8. A person paid £70..11..9. ,1764 for a debt due 15 months hence, he being allowed 5 per cent. for the discount, how much was the debt? *Ans.* £75.

III. S, P, T, are given, to find R.

RULE. $\dfrac{s - p}{tp} = R$.

EXAMPLES.

9. At what rate per cent. will £357..10..–. payable 9 months hence, produce £344..11..6. 3,168 qrs. for present payment? *Ans.* 5 per cent.

$$\dfrac{357.5 - 344.5783}{344.5783 \times .75} = .05 = 5 \text{ per cent.}$$

10. At what rate per cent. will £275..10..–. payable 7 months hence, produce £267..13..10. ,164d. for the present payment? *Ans.* 5 per cent.

11. At what rate per cent. will £875..5..6. payable 5 months hence, produce the present payment of £859..3..3. 3,2544 qrs.? *Ans.* 4½ per cent.

12. At what rate per cent. will £75. payable 15 months hence, produce the present payment of £70..11..9. ,1764? *Ans.* 5 per cent.

IV. When

ASSISTANT. *Equation of Payments.* 151

IV. *When* S, P, R, *are given to find* T.

Rule. $\dfrac{s-p}{rp}$ = T.

EXAMPLES.

13. The present worth of £357..10..—. due for a certain time to come, is £344..11..6. 3,168 qrs. at 5 per cent. in what time should the sum have been paid without any rebate?

Ans. 9 *months.*

$$\dfrac{357.5-344.57^83}{344.57^83 \times .05} = ,75 = 9 \; months.$$

14. The present worth of £275..10..—. due for a certain time to come, is £267..13..10.,164d. at 5 per cent. in what time should the sum have been paid without any rebate?

Ans. 7 *months.*

15. A person receives £859..3..3..3. 3,2544 qrs. for £875..5..6. due at a certain time to come, allowing 4½ per cent. discount, I desire to know in what time the debt should have been discharged without any rebate? *Ans.* 5 *months.*

16. I have received £70..11.9.,1752d. for a debt of £75. allowing the person 5 per cent. for prompt payment, I desire to know when the debt would have been payable without the rebate?

Ans. 15 *months.*

EQUATION of PAYMENTS.

To find the equated time for the Payment of a sum of money due at several times.

Rule. Find the present worth of each payment for its respective time, thus $\dfrac{s}{tr+1}$ = P.

And all the present worths together, then, $s-p=D$.

and $\dfrac{d}{pr}$ = E.

EXAMPLES.

152 *Compound Interest.* The TUTOR's

EXAMPLES.

1. D owes E £200. whereof £40. is to be paid at 3 months, £60. at 6 months, and £100. at 9 months; at what time may the whole debt be paid together, rebate being made at 5 per cent.? *Anf.* 6 months 26 days.

$$\frac{40}{1,0125}=39,5061 \quad \frac{60}{1,025}=58,5365 \quad \frac{100}{1,0375}=96,3855$$

then 200—39,5061+58,5365+96,3855=5,5719

$$\frac{5,5719}{194,4281\times,05}=,57315=6\ months\ 26\ days.$$

2. D owes F £800. whereof £200. is to be paid in 3 months, £200. at 4 months, and £400. at 6 months; but they agreeing to make but one payment in the whole, at the rate of 5 per cent. rebate, the true equated time is demanded? *Anf.* 4 *months*, 22 *days.*

3. E owes F £1200. which is to be paid as follows: £200. down, £500. at the end of 10 months, and the rest at the end of 20 months; but they agreeing to have one payment of the whole, rebate at 3 per cent. the true equated time is demanded? *Anf.* 1 *year*, 11 *days.*

COMPOUND INTEREST.

THE letters made use of in Compound Interest, are,

    A the Amount.
    P the principal.
    T the Time.
    R the Amount of £1. for 1 year, at any given rate: which is thus found:

As 100 : 105 :: 1 : 1,05. As 100 : 105,5 :: 1 : 1,055.

A TABLE of the amount of £1. for One Year.

Rates per cent.	Amts. of £1.	Rates per cent.	Amts. of £1.	Rates per cent.	Amts. of £1.
3	1,03	5½	1,055	8	1,08
3½	1,035	6	1,06	8½	1,085
4	1,04	6½	1,065	9	1,09
4½	1,045	7	1,07	9½	1,095
5	1,05	7½	1,075	10	1,1

ASSISTANT. Compound Interest. 153

A TABLE, shewing the amount of £1. for any number of years under 31, at 5 and 6 per cent. per annum.

Years.	5 Rates	6	Years.	5 Rates	6
1	1,05000	1,06000	16	2,18287	2,54035
2	1,10250	1,12360	17	2,29201	2,69277
3	1,15762	1,19101	18	2,40662	2,85434
4	1,21550	1,26247	19	2,52695	3,02559
5	1,27628	1,33822	20	2,65329	3,20713
6	1,34009	1,41852	21	2,78596	3,39956
7	1,40710	1,50363	22	2,92526	3,60353
8	1,47745	1,59384	23	3,07152	3,81975
9	1,55132	1,68948	24	3,22510	4,04893
10	1,62889	1,79084	25	3,38635	4,29187
11	1,71034	1,89829	26	3,55567	4,54938
12	1,79585	2,01219	27	3,73345	4,82234
13	1,88565	2,13292	28	3,92013	5,11168
14	1,97993	2,26040	29	4,11613	5,41838
15	2,07892	2,39655	30	4,32194	5,74340

NOTE, The above Table is thus made: As 100 : 105 :: 1 : 1,05 for the first year; then, As 110 : 105 :: 1,05 : 1,025, second year, &c.

. I. When P, T, R, are given, to find A.

RULE. $p \times rt = A$.

EXAMPLES.

1. What will £225. amount to in 3 years time, at 5 per cent. per annum? Ans. 1,05×1,05×1,05=1,157625, then 1,157625×225=£260..9..3. 3 qrs.

2. What will £200. amount to in 4 years, at 5 per cent. per annum? Ans. £243. 2,025s.

3. What will £450. amount to in 5 years, at 4 per cent. per annum? Ans. 547..9..10. 2,0538368 qrs.

4. What will £500. amount to in 4 years, at 5½ per cent. per annum? Ans. £619..8..2. 3,8323 qrs.

II. When A, R, T, are given, to find P.

RULE. $\dfrac{a}{rt} = P$.

EXAMPLES.

154 Compound Interest.   The Tutor's

EXAMPLES.

5. What principal being put to interest will amount to £260..9..3. 3 qrs. in 3 years, at 5 per cent. per annum?

$$1{,}05 \times 1{,}05 \times 1{,}05 = 1{,}157625. \quad \frac{260{,}465625}{1{,}157625} = £225.$$

6. What principal being put to interest will amount to £243. 2,02 5s. in 4 years, at 5 per cent. per annum?

                                              Ans. £200.

7. What principal will amount to £547..9..10. 2,0538368 qrs. in 5 years, at 4 per cent. per annum?

                                              Ans. 450.

8. What principal will amount to £619..8..2. 3,8323 qrs. in 4 years, at 5½ per cent.?   Ans. £500.

III. *When P, A, T, are given, to find R.*

RULE.—$\frac{a}{p} = rt$, which being extracted by the rule of extraction, (the time given to the question shewing the power) will give R.

EXAMPLES.

9. At what rate per cent. will £225. amount to £260..9..3. 3 qrs. in 3 years?   Ans. 5 per cent.

$$\frac{260{,}465625}{225} = 1{,}157625, \text{ the cube root of which}$$

(it being the 3d power) = 1,05 = 5 per cent.

10. At what rate per cent. will £200. amount to £243. 2,02 5s. in 4 years?   Ans. 5 per cent.

11. At what rate per cent. will £450. amount to £547..9..10. 2,0538368 qrs. in 5 years?   Ans. 4 per cent.

12. At what rate per cent. will £500. amount to £619..8..2. 3,8323 qrs. in 4 years?   Ans. 5½ per cent.

IV. *When P, A, R, are given, to find T.*

RULE.—$\frac{a}{p} = rt$, which being continually divided by R till nothing remains, the number of those divisions will be equal to T.

EXAMPLES.

ASSISTANT.   Compound Interest.   155

EXAMPLES.

13. In what time will £225. amount to £260..9..3. 3 qrs. at 5 per cent.?

$$\frac{260,465625}{225} = 1,157625 \quad \frac{1,157625}{1,05} = 1,1025 \quad \frac{1,1025}{1,05} = 1,05 \quad \frac{1,05}{1,05}$$

= 1. The number of divisions being 3 = time sought.

14. In what time will £200. amount to £243. 2,025s. at 5 per cent.? *Ans.* 4 years.

15. In what time will £450. amount to £547..9..10. 2,0538368 qrs. at 4 per cent.? *Ans.* 5 years.

16. In what time will £500. amount to £612..8..2. ,938323 qrs. at 5½ per cent.? *Ans.* 4 years.

ANNUITIES, or PENSIONS in ARREARS.

NOTE. U *represents the annuity, pension, or yearly rent;* A, R, T, *as before.*

A TABLE shewing the amount of £1. annuity for any number of years under 31, at 5 and 6 per cent. per annum.

Yrs.	5 Rates	6	Yrs.	5 Rates	6
1	1,00000	1,00000	16	23,65749	25,67252
2	2,05000	2,06000	17	25,84036	28,21288
3	3,15250	3,18360	18	28,13238	30,90565
4	4,31012	4,37461	19	30,53900	33,75999
5	5,52563	5,63709	20	33,06595	36,78559
6	6,80191	6,97532	21	35,71925	39,99272
7	8,14200	8,39383	22	38,50521	43,39229
8	9,54910	9,89746	23	41,43047	46,99582
9	11,02656	11,49131	24	44,50199	50,81557
10	12,57789	13,18079	25	47,72709	54,86451
11	14,20678	14,97164	26	51,11345	59,15638
12	15,91712	16,86994	27	54,66912	63,70576
13	17,71298	18,88213	28	58,40258	68,52811
14	19,59863	21,01506	29	62,32271	73,63979
15	21,57856	23,27597	30	66,43884	79,05818

NOTE. The above Table is made thus: take the first year's amount, which is £1. multiply it by 1,05 + 1 = 2,05 = second year's amount, which also multiply by 1,05 + 1 = 3,1525 = third year's amount. I. When

Compound Interest.

I. When U, T, R, are given, to find A.

RULE. $\dfrac{urt - u}{r - 1} = A$, or by the Table thus,

Multiply the amount of £1. for the number of years, and at the rate per cent. given in the question, by the annuity, pension, &c. and it will give the answer.

EXAMPLES.

17. What will an annuity of £50. per annum, payable yearly, amount to in 4 years, at 5 per cent.?

Ans. $1,05 \times 1,05 \times 1,05 \times 1,05 \times 50 = 60,77531250$

then $\dfrac{60,7753125 - 50}{1,05 - 1} = £215..10..1.\ 2\ qrs.$ or,

by the Table thus, $4,31012 \times 50 = £215..10..1.\ 1,76\ qrs.$

18. What will a pension of £45. per annum, payable yearly, amount to in 5 years, at 5 per cent.
Ans. 248..13..0. 3,27 qrs.

19. If a salary of £50. per annum, to be paid yearly, be forborne 6 years, at 6 per cent. what is the amount?
Ans. £279..0. 3,072d.

20. If an annuity of £75. per annum, payable yearly, be omitted to be paid for 10 years, at 6 per cent. what is the amount?
Ans. 988..11..0. 2,22d.

II. When A, R, T, are given, to find U.

RULE. $\dfrac{ar - a}{rt - r} = U$

EXAMPLES.

21. What annuity, being forborne 4 years, will amount to £215..10..1. 2 qrs. at 5 per cent.?

Ans. $\dfrac{215,50625 \times 1,05 - 215,50625}{1,05 \times 1,05 \times 1,05 \times 1,05 - 1} = £50.$

22. What

22. What pension being forborne 5 years will amount to £248..13..—. 3,27 qrs. at 5 per cent. ? Anf. £45.

23. What falary being omitted to be paid 6 years, will amount to £279..—.3,072d. at 6 per cent. ? Anf. £40.

24. If the payment of an annuity be forborne 10 years amount to £988..11..—. 2,22d. at 6 per cent. what is the annuity ? Anf. £75.

III. *When U, A, R, are given, to find T.*

RULE. $\dfrac{ar+u-a}{u}=rt$ which being continually divided by R, till nothing remains, the number of thofe divifions will be equal to T.

EXAMPLES.

25. In what time will £50. per annum amount to £215..10..1. 2 qrs. at 5 per cent. for non-payment ?

$$\dfrac{Anf.\ 215,50625 \times 1,05 + 50 - 215,50625}{50} = 1,21550625$$

which being continually divided by R, the number of thofe divifions will be = 4 years.

26. In what time will £45. per annum amount to £248..13..—. 3,27 qrs. allowing 5 per cent. for forbearance of payment ? Anf. 5 years.

27. In what time will £40. per annum amount to £279..—. 3,072, at 6 per cent. ? Anf. 6 years.

28. In what time will £75. per annum amount to £988..11. 2,22d. allowing 6 per cent. for forbearance of payment ? Anf. 10 years.

PRESENT

158 *Compound Interest.* *The* TUTOR's

PRESENT WORTH of ANNUITIES, PENSIONS, &c.

A TABLE shewing the present worth of £1. annuity for any number of years under 31, rebate at 5 and 6 per cent.

Yrs.	5 Rates	6	Yrs.	5 Rates	6
1	0,95238	0,94339	16	10,83777	10,10589
2	1,85941	1,83339	17	11,27406	10,47726
3	2,72324	2,67301	18	11,68958	10,82760
4	3.54595	3,46510	19	12,08532	11,15811
5	4,32947	4,21236	20	12,46221	11,46992
6	5,07569	4,91732	21	12,82115	11,76407
7	5,78637	5,58238	22	13,16300	12,04158
8	6,46321	6,20979	23	13,48857	12,30338
9	7,10782	6,80169	24	13,79864	12,55035
10	7,72173	7,36008	25	14,09394	12,78335
11	8,30641	7,88687	26	14,37518	13,00316
12	8,86325	8,38384	27	14,64303	13,21053
13	9,39357	8,85268	28	14,89812	13,40616
14	9,89864	9,29498	29	15,14107	13,59072
15	10,37965	9,71225	30	15,37245	13,76483

Note. *The above table is thus made:* divide £1. by 1,05 =,95238, *the present worth of the first year,* which ÷ 1,05, =90703, *added to the first year's present worth* = 1,85941, *the second year's present worth:* then, 90703 ÷ 105, *and the quotient added to* 1,85941=2,72324, *third year's present worth,* &c.

I. *When* U, T, R, *are given, to find* P.

RULE.
$$\dfrac{u - \dfrac{u}{rt}}{r - 1} = P.$$

or, by the Table, thus,

Multiply the present worth of £1. annuity for the time and rate per cent. given by the annuity, pension, &c. it will give the answer.

EXAMPLES.

29. What is the present worth of an annuity of £30. per annum, to continue 7 years, at 6 per cent.?

$$\text{Anf. } £167.9..5.,184d.$$

$$\frac{30}{1,50363}=19,9517. \quad 30-19,9517=10,0483 \quad \frac{10,0483}{1,06-1}$$

$= 167,4716.$ By the Table $5.53238 \times 30 = 167,4716.$

30. What is the present worth of a pension of £40. per annum, to continue 8 years, at 5 per cent.?

$$\text{Anf. } £258..10..6. \; 3,264 \, qrs.$$

31. What is the present worth of a salary of £35. to continue 7 years, at 6 per cent.? Anf. £195..7..7. 3,968 qrs.

32. What is the yearly rent of £50. to continue 5 years, worth in ready money, at 5 per cent.?

$$\text{Anf. } £216..9..5. \; 2,56 \, qrs.$$

II. *When P, T, R, are given to find U.*

$$\text{Rule.} \quad \frac{prt \times r - prt}{rt - 1} = U.$$

EXAMPLES.

33. If an annuity be purchased for £167..9..5.,184d. to be continued 7 years, at 6 per cent. what is the annuity?

$$\text{Anf. } \frac{167,4716 \times 1,50363 \times 1,06 - 167,4716 \times 1,50363}{1,50363 - 1} = £30.$$

34. If the present payment of £258..10..6. 3,64 qrs. be made for a salary 8 years to come, at 5 per. cent. what is the salary? Anf. £40.

35. If the present payment of £195..7..7. 3,968 qrs. were required for a pension for 7 years to come, at 6 per cent. what is the pension? Anf. £35.

36. If the present worth of an annuity, 5 years to come, be £216..9..5. 2,56 qrs. at 5 per cent. what is that annuity?
Anf. £50.

III. *When*

III. When U, P, R, *are given to find* T.

RULE. $\dfrac{u}{p+u-fr} = rt$ which being continually divided by R, till nothing remains, the number of those divisions will be equal to T.

EXAMPLES.

37. How long may a lease of £30. yearly rent be had for £167..9..5. ,184*d*. allowing 6 per cent. to the purchaser?

Ans. $\dfrac{30}{167,4716+30-177,5198} = 1,50363$ which being continually divided, the number of those divisions will be =to T.=7 years.

38. If £258..10..6. 3,264 *qrs*. is paid down for a lease of £40. per annum, at 5 per cent. how long is the lease purchased for? Ans. 8 years.

39. If a house is let upon lease for £35. per annum, and the lessee makes present payment of £195..7..8. he being allowed 6 per cent. I demand how long the lease is purchased for? Ans. 7 years.

40. For what time may a lease of £50. per annum be purchased, when present payment is made of £216..9..5. 2,56 *qrs*. at 5 per cent.? Ans. 5 years.

ANNUITIES, LEASES, &c. taken in REVERSION.

To find the present worth of annuities, leases, &c. taken in reversion.

RULE. Find the present worth of the annuity, &c. at the given rate, and for the time of its continuance; thus, $u - \dfrac{u}{rt} = P$.

2. Change P into A, and find what principal being put to interest will amount to P at the same rate, and for the time to come, before the annuity commences, which will be the present worth of the annuity &c. thus, $\dfrac{a}{rt} = R$.

EXAMPLES.

ASSISTANT. *Compound Interest.*

EXAMPLES.

41. What is the present worth of a reversion of a lease of £40. per annum, to continue for 6 years, but not to commence till the end of 2 years, allowing 6 per cent. to the purchaser? *Ans.* £175..1..1. 2048 *qrs.*

$$\frac{40}{1,41852} = 28,1984. \qquad \frac{40 - 28,1984}{1,06 - 1} = 196,6933. \qquad \frac{196,6933}{1,1236}$$
$$= 175,0563.$$

42. What is the present worth of a reversion of a lease of £60. per annum, to continue 7 years, but not to commence till the end of 3 years, allowing 5 per cent. to the purchaser?
Ans. £299..18.. 2, 4*d.*

43. There is is a lease of a house at £30. per annum, which is yet in being for 4 years, and the lessee is desirous to take a lease in reversion for 7 years, to begin when the old lease shall be expired, what will be the present worth of the said lease in reversion, allowing 5 per cent. to the purchaser? *Ans.* £142..16..3. 2,688. *qrs.*

To find the yearly income of an annuity, &c. taken in reversion.

RULE. Find the amount of the present worth, at the given rate, and for the time before the annuity commences, thus, $prt = A.$

Change A into P, and find what yearly rent being sold will produce P, at the same rate, and for the time of its continuance, which will be the yearly sum required. thus, $\dfrac{prt \times r - prt}{rt - 1} = U.$

EXAMPLES.

44. What annuity to be entered upon 2 years hence, and then to continue 6 years, may be purchased for £175..1..1. 2,048 *qrs.* at 6 per cent.?
Ans. $175,0563 \times 1,1236 = 196,6933$
then $\dfrac{196,6933 \times 1,41852 \times 1,06 - 279,01337}{1,41852 - 1} = £40.$

162   *Compound Interest.*   *The* TUTOR'S

45. The present worth of a lease of a house is £299..18. 2,4*d.* taken in reversion for 7 years, but not to commence till the end of three years, allowing 5 per cent. to the purchaser, what is the yearly rent?   *Ans.* £60.

46. There is a lease of a house in being for 4 years, and the lessee being minded to take a lease in reversion for 7 years, to begin when the old lease shall be expired, paid down £142..16..3. 2,688 *qrs.* what was the yearly rent of the house, when the lessee was allowed 5 per cent. for present payment?   *Ans.* 30.

Purchasing FREEHOLD or REAL ESTATES,
is such as is bought to continue for ever.

I. When U, R, are given, to find W.

RULE. $\dfrac{u}{r-1} = W.$

EXAMPLES.

47. What is the worth of a freehold estate of £50. per annum, allowing 5 per cent. to the buyer?

$$Ans. \frac{50}{1,05-1} = £1000.$$

48. What is an estate of £140. per annum, to continue for ever, worth in present money, allowing 4 per cent. to the buyer?   *Ans.* £3500.

49. If a freehold estate of £75. yearly rent was to be sold, what is the worth, allowing the buyer 6 per cent. *Ans.* £1250.

II. When W, R, are given, to find U.

RULE. $w \times r - 1 = U.$

EXAMPLES.

50. If a freehold estate is bought for £1000. and the allowance of 5 per cent. is made to the buyer, what is the yearly rent?   *Ans.* 1,05—1=,05. *then* 1000×,05=£50.

51. If an estate be sold for £3500. and 4 per cent. allowed to the buyer, what is the yearly rent?   *Ans.* £140.

52. If a freehold estate is bought for £1250. present money, and an allowance of 6 per cent. made to the buyer for the same, what is the yearly rent?   *Ans.* 75.

III. When W, U, are given, to find R.

RULE. $\dfrac{u+w}{w} = R.$

EXAMPLES.

53. If an estate of £50. per annum be bough for £1000. what is the rate per cent.?

$$\text{Anf. } \frac{1000+50}{1000} = 1,05 = 5 \text{ per cent.}$$

54. If a freehold estate of £140. per annum be bought for £3500. what was the rate per cent. allowed? *Anf.* 4 per cent.

55. If an estate of £75. per annum is sold for £1250. what is the rate per cent. allowed? *Anf.* 6 per cent.

Purchasing FREEHOLD ESTATES in REVERSION.

To find the worth of a freehold estate in reversion.

RULE. Find the worth of the yearly rent, thus, $\frac{u}{r-1} = W$.

Change W into A, and find what principal being put to interest, will amount to A at the same rate, and for the time to come, before the estate commences, and that will be the worth of the estate in reversion; thus, $\frac{a}{rt} = P$.

EXAMPLES.

56. If a freehold estate of £50. per annum, to commence 4 years hence, is to be sold, what is it worth, allowing the purchaser 5 per cent. for present payment?

$$\text{Anf. } \frac{50}{1.05-1} = 1000. \text{ then } \frac{1000}{1,2155} = £822..14..1..2 \text{ qrs.} +$$

57. What is an estate of £200. to continue for ever, but not to commence till the end of 2 years, worth in ready money, allowing the purchaser 4 per cent.?

Anf. £4622..15..7. ,44 qrs.

58. What is an estate of £240. per annum worth in ready money, to continue for ever, but not to commence till the end of 3 years, allowance being made at 6 per cent.?

Anf. £3358..9..6. 2,24 qrs.

To find the yearly rent of an estate taken in reversion.

RULE. Find the amount of the worth of the estate, at the given rate and time before it commences; thus, $urt = A$.

Change A into W, and find what yearly rent being sold will produce U, at the same rate; thus, $\frac{wr \times r - wr}{r} = U$.

which will be the yearly rent required.

EXAMPLES.

164 *Rebate or Discount.*   *The Tutor's*

EXAMPLES.

59. If a freehold estate, to commence 4 years hence, is sold for £822..14..1..2 *qrs.* allowing the purchaser 5 per cent. what is the yearly income?

Ans. 822,70625×1,2155=1000.
$$\frac{then\ 1000\times1,05\times1,05-1050}{10,05}=£50.$$

60. A freehold estate is bought for £4622..15..7..4¾*d.* which does not commence till the end of 2 years, the buyer being allowed 4 per cent. for his money; I desire to know the yearly income?   *Ans.* £200.

61. There is a freehold estate sold for £3358..9..6. 2,24 *qrs.* but not to commence till the expiration of 3 years, allowing 6 per cent. for present payment; what is the yearly income?   *Ans.* £240.

REBATE or DISCOUNT.

A TABLE shewing the present worth of £1. due any number of years, to commence under 31, rebate at 5 and 6 per cent.

Years.	5 Rates 6		Years.	5 Rates 6	
1	,952381	,943396	16	,458111	,393647
2	,907030	,889996	17	,436296	,371364
3	,863838	,839619	18	,415520	,350343
4	,822702	,792093	19	,395734	,330513
5	,783526	,747258	20	,376889	,311804
6	,746215	,704960	21	,358942	,294155
7	,710682	,665057	22	,341849	,277505
8	,676839	,627412	23	,325571	,261797
9	,644609	,591898	24	,310067	,246978
10	,613913	,558394	25	,295302	,232998
11	,584679	,526787	26	,281240	,219810
12	,556837	,496969	27	,267848	,207368
13	,530321	,468839	28	,255093	,195630
14	,505068	,442301	29	,242946	,184556
15	,481017	,417265	30	,231377	,174110

Note. The above Table is thus made: 1÷1,05=,952381 first year's present worth; and ,952381÷1,05=,90703 second year; and ,90703÷1,05=,863838 third year, &c.

L. When

I. *When S, T, R, are given, to find P.*

RULE. $\frac{s}{rt} = P$.

EXAMPLES.

1. What is the present worth of £315..12..4. 2d. payable 4 years hence, at 6 per cent.?

Ans. 1,06 × 1,06 × 1,06 × 1,06 = 1,26247. then by the Table.

$$\frac{315,6175}{1,26247} = £250$$

$$\begin{array}{r} 315,6175 \\ ,792093 \\ \hline 249,9984124275 \end{array}$$

2. If £344..14..9. 1,92 qrs. be payable in 7 years time, what is the present worth, rebate being made at 5 per cent.?
Ans. 245.

3. There is a debt of £441..17..3. 1,92 qrs. which is payable 4 years hence, but it is agreed to be paid in present money; what sum must the creditor receive, rebate being made at 6 per cent.? Ans. £350.

II. *When P, T, R, are given, to find S.*
RULE. $p \times rt = S$.

EXAMPLES.

4. If a sum of money due 4 years hence produce £250. for the present payment, rebate being made at 6 per cent. what was the sum first due?
Ans. £250 × 1,26247 = £315..12..4d. ,2d.

5. If £245. be received for a debt payable 7 years hence, and an allowance of 5 per cent. to the debtor for present payment, what was the debt? Ans. £344..14. 9 1,92 qrs.

6. There is a sum of money due at the expiration of 4 years, but the creditor agrees to take £350. for present payment, allowing 6 per cent. what was the debt?
Ans. £441..17..3. 1,92 qrs.

III. *When S, P, R, are given, to find T.*

RULE. $\frac{s}{p} = rt$ which being continually divided by R, till nothing remains, the number of those divisions will be equal to T.

EXAMPLES.

166 Rebate or Discount. The TUTOR's ASSISTANT.

EXAMPLES.

7. The present payment of £250. is made for a debt of £315..12..4. ,2d. rebate at 6 per cent. in what time was the debt payable?

Anſ. $\dfrac{315,6175}{250} = 1,26247$ which being continually divided, those divisions will be equal to 4 = the number of years.

8. A person receives £245. now for a debt of £344..14..9. 1,92 qrs. rebate being made at 5 per cent. I demand in what time the debt was payable? Anſ. 7 years.

9. There is a debt of £441..17..3. 1,92 qrs. due at a certain time to come, but 6 per cent. being allowed to the debtor for the present payment of £350. I desire to know in what time the sum should have been made without any rebate? Anſ. 4 years.

IV. When S, P, T, are given, to find R.

RULE.—$\dfrac{S}{P} = rt$ which being extracted by the rules of extraction, (the time given in the question shewing the power) will be equal to R.

EXAMPLES.

10. A debt of £315..12..4. ,2d. is due 4 years hence, but it is agreed to take £250. now, what is the rate per cent. that the rebate is made at?

Anſ. $\dfrac{315,6175}{250} = 1,26247$; $\sqrt[4]{1,26247} = 1,06 = 6$ per cent.

11. The present worth of £344..14..9. 1,22 qrs. payable 7 years hence, is £245. at what rate per cent. is rebate made? Anſ. 5 per cent.

12. There is a debt of £441..17..3. 1,92 qrs. payable in 4 years time, but is agreed to take £350. present payment, I desire to know what rate per cent. rebate is made at? Anſ. 6 per cent.

THE

THE
TUTOR's ASSISTANT.

PART IV.

DUODECIMALS:

OR, WHAT IS GENERALLY CALLED,

Cross Multiplication and Squaring of Dimensions by ARTIFICERS *and* WORKMEN.

RULE *for* Multiplying DUODECIMALLY.

1. UNDER the Multiplicand write the corresponding denominations of the Multiplier.

2. Multiply each term in the Multiplicand (beginning at the lowest) by the feet in the Multiplier; write each result under its respective term, observing to carry an unit for every 12, from each lower denomination to its next superior.

3. In the same manner multiply the Multiplicand by the primes in the Multiplier, and write the result of each term one place more to the right hand of those in the Multiplicand.

4. Work in the same manner with the seconds in the Multiplier, setting the result of each term two places to the right hand of those in the Multiplicand, and so on for thirds, fourths, &c.

EXAMPLES.

EXAMPLES.

1. Multiply 7 f. 9 in. by 3 f. 6 in.

Cross Multiplication.	Practice.	Duodecimals.	Decimals.
7 × 9	6½ 7 . 9	7 . 9	7,75
3 × 6	3 . 6	3 . 6	3,5
21.-.- = 7×3	23 . 3	23 . 3 ×3	3875
2.3.- = 9×3	3 . 10.6	3 . 10.6 ×6	2325
3.6.- = 7×6	27 . 1 .6	27 . 1 . 6	27,125
-.4.6 = 9×6			

27.1.6

	f. in.		f. in.		f. in.
2. Multiply	8.5.	by	4. 7.	Facit	38. 6.11.
3. Multiply	9.8.	by	7. 6.	Facit	72. 6.
4. Multiply	8.1.	by	3. 5.	Facit	27. 7. 5.
5. Multiply	7.6.	by	5. 9.	Facit	43. 1. 6.
6. Multiply	4.7.	by	3.10.	Facit	17. 6.10.
7. Multiply	7.5.9″	by	3. 5.3″	Facit	25. 8.6.2.3.
8. Multiply	10.4.5.	by	7. 8.6.	Facit	79.11.0.6.6.
9. Multiply	75.7	by	9. 8.	Facit	730. 7.8.
10. Multiply	97.8.	by	8. 9.	Facit	854. 7.
11. Multiply	57.9.	by	9. 5.	Facit	543. 9.9.
12. Multiply	75.9.	by	17. 7.	Facit	1331.11.3.
13. Multiply	87.5.	by	35. 8.	Facit	3117.10.4.
14. Multiply	179.3.	by	38.10.	Facit	6960.10.6.
15. Multiply	259.2.	by	48.11.	Facit	12677.6.10.
16. Multiply	257.9.	by	39.11.	Facit	10288.6.3.
17. Multiply	311.4.7.	by	36. 7.5.	Facit	11402.2.4.11.11.
18. Multiply	321.7.3.	by	9. 3.6.	Facit	2988.2.10.4.6.

The APPLICATION.

Artificer's work is computed by different measures, viz.

1. Glazing and mason's flat-work by the foot.
2. Painting, plaistering, paving, &c. by the yard.
3. Partitioning, flooring, roofing, tyling, &c. by the square of 100 feet.
4. Brickwork, &c. by the rod or 16 feet ½, whose square is 272¼.

MEASURING *by the* FOOT SQUARE, *as* GLAZIERS *and* MASON's *Flatwork.*

EXAMPLES.

19. There is a house with 3 tier of windows, 3 in a tier, the height of the first tier 7 feet 10 inches, the second 6 feet 8 inches, and the third 5 feet 4 inches, the breadth of each is 3 feet 11 inches, what will the glazing come to at 14d. per foot?

Duodecimals.
7 . 10 *the*
6 . 8 *heights*
5 . 4 *added*
―――――
19 . 10
    3=*windows*
―――――
59 . 6 *in a tier.*
  3 . 11 *in breadth.*
―――――
178 . 6
54 . 6 . 6
―――――
233 . — . 6

feet. in. pts.
233.—..6 *at* 14d. *per foot.*
―――――
2d.⅙ 233   = 1s.
    38..10 = 2d.
        ⅙ = 6 *parts.*
―――――
2|0)27|1..10½
£ 13..11..10½ *Anſ.*

20. What is the worth of 8 squares of glass, each measuring 4 feet 10 inches long, and 2 feet 11 inches broad, at 4d. ¼ per foot?   *Anſ.* £1..18..9.

21. There are 8 windows to be glazed, each measures 1 foot 6 inches wide, and 3 feet in height, how much will they come to at 7d. ¼ per foot?   *Anſ.* £1..3..3.

22. What is the price of a marble slab, whose length is 5 feet 7 inches, and the breath 1 foot 10 inches, at 6s. per foot?   *Anſ.* £3..1..5.

MEASURING *by the* YARD SQUARE, *as* PAVIORS, PAINTERS, PLASTERERS, *and* JOINERS,

NOTE *Divide the square feet by* 9, *and it will give the number of square yards.*

EXAMPLES.

23. A room is to be ceiled, whose length is 74 feet 9 inches, and width 11 feet 6 inches, what will it come to at 3s. 10d. per yard.   *Anſ.* £18..10..1.

24. What

24. What will the paving of a court-yard come to, at 4*l*.¾ per yard, the length being 58 feet 6 inches, and breadth 54 feet 9 inches? *Anſ.* £7..—..10-

25. A room painted 97 feet 8 inches about, and 9 feet 10 inches high, what does it come to at 2*s*. 8*d*.¼ per yard? *Anſ.* £14..11..1.

26. What is the content of a piece of wainſcotting in yards ſquare, that is 8 feet 3 inches long, and 6 feet 6 inches broad, and what will it come to at 6*s*. 7*d*.½ per yard? *Anſ.* £1..19..5.

27. What will the paving a court-yard come to, at 3*s*. 2*d*. per yard, if the length be 27 feet 10 inches, and the breadth 14 feet 9 inches? *Anſ.* £7..4..5.

28. A perſon has paved a court-yard 42 feet 9 inches in front, and 68 feet 6 inches in depth, and in this he laid a foot-way the depth of the court, of 5 feet 6 inches in breadth: the foot-way is laid with Purbeck ſtone, at 3*s*. 6*d*. per yard, and the reſt with pebbles, at 3*s*. per yard, what will the whole come to? *Anſ.* £49..17..—.

29. What will the plaiſtering a ceiling, at 10*d*. per yard, come to, ſuppoſing the length 21 feet 8 inches, and the breadth 14 feet 10 inches? *Anſ.* £1..9..9.

30. What will the wainſcotting a room come to, at 6*s*. per ſquare yard, ſuppoſing the height of the room (taking in the cornice and moulding) is 12 feet 6 inches, and the compaſs 83 feet 3 inches, the three window ſhutters each 7 feet 8 inches, by 3 feet 6 inches, and the door 7 feet by 3 feet 6 inches; the ſhutters and door being worked on both ſides, is reckoned work and half work. *Anſ.* £36..12..2½

MEASURING *by the* SQUARE *of* 100 *feet, as* FLOORING, PARTITIONING, ROOFING, TYLING, *&c.*

EXAMPLES.

31. In 173 feet 10 inches in length, and 10 feet 7 inches in height of partitioning, how many ſquares?

Anſ. 18 ſquares, 39 feet, 8 inches, 10 p.

32. If a houſe of 3 ſtories, beſides the ground floor, was to be floored at £6..10..—. per ſquare, and the houſe meaſured 20 feet 8 inches, by 16 feet 9 inches: there are 7 fire places, whoſe meaſures are two of 6 feet, by 4 feet 6 inches each, two of 6 feet by 5 feet 4 inches each; and two of 5 feet 8 inches, by 4 feet 8 inches, and the ſeventh of 5 feet 2 inches, by 4 feet, and the well-hole for the ſtairs

stairs is 10 feet 6 inches, by 8 feet 9 inches, what will the whole come to? *Anſ.* £53..13..3¼.

33. If a houſe meaſures within the walls 52 feet 8 inches in length, and 30 feet 6 inches in breadth, and the roof be of a true pitch, what will it come to roofing at 10s. 6d. per ſquare? *Anſ.* £12..12..11¾

Note. *In tyling, roofing, and ſlating, it is cuſtomary to reckon the flat, and half of any building within the wall, to be the meaſure of the roof of that building, when the ſaid roof is of a true pitch, i. e. when the rafters are ¾ of the breadth of the building; but if the roof is more or leſs than the true pitch, they meaſure from one ſide to the other, with a rod or ſtring.*

34. What will the tyling of a barn coſt, at 25s. 6d. per ſquare, the length being 43 feet 10 inches, and breadth 27 feet 5 inches on the flat, the eave boards projecting 16 inches on each ſide? *Anſ.* 24..9..5½.

Measuring by the Rod.

Note. *Bricklayers always value their work at the rate of a brick and a half thick; and if the thickneſs of the wall is more or leſs, it muſt be reduced to that thickneſs by this*

Rule. Multiply the area of the wall by the number of half bricks the thickneſs of the wall is of; the product, divided by 3, gives the area.

Examples.

35. If the area of a wall be 4085 feet, and the thickneſs two bricks and a half, how many rods doth it contain? *Anſ.* 25 rods.

36. If a garden wall be 254 feet round, and 12 feet 7 inches high, and 3 bricks thick, how many rods doth it contain? *Anſ.* 23 rods, 136 feet.

37. How many ſquare rods are there in a wall 62½ feet long, 14 feet 8 inches high, and 2½ bricks thick? *Anſ.* 5 rods, 167 feet.

38. If the ſide walls of a houſe be 28 feet 10 inches in length, and the height of the roof from the ground 53 feet 8 inches, and the gable (or triangular part at top) to riſe 42 courſe of bricks, reckoning 4 courſe to a foot. Now, 20 feet high is 2½ bricks thick, 20 feet more, at 2 bricks thick, 15 feet 8 inches more, at 1½ brick thick, and the gable at 1 brick thick, what will the whole work come to, at £5..18..—. per rod? *Anſ.* £48..13..5½.

Multiplying several figures by several, and the product to be produced in one line only.

Rule. Multiply the units of the multiplicand by the units of the multiplier, setting down the units of the product, and carry the tens; next multiply the tens in the multiplicand by the units of the multiplier, to which add the product of the units of the multiplicand multiplied by the tens in the multiplier, and the tens carried; then multiply the hundreds in the multiplicand by the units of the multiplier, adding the product of the tens in the multiplicand multiplied by the tens in the multiplier, and the units of the multiplicand by the hundreds in the multiplier; and so proceed till you have multiplied the multiplicand all through, by every figure in the multiplier.

Examples.

```
Multiply —  35234            35234
      by —  52424            52424
            ─────            ─────
         1847107216         140936
                             70468
                            140936
                             70468
                            176170
                            ──────
                          1847107216
```

Explanation.

First, $4 \times 4 = 16$, that is 6 and carry 1. *Secondly*, $3 \times 4 + 4 \times 2$, and 1 that is carried is 21, set down 1 and carry 2. *Thirdly*, $2 \times 4 + 3 \times 2 + 4 \times 4 + 2$ carried $= 32$; that is, 2 and carry 3. *Fourthly*, $5 \times 4 + 2 \times 2 + 3 \times 4 + 4 \times 2 + 3$ carried $= 47$; set down 7 and carry 4. *Fifthly*, $3 \times 4 + 5 \times 2 + 2 \times 4 + 3 \times 2 + 4 \times 5 + 4$ carried $= 60$; set down 0 and carry 6. *Sixthly*, $3 \times 2 + 5 \times 4 + 2 \times 2 + 3 \times 5 + 6$ carried $= 51$; set down 1 and carry 5. *Seventhly*, $3 \times 4 + 5 \times 2 + 2 \times 5 + 5$ carried $= 37$, that is 7 and carry 3. *Eighthly*, $3 \times 2 + 5 \times 5 + 3$ carried $= 34$; set down 4 and carry 3. *Lastly*, $3 \times 5 + 3$ carried $= 18$; which being multiplied by the last figure in the multiplier, set the whole down, and the work is finished.

THE TUTOR's ASSISTANT.

PART V.

The Mensuration of Circles, &c.

A Circle is a plain figure, contained under one line, which is called a circumference, unto which all lines drawn from a point in the middle of the figure, called the centre, and falling upon the circumference, are equal the one to the other. The circle contains more space than any plain figure of equal compass.

Problem 1. *The diameter of a circle being given to find the circumference; or the circumference being given, to find the diameter.*

RULE 1. As 7 is to 22, so is the diameter to the circumference. Or, as 22 is to 7, so is the circumference to the diameter.

EXAMPLES.

1. If the diameter of a circle be 7, what is the circumference? As 7 : 22 :: 7

$$\begin{array}{r} 7 \\ \hline 7)\,154 \\ \hline \end{array}$$

Ans. 22 per rule.

2. If the circumference of a circle be 22, what is the diameter? As 22 : 7 :: 22

$$\begin{array}{r} 7 \\ \hline 22)\,154(7\ \textit{Ans.} \\ 154 \\ \hline \cdots \end{array}$$

174 *Menſuration.*   *The* Tutor's

   3. If the diameter of a circle be 4, what is the circumference?   *Anſ.* 12,75 *the circumference.*

   4. If the circumference of a circle be 12,57, what is the diameter?   *Anſ.* 3,999=4, *nearly the diam.*

   Rule 2. As 113 is to 355, ſo is the diameter to the circumference. Or, as 355 is to 113, ſo is the circumference to the diameter.

   1. If the diameter of a circle be 5 feet, what is the circumference?

$$\text{As } 113 : 355 :: 5$$

$$\underline{5}$$

$$113)1775(15,7 \textit{ feet, the circumference.}$$
$$\underline{113}$$
$$645$$
$$\underline{565}$$
$$800$$
$$\underline{791}$$
$$9$$

   2. What is the diameter of that circle, whoſe circumference is 15,7?

$$\text{As } 355 : 113 :: 15,7$$
$$\underline{15,7}$$
$$791$$
$$565$$
$$113$$
$$\underline{}$$
$$355)1774,1(4,99(=5, \textit{ nearly the diam.}$$
$$\underline{1420}$$
$$3541$$
$$\underline{3195}$$
$$3460$$
$$\underline{3195}$$
$$265$$

Rule

RULE 3. Multiply the diameter by 3,1416, and the product will be the circumference. Or, divide the circumference by 3,1416, and the quotient will be the diameter.

EXAMPLES.

1. If the diameter of a circle be 10, what is the circumference?

$$3,1416$$
$$10$$
———
Anf. 31,416 = *the circumference.*

2. If the circumference of a circle be 31,416, what is the diameter? 3,1416)31,4160(10 = *the diameter.*
  31416
  ———
  0

3. If the diameter of a circle be 100 inches, what is the circumference?   Anf. 314,16 *the circumference.*

4. The circumference of the earth is known to be 25020 miles, what is the diameter?   Anf. 7964 Miles, the diam.

Problem 9. *To find the area of a circle.*

RULES.

1. Multiply half the circumference by half the diameter, and the product will be the area.
2. Multiply the square of the diameter by ,7854, the product will be the area.
3. Multiply the square of the circumference by ,079574, the product is the area.
4. Multiply the square of the femi-diameter by 3,1416, the product will be the area.
5. Multiply the circumference by the diameter, and a fourth part of the product will be the area.

Note. ,7854, and 3,1416, are areas of circles, whofe diameters are 1 and 2, and ,079577, is the area of a circle, whofe circumference is 1, likewife 432, and 1,273939, are
squares

176 *Mensuration.* The Tutor's

squares of the diameters of circles, whose areas are 355, and 1, and 1,12831 is the diameter of a circle, whose area is equal to a square, whose side is 1.

Examples.

1. What is the area of a circle, whose diameter is 100 inches, and circumference 314,16?

By rule 2, 100
           100
           ─────
           10000
           ,7854
           ─────
           Ans. 7854 area.

Or thus, by rule 4, 50×50=2500. Then 3,1416× 2500=7854, the area, as before.

By rule 1, 2)314,16
           ─────────
           157,08 = Half circumference
            50   = Half diameter

           Ans. 7854,00 Area, as before.

2. What is the area of a circle, whose diameter is 17, and circumference 53,4072 inches?

By rule 1, 2)53,4072
           ─────────
           26,7036 = Half circumference
            8,5   = Half diameter

           1335180
           2136288
           ─────────
           Ans. 226,98060 inches.

3. What is the area of a circle whose diameter is 3 feet?
           By rule 2, ,7854
                       9 = square of the diameter
                      ─────
           Ans. 7,0686 = 7 feet, 0 inches, 9 parts.

4. If the diameter of a circle be 4 inches, what is the area?

By rule 2, ,7854
            16 = *square of the diameter*
            ⎯⎯⎯⎯
Anſ. 12,5664 inches.

5. What is the area of a circle, whoſe diameter is 4, and circumference 12,5664 inches?

By rule 1,   2)12,5664
            ⎯⎯⎯⎯⎯⎯⎯
            6,2832 = *Half the circumference.*
            2
            ⎯⎯⎯⎯⎯⎯⎯
Anſ. 12,5664 inches, the area.

Note. In this example it may be obſerved, that when the diameter is 4, the circumference and area are equal.

THE
TUTOR's ASSISTANT.

PART VI.

A Collection of QUESTIONS *set down promiscuously, for the greater Trial of the foregoing* RULES.

1. WRITE down two millions, five hundred and two thousand, two hundred and five.

2. What is the value of 14 barrels of soap, at 4*d.*½ per lb. each barrel containing 254lb? *Ans.* £66..13..6.

3. If £100. principal gain £5. interest in 12 months, what principal will gain £20. in 8 months? *Ans.* £600.

4. What number is that from which, if the square of 14 be deducted, and to the remainder the square of 12 be added, the sum will be 250.? *Ans.* 302.

5. A and B trade together; A put in £320. for 5 months, B £460. for 3 months, and they gained £100. what must each man receive? *Ans.* A £53..13..9 $\frac{170}{298}$.
and B £46..6..2 $\frac{78}{398}$.

6. How many yards of cloth at 17*s.* 6*d.* per yard, can I have for 13 cwt. 2 qrs. of wool, at 14*d.* per lb.?
Ans. 100 yards 3 qrs. $\frac{1}{5}$

7. What number added to the cube of 21, will make the sum equal to 113 times 147? *Ans.* 7350

8. If I buy 1000 ells of Flemish linen for £90. what may I sell it per ell in London, to gain £10. by the whole?
Ans. 3*s.* 4*d.* per ell.

9. A has 648 yards of cloth, at 14*s.* per yard, ready money, but in barter will have 16*s.* B has wine at £42. per tun, ready money; the question is, how much wine must be given for the cloth, and what is the price of a tun of wine in barter? *Ans.* £48. the tun, and
10 tun, 3 hhds. 12. gal. of wine must be given for the cloth.

10. A jeweller sold jewels to the value of £1200. for which he received in part 876 French pistoles, at 16*s.* 6*d.* each, what sum remains unpaid? *Ans.* £447..6..—.

11. An

11. An oilman bought 417 cwt. 1 qr. 15 lb. gross weight of train oil, tare 20lb. per 112 lb. how many neat gallons were there, allowing $7\frac{1}{2}$ lb. to a gallon? *Ans.* 5120 *gallons.*

12. I bought threescore pieces of Holland for three times as many pounds, and sold them again for four times as much: but if they had cost me as much as I sold them for, what should I have sold them for to gain after the same rate? *Ans.* £320.

13. What number taken from the square of 54 will leave 19 times 46? *Ans.* 2042.

14. If I buy a yard of cloth for 14*s.* 6*d.* and sell it for 16*s.* 9*d.* what do I gain per cent? *Ans.* £15..10..4 $\frac{24}{174}$.

15. Bought 27 bags of ginger, each weighing gross 84lb.$\frac{1}{4}$, tare 1lb.$\frac{3}{8}$ per bag, trett 4lb. per 104lb. what do they come to at 8*d*$\frac{1}{2}$. per lb.? *Ans.* £76..13..3$\frac{1}{2}$.

16. If $\frac{2}{3}$ of an ounce cost $\frac{7}{8}$ of a shilling, what will $\frac{5}{6}$ of a lb cost? *Ans.* 17*s.* 6*d.*

17. If $\frac{5}{6}$ of a gallon cost $\frac{3}{8}$ of a £. what will $\frac{5}{9}$ of a tun cost? *Ans.* £105.

18. A young man received £210. which was $\frac{2}{3}$ of his elder brother's portion; now three times the eldest brother's portion was half of the father's estaae, I demand how much the estate was? *Ans.* £1890.

19. If the salary of an officer be £48. per annum, what must he receive for 232 days? *Ans.* £30..10..2$\frac{1}{4}$.

20. A gentleman spends one day with another £1..7..10$\frac{1}{2}$. and at the year's end layeth up £340. what is his yearly income? *Ans.* £848..14..4$\frac{1}{2}$.

21. A lady's fortune consisted of a cabinet, worth £200. containing 16 drawers, each having two partitions, each of which contained £37. and 2 crowns, pray what was her portion? *Ans.* £1400.

22. A has 13 fother of lead to send abroad, each being 19$\frac{1}{2}$ times 112lb. B has 39 casks of tin, each 388lb. how many ounces difference is there in the weight of these commodities? *Ans.* 212160 *oz.*

23. A captain and 160 sailors took a prize worth £1360. of which the captain had $\frac{1}{5}$ for his share, and the rest was equally divided among the sailors, what was each man's part?

Ans. The captain had £272. *ane each sailor* £6..16..--.

24. What number is that, to which if you add $7\frac{2}{3}$, the whole will be $12\frac{1}{4}$. *Ans.* $4\frac{7}{12}$.

25. An usurer put out £75. for 12 months, and received for principal and interest £81. I demand at what rate per cent he received interest? *Ans.* 8 *per cent.*

26. What will £956. amount to in 7½ years, at 5 per cent. simple interest? *Anf.* £1314..10..—.

27. At what rate per cent. will £956. amount to £1314. 10s, in 7½ years, at simple interest? *Anf.* 5 per cent.

28. If for £1..4..—. I have 1200lb. weight carried 36 miles, how many lb. weight can I have carried 24 miles for the same money? *Anf.* 1800 lb.

29. If 8 cannons in one day spend 48 barrels of powder, I demand how many barrels 24 cannons will spend in 22 days? *Anf.* 3168.

30. What number is that, which being multiplied by ⅔, will produce ¼? *Anf.* ⅜.

31. A hath 24 cows worth 72s. each, and B 7 horses worth £13. a piece, how much will make good the difference, in case they interchange their said drove of cattle?
Anf. £4..12..—.

32. A man dies and leaves £120. to be given to three persons, viz. A, B, and C; to A share unknown; B twice as much as A, and C as much as A and B; what was the share of each? *Anf.* A £20. B £40, and C £60.

33. A person dying, left his widow £1780. and £1250. to each of his four children; he had been 25½ years in trade, and had cleared (at an average) £126. a year, what had he to begin with? *Anf.* £3567.

34. There is a sum of £1000. to be divided among 3 men, in such manner that if A has £3. B shall have £5. and C £8. how much must each man have?
Anf. A £187..10..—. B £312..10..—. and C £500.

35. A piece of wainscot is 8 feet 6 inches and ¼ long, and 2 feet 9 inches ½ broad, what is the superficial content?
Anf. 24 feet 0..3 ..4..6.

36. How many changes may be rung on 6 bells? *Anf.* 720.

37. A merchant at Amsterdam is indebted to another in London £642. and would pay it in Spanish guilders, at 2s. per piece, how many must the English merchant receive?
Anf. 6420.

38. If 360 men be in garrison, and have provision for 6 months, but hearing of no relief at the end of five months, how many men must depart, that the provisions may last so much the longer? *Anf.* 288 men.

39. The less of two numbers is 187, their difference 84, the square of the product is required? *Anf.* 1707920929.

40. A butcher sends his man with £216. to a fair to buy cattle; oxen at £11. cows at 40s. colts at £1..5..—. and hogs

hogs at £1..15..—. per piece, and of each a like number, how many of each sort did he buy?

Anſ. 13 of each ſort, and 8 over.

41. What number added to $11\frac{5}{7}$, will produce $36\frac{1}{6}\frac{1}{7}$?
Anſ. $24\frac{5}{6}\frac{1}{7}\frac{3}{6}$.

42. What number multiplied by $\frac{3}{7}$ will produce $11\frac{9}{17}$?
Anſ. $26\frac{46}{51}$.

43. A man had 12 ſons; the youngeſt was three years old, and the eldeſt 58; they increaſed in arithmetical progreſſion, what was the common difference of their ages?
Anſ. 5 years.

44. What is the value of 179 hogſheads of tobacco, each weighing 13 cwt. at £2..7..1. per cwt.? Anſ. £5478..2..11.

45. My factor ſends me word he has bought goods to the value of £500..13..6. upon my account, what will his commiſſion come to at $3\frac{1}{2}$ per cent.? Anſ. 17..10..5. 2 qrs. $\frac{68}{100}$.

46. Miſs Kitty told her ſiſter Charlotte, whoſe father had before left them £13200. a-piece, that their grandmother by will had raiſed her fortune to 15000. and had made her own £20000. what did the old lady leave them? Anſ. £8600.

47. A ſnail, in getting up a may-pole only 20 feet high, was obſerved to climb 8 feet every day, but every night he came down again 4 feet; in what time by this method did he reach the top of the pole? Anſ. 4 days.

48. If the $\frac{1}{5}$ of 6 be 3, what will $\frac{1}{4}$ of 20 be? Anſ. $7\frac{1}{2}$.

49. What is the difference between 14676, and the fourth of itſelf? Anſ. 11007.

50. There is in three bags the ſum of £1468. viz. in the firſt bag £461. in the ſecond £581. what was in the third bag? Anſ. £426.

51. What is the decimal of 3 qrs. 14 lb. of an cwt.? Anſ. 875.

52. How many lb. of ſugar, at $4d\frac{1}{2}$ per lb. muſt be given in barter for 60 groſs of incle, at 8s. 8d. per groſs?
Anſ. $1380\frac{2}{3}$.

53. If I buy yarn for 9d. the lb. and ſell it again for $13d\frac{1}{2}$. per lb. what is the gain per cent.? Anſ. £50.

54. A tobacconiſt would mix 20 lb. of tobacco, at 9d. per lb. with 60 lb. at 12d. per lb. 40 lb. at 18d. per. lb. and with 12 lb. at 2s. per lb. what is a lb. of this mixture worth?
Anſ. 1s. 2d. $\frac{1}{4}\frac{7}{11}$.

55. What is the value of 14 barrels of ſoap, at $4d\frac{1}{2}$. per lb. each barrel containing 254 lb.? Anſ. £66..13..6.

56. Two perſons, A and B, owe ſeveral debts; the leſſer debt being that of A, is £2173. the difference is £371. what is the debt of B? Anſ. £2544.

57. What is the difference between twice eight and twenty and twice twenty-eight: as also between twice five and fifty and twice fifty-five. *Anſ.* 20 *and* 50.

58. What number taken from the ſquare of 54 will leave 19 times 46? *Anſ.* 2042.

59. A ſchoolmaſter being aſked how many ſcholars he had, ſaid, if I had as many more, half as many, and 1 quarter as many, I ſhould have 99, how many had he? *Anſ.* 36.

60. An ancient lady being aſked how old ſhe was, to avoid a direct anſwer, ſaid, I have 9 children, and there are 3 years between the birth of each of them; the eldeſt was born when I was 19 years old, which is now exactly the age of the youngeſt; how old was the lady? *Anſ.* 62.

61. What number is that which being added to 168 makes the ſum to be 706? *Anſ.* 538.

62. From £100. borrowed, take £72. paid;
'Twas a virgin that lent it, what's due to the maid? *Anſ.* £28.

63. If when wheat is 4s. the buſhel, the 20 penny loaf weighs 18 lb. what muſt the ſaid 20 penny loaf weigh, when wheat is 6s. the buſhel? *Anſ.* 12 lb.

64. Whereas a noble and a mark juſt 15 yards did buy; How many ells of the ſame cloth for £50. had I? *Anſ.* 600.

65. A broker bought for his principal in the year 1720, £400. capital ſtock in the South Sea, at £650. per cent. and ſold it again when it was worth but £130. per cent. how much was loſt in the whole? *Anſ.* £2080.

66. What number added to the 43d part of 4429, will make the ſum 240? *Anſ.* 137.

67. What number deducted from the 26th part of 2262, will leave the 87th part of the ſame? *Anſ.* 61.

68. A gentleman went to ſea at 17 years of age; 8 years after that he had a ſon born, who lived 46 years, and died before his father; after whom the father lived twice 20 years, and then died alſo; what was the age of the father when he died? *Anſ.* 111.

69. C hath candles at 6s. per dozen ready money, but in barter will have 6s. 6d. per dozen; D hath cotton at 9d. per lb. ready money; I demand what price the cotton muſt be at in barter; alſo how much cotton muſt be bartered for 100 dozen of candles? *Anſ. The cotton at* 9d. 3 qrs. per lb. and 7 cwt. 16 lb. of cotton muſt be given for 100 dozen of candles.

70. The ſum of two numbers is 380, the leſs 114, what is their difference, product, and larger quota?
Anſ. 132 diff. 28044 prod. 2 $\frac{2}{19}$.

ASSISTANT.   *A Collection of Questions.*   183

71. A brigade of horse, consisting of 384 men, is to be formed into a square body, having 32 men in front, how many ranks will there be?   *Ans.* 12.

72. If a clerk's salary be £73. a year, what is that per day?   *Ans.* 4s.

73. B hath an estate of £53. per annum, and payeth 5s. 10d. to the subsidy, what must C pay, whose estate is worth £100. per annum?   *Ans.* 11s. 0d. $\frac{4}{53}$.

74. If I buy 100 yards of ribbon, at 3 yards for a shilling, and 100 more at 2 yards for a shilling, and sell it at the rate of 5 yards for 2 shillings, whether do I get or lose, and how much?   *Ans. lose* 3s. 4d.

75. What is the value of $\frac{5}{8}$ of 20s.   *Ans.* 12s. 6d.

76. What number is that, from which if you take $\frac{3}{5}$, the remainder will be $\frac{1}{8}$?   *Ans.* $\frac{29}{40}$.

77. My purse and money, quoth Dick, are worth 12s. 8d. but the money is worth 7 of the purse, pray what is the sum therein?   *Ans.* 11s. 1d.

78. What number is that which maketh 9 to be the $\frac{2}{3}$ of it?   *Ans.* 13$\frac{1}{2}$.

79. A maltster has several sorts of malt, one at 4s. 6d. another at 4s. and a third at 3s. 6d. a bushel; to mix an equal quantity of each, what must be the price of a bushel? *Ans.* 4s.

80. A farmer is willing to make a mixture of rye at 4s. a bushel, barley at 3s. and oats at 2s. how much must he take of each to sell it at 2s. 6d. the bushel?

Ans. 6 *of rye,* 6 *of barley, and* 24 *of oats.*

81. If $\frac{3}{8}$ of a ship be worth £3740. what is the worth of the whole?   *Ans.* £9973..6.8.

82. A person said he had 20 children, and that it happened there was a year and a half between each of their ages; his eldest son was born when he was 24 years old, and the age of his youngest is 21, what was the father's age? *Ans.* 73$\frac{1}{2}$ *years.*

83. Bought a cask of wine for £62..8..—. how many gallons were in the same, when a gallon was valued at 5s. 4d.?
   Ans. 234.

84. B owes C £269..17..—. but he compounds for 7s. 6d. in the pound, what must C receive for his debt?
   Ans. 111..6..4$\frac{1}{2}$.

85. How many dozen of stockings, at 11 groats per pair, may I buy for £190..12..—?   *An.* 86 doz. 7 pair $\frac{28}{44}$.

86. A sheepfold was robbed 3 nights successively; the first night half the sheep were stolen, and half a sheep more;

184 *A Collection of Questions.* The Tutor's

the second night half the remainder were lost, and half a sheep more; the last night they took half that were left, and half a sheep more; by which time they were reduced to 20; how many were they at first? *Ans.* 167.

87. The Spectator's club of fat people, though it consisted but of 15 persons, is said to weigh no less than 3 tons, how much at an equality was that per man? *Ans.* 4 cwt.

88. A merry young fellow in a small time got the better of $\frac{1}{3}$ of his fortune; by advice of his friends, he gave £2200. for an Exempt's place in the guards; his profusion continued till he had no more than 880 guineas left, which he found by computation was $\frac{3}{20}$ part of his money after the commission was bought; pray what was his fortune at first? *Ans.* £10450.

89. B owes C £395..18..–. but compounds the whole debt for £100..12..–. what is that in the pound? *Ans.* 5..0d. $\frac{3}{4}\frac{7544}{7978}$.

90. How many dollars at 4s. 4d. each, must be given for 360 guilders, at 2s. 2d. each? *Ans.* 180.

91. Four men have a sum of money to be divided amongst them in such a manner, that the first shall have $\frac{1}{2}$ of it, the second $\frac{1}{4}$, the third $\frac{1}{6}$, and the fourth the remainder, which is 28, what is the sum? *Ans.* 112.

92. What is the amount of £1000. for 5 years $\frac{1}{2}$, at $4\frac{1}{4}$ per cent. simple interest? *Ans.* £1261..5..–.

93. Sold goods amounting to the value of £700. for two 4 months, what is the present worth, at 5 per cent. simple interest? *Ans.* £682..10..–.

94. A room 30 feet long, and 18 feet wide, is to be covered with painted cloth, how many yards of $\frac{3}{4}$ wide will cover it? *Ans.* 80 yards.

95. There are two numbers, the one 48, the other twice as much, what is the difference between their sum and difference? *Ans.* 96.

96. Hetty told her brother George, that though her fortune on her marriage took £19312. out of her family, it was but $\frac{3}{5}$ of 2 years rent. Heaven be praised! of his yearly income, pray what was that? *Ans.* £16093..6..8. a year.

97. There are two numbers, the one 25, the other the square of 25, I demand the square root of the sum of their squares? *Ans.* 625.4998.

98. Says B to C, if I had 4 of your sheep, I should have as many as you; and says C to B, if I had 4 of yours, I should have twice as many as you; how many had each? *Ans.* B 20, C 28.

99. B, C, and D, trading together gained £120. which is to be shared according to each man's stock; B put in £140. C £300. and D £160. what is each man's share?
Ans. B £28. C £60. D £32.

100. A gentleman having 50s. to pay among his labourers for a day's work, would give to every boy 6d. to every woman 8d. and to every man 16d. the number of boys, women and men, was the same, I demand the number of each?
Ans. 20 of each.

101. There are 3 numbers, 17, 19, and 48, I demand the difference between the sum of the squares of the first and last, and the cube of the middlemost?
Ans. 4266.

102. A stone that measures 4 feet 6 inches long, 2 feet 9 inches broad, and 3 feet 4 inches deep, how many solid feet doth it contain?
Ans. 41 feet 3 inches.

103. What does the whole pay of a man of war's crew of 640 sailors amount to for 32 months service, each man's pay being 22s. 6d. per month?
Ans. £23040.

104. If I have an estate of £470. per annum, what may I expend daily, and yet lay up £130. per annum?
Ans. 18s. 7d. $\frac{1}{2} \frac{9}{365}$.

105. What number is that, which being divided by 19, the quotient will be 72?
Ans. 1368.

106. Reduce 13 ½ bushels of coals to the fraction of a chaldron.
Facit ⅜.

107. Bought 28 qrs. 2 bushels of wheat at 4s. 6d. per bushel, what does it come to?
Ans. £50..17..—.

108. How many pounds of coffee, at 5s. 9d. per lb. is equal in value to 426 lb. of tea, at 13s. 4d. per lb.?
Ans. £937 $\frac{57}{69}$.

109. What is the value of 27 dozen, 10 lb. of candles, at 5d. per lb?
Ans. £6..19..2.

110. A traveller would change 500 French crowns at 4s. 6d. per crown, into sterling money, but he must pay a halfpenny per crown for change, how much must he receive?
Ans. £111..9..2.

111. There are two numbers, the one 63, and the other ⅔ as much, I demand the product of their squares, and the difference of their product and sum?
Ans. Product of their squares 3938240, 25. difference 1890.

112. B and C traded together, and gained £100.; B put in £640.; C put in so much that he might receive £60. of the gain, I demand how much C put in?
Ans. £960.

113. Of

113. Of what principal sum did £20. interest arise in one year, at the rate of 5 per cent. per annum? Ans. £400.

114. Having bought 40 yards of cloth, at 8s. per yard, and 79 yards at 12s. what is the value of both pieces?
Ans. £58.

115. Two men depart both from one place, the one goes North, the other South; the one goes 7 miles, and the other 11 miles a day, how far are they distant at the 12th day of their departure? Ans. 216 miles.

116. In 672 Spanish guilders of 2s. each, how many French pistoles, at 17s. 6d. per piece? Ans. $76\frac{28}{35}$.

117. In 7 cheeses, each weighing 1 cwt. 2 qrs. 5 lb. how many allowances for seamen may be cut, each weighing 5 oz. 7 drams? Ans. $3563\frac{3}{87}$.

118. If 48 taken from 120 leaves 72, and 72 taken from 91 leaves 19, and 7 taken from thence leaves 12, what number is that, out of which, when you have taken 48, 72, 19, and 7, leaves 12? Ans. 158.

119. A farmer, ignorant of numbers, ordered £500. to be divided among his five sons, thus: give A, says he $\frac{1}{3}$, B $\frac{1}{4}$, C $\frac{1}{5}$, D $\frac{1}{6}$, E $\frac{1}{7}$ part; divide this equitably among them, according to the father's intention.

Ans. A £$152\frac{1392}{2734}$, B £$114\frac{1014}{2734}$, C £$91\frac{1386}{2734}$, D £$76\frac{696}{2734}$, E £$65\frac{96}{2734}$.

120. When first the marriage knot was ty'd
Between my wife and me,
Her age did mine as far exceed,
As three times three does three:
But when seven years, and half seven years,
We man and wife had been,
My age came then as near to her's,
As eight is to sixteen.

Quest. What was each of our ages when we married?
Ans. $10\frac{1}{2}$ years the man, $31\frac{1}{2}$ the woman.

121. If 12 oxen will eat $3\frac{1}{3}$ acres of grass in four weeks, and 21 oxen will eat 10 acres in 9 weeks, how many oxen will eat 24 acres in 18 weeks, the grass being allowed to grow uniformly? Ans. 36.

122. A lady was asked her age, who replied thus:
My age if multiplied by three,
Two sevenths of that product tripled be,
The square root of two ninths of that is four;
Now tell my age, or never see me more?
Ans. 28 years.

A TABLE for finding the INTEREST of any fum of Money for any number of months, weeks, or days, at any rate PER CENT.

Year. £.	Calen.Mon. £. s. d.	Week. £. s. d.	Day. £. s. d.
1	..—.. 1..8	..—..—.. 4½	—..—..—½
2	..—. 3..4	..—..—.. 9	—..—.. 1¼
3	..—.. 5..—	..—.. 1.. 1¾	—..—.. 2
4	..—.. 6..8	..—.. 1.. 6½	—..—.. 2½
5	..—.. 8..4	..—.. 1.. 11	—..—.. 3¼
6	..—..10..—	..—.. 2.. 3¾	—..—.. 4
7	..—..11..8	..—.. 2.. 8¼	—..—.. 4½
8	..—..13..4	..—.. 3.. 1	—..—.. 5¼
9	..—..15..—	..—.. 3.. 5½	—..—.. 6
10	..—..16..8	..—.. 3.. 10¼	—..—.. 6½
20	.. 1..13..4	..—.. 7.. 8¼	—. 1.. 1¼
30	.. 2..10..—	..—.. 11..6½	—.. 1.. 7¾
40	.. 3.. 6..8	..—.. 15..4½	—.. 2.. 2¼
50	.. 4.. 3..4	..—.. 19..2¾	—.. 2.. 9
60	.. 5..—..—	.. 1.. 3.. ¼	—.. 3.. 3½
70	.. 5..16..8	.. 1.. 6..11	—.. 3..10
80	.. 6..13..4	.. 1.. 10..9¼	—.. 4.. 4½
90	.. 7..10..—	.. 1.. 14..7¼	—.. 4..11¼
100	.. 8.. 6..8	.. 1.. 18..5½	—.. 5.. 5¾
200	..16..13..4	.. 3..16..11	—..10..11½
300	..25..—..—	.. 5..15.. 4½	—..16.. 5¼
400	..33.. 6..8	.. 7..13..10	1.. 1..11
500	..41..13..4	.. 9..12.. 3½	1.. 7.. 4¾
600	..50..—..—	.. 11..10..9	1..12..10½
700	..58.. 6..8	.. 13..9.. 2¾	1..18.. 4¼
800	..66..13..4	.. 15..7.. 8¼	2.. 3..10
900	..75..—..—	.. 17..6.. 1¾	2.. 9.. 3¾
1000	..83. 6..8	.. 19. 4.. 7½	2..14.. 9½
2000	.166..13..4	.. 38..9.. 2¾	5.. 9.. 7
3000	.250..—..—	..57..13..10	8.. 4.. 4½
4000	.333.. 6..8	..76..18.. 5½	10..19.. 2
5000	.416..13..4	..96.. 3..—¾	11..13..11½
6000	.500..—..—	.115.. 7.. 8¼	16.. 8.. 9
7000	.583.. 6..8	.134..12.. 3½	19.. 3.. 6½
8000	.666..13..4	.153..16..11	21..18. 4¼
9000	.750..—..—	.173.. 1.. 6¼	24..13.. 1½
10,000	.833.. 6..8	.192.. 6.. 1¾	27.. 7..11¼
20,000	1666..13..4	..384..12..3½	54..15..10½
30,000	.2500..—..—	.576..18.. 5½	82.. 3..10

RULE. Multiply the principal by the rate *per cent.* and the number of months, weeks, or days, which are required, cut off two figures on the right-hand fide of the product, and collect from the table the feveral fums againft the different numbers as when added will make the number remaining. Add the feveral fums together it will give the intereft required.

N. B. For every 10 that is cut off in months, add 2d; for every 10 cut off in weeks, add a halfpenny; and for every 40 in the days 1 farthing.

(188)

EXAMPLES.

1. What is the intereſt of £2467..10..0. for 10 months at 4 per cent. per annum?

```
    2467..10        900=75..—..—
         4          80= 6..13..4
    ─────           7=—..11..8
    9370..—         ─────────
        10          987=82.. 5..—
    ─────
     937 00
```

2. What is the intereſt of £2467..10..—. for 12 weeks, at 5 per cent.?

```
    2467..10        1000=19.. 4.. 7¼
         5          400= 7..13..10
    ─────           80= 1..10.. 9¼
   12337..10        50=   —.. 2¼
        12          ──────────
    ─────           1480|50=28.. 9.. 5
    1480|50..—
```

3. What is the intereſt of £2467..10..—. for 50 days at 6 per cent.?

```
    2467..10        7000=19..3.. 6¼
         .6         400= 1..1..11
    ─────           2=—..—.. 1¼
    14805..—        50=—..—.. —¼
        50          ──────────
    ─────           7402|50=20 .5..7
    7402|50
```

To find what any eſtate, from 1 to £60,000 per annum, will come to for 1 day.

RULE. Collect the annual rent or income from the table for one year, againſt which take the ſeveral ſums for one day, add them together, it will give the anſwer.

An eſtate of £367. per annum, what is that per day?

```
    300=—..16.. 5¼
    70=—.. 3..10
    6=—..—.. 4
    ─────────
    367=1..—.. 7¼
```

To find the amount of any income, ſalary, or ſervant's wages, for any number of months, weeks, or days.

RULE. Multiply the yearly income or ſalary by the number of months, weeks, or days, and collect the product from the table.   What

What will £270. per annum come to for 11 months, for 3 weeks, and for 6 days?

```
        For 11 months.                      For 3 weeks.
270    2000=166..13..4              270    800=15.. 7.. 8¼
 11     900= 75.. 0..0                3     10= 0.. 3..10
        70=   5..16..8                      ───────────────
2970   ─────────────                 810  =  15..11.. 6¼
       2970=247..10..0

        For 6 days.                      For the whole Time.
270    1000=2..14.. 9¼                      247..10..0
  6     600=1..12..10½                       15..11..6¼
        20=0.. 1.. 1                          4.  8..9
1620   ─────────────                        ─────────────
       1620=4..8.. 9                        267..10..3¼
```

A TABLE, shewing the number of days from any day in the month to the same day in any other month, through the year.

To / from	Jan.	Feb.	Mar.	Apr	May	June	July	Aug.	Sept.	Oct.	Nov.	Dec.
Jan.	365	31	59	90	120	151	181	212	243	273	304	334
Feb.	334	365	28	59	89	120	150	181	212	242	273	303
Mar.	306	337	365	31	61	92	122	153	184	214	245	275
Apr.	275	306	334	365	30	61	91	122	153	183	214	244
May	245	276	304	335	365	31	61	92	123	153	184	218
June	214	245	273	304	334	365	30	61	91	122	153	183
July	184	215	243	274	304	335	65	31	62	92	123	153
Aug.	153	184	212	243	273	304	334	365	31	61	92	122
Sept	122	153	181	212	242	273	303	334	365	30	61	91
Oct.	92	123	151	182	212	243	273	304	335	365	31	61
Nov	61	92	120	151	181	212	242	273	304	334	365	30
Dec.	31	62	90	121	151	182	212	243	274	304	335	365

EXAMPLE.

How many days are there from the 5th of July to the 5th of March?

Find July in the first column towards the left hand, and March at the head of the table, and in the angle of meeting you will find 243, the number of days required.

NOTE. In Leap year, if February be included, you must add one day to the number found in the table.

A COURSE of BOOK-KEEPING,

According to the method of Single Entry;

With a description of the Books, and directions for using them.

PART VII.

BOOK-KEEPING, by SINGLE ENTRY.

IN book-keeping by single entry, two books are indispensibly necessary, viz. Day-book and Ledger; the forms of which may be sufficiently known by inspection.

In the Day-Book every person is written down Debtor to the things he receives from you on trust, and Creditor by those which you receive from him.—In the margin of the Day-Book are written the pages where the accounts stand in the Ledger.—Instead of these marginal figures, some make only a dash with the pen, to shew that the account has been posted, that is, entered in the Ledger; but it is better to use the figures, for they shew not only that the account has been posted, but likewise where to find it in the Ledger, without looking in the alphabet.—I have entered in the Day-Book what is received, as well as what is delivered, which is very necessary in teaching; for the learner ought to make out his Ledger from his Day-Book.

There are several other Books kept by most merchants, as the Cash-Book, the Book of House Expences, the Invoice Book, the Bill Book, &c. &c.

DIRECTIONS

DIRECTIONS FOR THE READER.

YOUR Books being ruled in the proper form, copy into your Day-Book one month's accounts; then calculate them upon your slate, to find if they be rightly cast up. Next, rule your slate in the form of the Ledger, and upon it post the accounts that were copied in the Day-Book, with their dates prefixed, observing to put on the Debtor side of each person's account, those accounts to which he is debtor in the Day-Book, and on the Creditor side, those by which he is Creditor, and if any accounts consist but of one article, you are to express it particularly with its money in the columns; but if of several, write *to* or *by* sundries, placing the sum of the amounts of all the articles in the columns. After the accounts are properly placed, transcribe them into your Ledger, leaving a proper space under each person's name, to receive more accounts.

Then under the proper letters in the alphabet, enter those names with the pages where they stand in the Ledger; and lastly, write the Ledger pages to the several accounts in the Day-Book.

Do the same with the next month's accounts, and so on till the whole be finished: You must not enter any person's name down again, which has been entered before, till the space first assigned to it shall be filled with articles, and then the account must be transferred to a new place; and at the end of the old Ledger, draw out a balance account, placing your Debts on one side, and your Credits on the other.

THE DAY-BOOK.

		£	s	d
	January 1, 1792,			
1	Mr. John Holland, of York, Dr.			
	To 7 yards of fine broad cloth, at 18s. 6d.	6	9	6
	—20 ———— superfine ditto, — 19s. 8d.	19	13	4
	————— 1. —————	26	2	10
1	George Birch, Esq. of Bath, Dr.			
	To 6 gallons palm sack, at 8s. 6d. per gal.	2	11	0
	— 9 ———— port, red, — 5 8 ———	2	11	0
	— 9 ———— claret, ——— 8 9 ———	3	18	9
	————— 4. —————	9	0	9
1	Mrs. Sarah Moore, Dr.			
	To 2 lb. green tea, at 18s. 0d. —	1	16	0
	— 2½ ———— congou, — 9 6	1	3	9
	— ¼ stone of sugar, 5 0 per stone	0	2	6
	— A lump sugar, wt. 20lb. at 10d. per lb.	0	16	8
	————— 9. —————	3	18	11
2	Sir Joseph Johnson, Dr.			
	To a silver punch bowl, wt. 23 oz. at } 5s. 10d. per oz. — }	6	14	0
	— a tankard, — 10 10 at 6s. per oz.	3	3	0
	————— 20. —————	9	17	2
1	Sir John Mosley, Dr.			
	To a ream of fine post paper —	1	5	0
	————— 27. —————			
2	Mr. John Summers, schoolmaster, Dr.			
	To 6 cyphering books, at 1s. 2d. each	0	7	0
	— 3 dozen copy books, 2 4 per doz.	0	7	0
	— 4 quires of fool's cap, 0 9 per qr.	0	3	0
	— 1 quire thin post, — —	0	0	8
	————— February 5. —————	0	17	8
1	Mr. Anthony Archer, Dr.			
	To a ledger, ruled, — —	1	0	0
	— 5 hundred quills, at 2s. per hund.	0	10	0
	— 4 reams thick post, 1l. 2s. 4d. per rm.	4	9	4
	— 8 reams fool's cap, 1 1 0 —	8	8	0
		14	7	4

DAY-BOOK.

		£	s.	d.
2	——— 12. ——— Mr. William Grove, Dr. To 4 gallons rum, 12s. 0d. per gallon — 2 ——— brandy, 8 0 ——— — 3 ——— Eng. gin, 4 6 ———	2 0 0	8 16 13	0 0 6
2	——— 20. ——— William Warner, Esq. Dr. To 10 oz. nutmegs, at 1s. 2d. per oz. — 4 pounds coffee, 4 0 per lb. — 5 ——— almonds, 1 2 ——— — 8 ——— raisins, 0 8 ———	3 0 0 0 0	17 11 16 5 5	6 8 0 10 4
1	——— 27. ——— Sir John Mossey, Cr. By cash received of him in full —	1 1	18 5	10 0
1	——— March 22. ——— George Birch, Esq. of Bath, Dr. To 8 gallons sherry, at 6s. 4d. per gallon — 12 ——— rhenish, 6 6 ——— — 8 ——— Lisbon, 4 2 ———	2 3 1	10 18 13	8 0 4
1	——— April 24. ——— Mrs. Sarah Moore, Cr. By cash received of her in full —	8 3	2 18	0 11
1	——— May 3. ——— Mr. John Holland of York, Dr. To 25 yds. yd. wide cloth, 5s. 2d. per yd. — 8 ditto drugget, 5 8 ——— — 9 ——— serge, — 2 6 ——— — 36 ——— shalloon 1 8 ———	6 2 1 3	9 5 2 0	2 4 6 0
3	——— 14. ——— Mr. John Flint, of Nottingham, Dr. To 12 pr worsted stockings, 4s. 2d. per pr — 5 — silk ditto, 16 4 ——— — 16 — thread ditto, 5 0 ———	12 2 4 4	17 10 1 0	0 0 8 0
2	——— June 3. ——— Sir Joseph Johnson, Cr. By a bank note, received of his servant	10 5	11 0	8 0

S

Book-keeping by Single Entry.
DAY-BOOK.

		£.	s.	d.
	June 12.			
3	Mr. *James Davies*, Dr.			
	To 8 qrs. Wheat, at 2l. 8s. 0d. per qr.	19	4	0
	— 4 — rye, 1 8 2	5	12	8
	— 20 — oats, 0 10 9	10	15	0
		35	11	8
	—————— 17. ——————			
1	Mrs. *Sarah Moore*, Dr.			
	To 6 lb. hard soap, at 6½d. per lb.	0	3	3
	— 4 — soft ditto, 6	0	2	0
	— 5 — starch, 5	0	2	1
	— 4 dozen candles, 6 per dozen	1	4	0
		1	11	4
	—————— June 21. ——————			
1	Mrs. *Sarah Moore*, Cr.			
	By cash received in full	1	11	4
	—————— July 7. ——————			
2	Mr. *John Summers*, schoolmaster. Cr.			
	By cash received in full	0	17	8
	—————— 28. ——————			
3	Mr. *James Davies*, Dr.			
	To 12 bushels of Peas, 2s. 6d. per bushel	1	10	0
	— 8 ———— beans, 2 2	0	17	4
	— 10 ———— malt, 5 0	2	10	0
		4	17	4
	—————— August 1. ——————			
2	*William Warner*, Esq. Dr.			
	To 9 gross bottles, at 3s. per gross	1	7	0
	— 2 ——— small ditto, 2 0	0	4	0
	— 4 decanters, — 1 4 each	0	5	4
		1	16	4
	—————— 7. ——————			
1	Mr. *Anthony Archer*, Cr.			
	By a note upon Mr. *John Steventon*, for	10	0	0
	— cash in full	4	7	4
		14	7	4
	—————— 21. ——————			
2	Mr. *Charles Jones*, of *Shrewsbury*, Dr.			
	To 24 lb. cochineal, at 1l. 2s. 6d. per lb.	27	0	0
	— 3 opium, 0 8 0	1	4	0
		28	4	0

Book-keeping by Single Entry
DAY-BOOK.

		£	s.	d.
	September 4.			
2	Mr. John Summers, schoolmaster, Dr.			
	To 12 schoolmaster's guides, 2s. 2d. each	1	6	0
	— 3 dozen copy-books, 2 6 dozen	0	7	6
	— 1 ream fool's cap,	1	0	0
		2	13	6
	9.			
3	Mr. John Flint, Cr.			
	By a bank note for	5	0	0
	12.			
2	Mr. John Summers, Dr.			
	To 6 doz. spelling books, 10s. per doz.	3	0	0
	October 2.			
3	Mr. Samuel Taylor, Dr.			
	To 20lb. of flax at 1s. per lb.	1	0	0
	15.			
3	Mr. John Johnson, of Great Haywood, Dr.			
	To 4½ cwt. iron, at 18s. per cwt.	4	1	0
	21.			
3	Mrs. Phebe Young, Cr.			
	By 60 yards of Irish cloth, 2s. 6d. yard	7	10	0
	27.			
1	George Birch, Esq. Cr.			
	By cash in full	17	2	9
	30.			
3	Mr. Samuel Taylor, Dr.			
	To 12lb. of flax, at 1s. 0d. per lb.	0	12	0
	— 10 0 6	0	5	0
		0	17	0
	November 13.			
1	Mr. John Holland, Cr.			
	By a bill for	20	0	0
	15.			
3	Mr. James Davies, Cr.			
	By cash in full	40	9	0
	22.			
4	Mr. Thomas Green, Dr.			
	To 2 doz. knives and forks, 12s. per doz.	1	4	0
	— a set of china	3	10	6
	— a mahogany tea board	0	12	0
		5	6	6

S.2

Book-keeping by Single Entry.

DAY-BOOK.

	£.	s.	d.
November 26.			
Mr. Thomas Green, Cr.			
By 30 ells of holland, at 5s. 2d. per ell	7	15	0
———— 28. ————			
Sir Joseph Johnson, Cr.			
By cash in full	4	17	2
———— December 1. ————			
Mr. John Summers, schoolmaster, Cr.			
By cash in full	5	13	6
———— 3. ————			
Mr. Anthony Archer, Dr.			
To a cask of rum	10	0	0
———— 6. ————			
William Warner, Esq. Cr.			
By cash in full	3	15	2
———— 8. ————			
Mr. John Hunter, of Friesely, Dr.			
To 4 tons of coals, at 7s. 6d. per ton	1	10	0
———— 10. ————			
Mr. William Grove, Cr.			
By cash in full	3	17	6
———— 12. ————			
Mr. Carless, Dr.			
To 3 ton of oil, 236 gals. 2s. 6d. per gal.	29	10	0
———— 13. ————			
Mr. John Johnson, Cr.			
By cash in full	4	1	0
———— 18. ————			
Mrs. Hill, Dr.			
To a lump sugar, wt. 26 lb. at 12d. per lb.	1	6	0
———— 23. ————			
Mr. John Young, Dr.			
To 4 cwt. 2 qrs. cheese, at 32s. per cwt.	7	4	0
Mrs. Hill, Cr.			
By cash in full	1	6	0

LEDGER.

LEDGER.

The ALPHABET.

A	B	C
Mr. Anth. Archer 1	George Birch Esq. 1	Mr. Careless 4

D	E	F
Mr. Jas. Davies 3		Mr. John Flint 3

G	H	I
Mr. Wm. Grove 2	Mr. John Holland 1	Sir Jos. Johnson 2
Mr. Thos. Green 4	Mrs. Hill — 3	Mr. Charles Jones 2
	Mr. John Hunter 4	Mr. Jno. Johnson 3

K	L	M
		Mrs. Sarah Moore 1
		Sir John Moseley 1

N	O	P

Q	R	S
		Mr. J. Summers 2

T	V	W
Mr. Sam. Taylor 3		W. Warner, Esq. 2

X	Y	Z
	Mrs. Phebe Young 3	
	Mr. John Young 4	

S 3

Book-keeping by Single Entry.

Dr.	Mr. John ———		£.	s.	d.		Cr.	Holland of York, ———		£.	s.	d.
1792							1792					
January 1	To sundries —		26	2	10		Nov. 13	By a bill for		20	0	0
May 3	To sundries —		12	17	0			By cash remains to balance		18	19	10
			38	19	10					38	19	10

Dr.	George ———		£.	s.	d.		Cr.	Birch, Esq. of Bath, ———		£.	s.	d.
1793							1792					
January 1	To sundries —		9	0	9		Oct. 27	By cash in full —		17	2	9
March 22	To sundries —		8	2	0							
			17	2	9							

Dr.	Mrs. Sarah ———		£.	s.	d.		Cr.	Moore, ———		£.	s.	d.
1792							1792					
January 4	To sundries —		3	18	11		April 24	By cash in full —		3	18	11
June 17	To sundries —		1	11	4		June 21	By cash in full —		1	11	4
			5	10	3							

Dr.	Sir John ———		£.	s.	d.		Cr.	Moseley, ———		£.	s.	d.
1792							1792					
Jan. 20	To a ream of paper —		1	5	0		Feb. 27	By cash in full —		1	5	0

Dr.	Mr. Anthony ———		£.	s.	d.		Cr.	Archer, ———		£.	s.	d.
1792							1792					
Feb. 5	To sundries —		14	7	4		August 7	By sundries —		14	7	4
Dec. 3	To a cask of rum —		10	0	0			By cash remains to balance		10	0	0
			24	7	4					24	7	4

Book-keeping by Single Entry.

(2) Mr. William

1792	Dr.		£	s.	d.	1792		Cr.	£	s.	d.
Feb. 12	To sundries.		3	17	6	Dec. 10	*Grove.* By cash in full		3	17	6

Mr. Charles

1792	Dr.		£	s.	d.			Cr.	£	s.	d.
August 21	To sundries		28	4	0		*Jones of Shrewsbury,* Cr. By cash remains to balance		28	4	0

Mr. John

1792	Dr.		£	s.	d.	1792		Cr.	£	s.	d.
Jan. 27	To sundries		0	17	8	July 7	*Summers,* By cash in full		0	17	8
Sept. 4	To sundries		2	13	6	Dec. 1	By cash in full		5	13	6
— 12	To 6 doz spelling books, 10s.		3	0	0						
			6	11	2				6	11	2

William

1792	Dr.		£	s.	d.	1792		Cr.	£	s.	d.
Feb. 10	To sundries		1	18	10	Dec. 6	*Warner, Esq.* By cash in full		3	15	2
August 1	To sundries		1	16	4						
			3	15	2						

Sir Joseph

1792	Dr.		£	s.	d.	1792		Cr.	£	s.	d.
Jan. 9	To sundries		9	17	2	June 8	*Johnson,* By a bank note		5	0	0
						Nov. 28	By cash in full		4	17	2
									9	17	2

200   Book-keeping by Single Entry.

		£.	s.	d.				£.	s.	d.
3) 1792	Mr. John					Flint, of Nottingham, Cr.				
May 14	Dr. To sundries	10	11	8		By a bank note		6	0	8
						Cash remains to balance		5	11	0
								10	11	8
1792	Mrs.					Hill, Cr.				
Dec. 18.	Dr. To a lump of sugar, 26lb. 12d.	1	6	0		By cash in full		1	6	0
1792	Mr. John					Johnson, Cr.				
Oct. 15	Dr. To 4½ cwt. of iron, at 18s.	4	1	0		By cash in full		4	1	0
1792	Mr. James					Davies, Cr.				
June 12	Dr. To sundries	35	11	8		By cash in full		40	9	0
July 28	To sundries	4	17	4						
		40	9	0						
1792	Mr. Samuel					Taylor, Cr.				
October 2	Dr. To 20lb. of flax, at 1s.	1	0	0		Cash remains		1	17	0
30	To sundries	0	17	0						
		1	17	0						
1792	Mrs. Phebe					Young, Cr.				
Oct. 24	Dr. To balance	7	10	0		By 60 yds Irish cloth, 2s. 6d.		7	10	0

Book-keeping by Single Entry.

4) 1792	Dr. Mr. Thomas	£	s.	d.	1792	Green, Cr.	£	s.	d.
Nov. 22	To sundries	5	6	6	Nov. 26	By 30 ells Holland, at 5s. 2d.	7	15	0
	Cash remains to balance	2	8	6					
		7	15	0					
1792	Dr. Mr. John					Hunter, Cr.			
Dec. 8	To 4 tons of coals, at 7s. 6d.	1	10	0		Cash remains to balance	1	10	0
1792	Dr. Mr.					Carless, Cr.			
Dec. 12	To a ton of oil	29	10	0		Cash remains to balance	29	10	0
1792	Dr. Mr. John					Young, Cr.			
Dec. 23	To 4 cwt. 2 qrs. cheese, at 32s.	7	4	0		Cash remains to balance	7	4	0

BALANCE.

1792	Dr. Balance	£	s.	d.		Cr.	£	s.	d.
	To Mr. John Holland, due to me	18	19	10		By Mrs. Phebe Young	7	10	0
	To Mr. Anthony Archer	10	0	0		By Mr. Thomas Green	2	8	6
	To Mr. John Flint	5	11	8			9	13	6
	To Mr. Samuel Taylor	1	17	0					
	To Mr. John Hunter	1	10	0					
	To Mr. Carless	29	10	0					
	To Mr. John Young	7	4	0					
		74	12	6					

BOOKS,
LATELY PRINTED AND PUBLISHED BY
SWINNEY AND *WALKER,*
Birmingham.

SACRED LITERATURE: shewing the Holy Scriptures to be superior to the most celebrated Writings of Antiquity, by the testimony of above five hundred witnesses, and also by a Comparison of their several kinds of Composition. In 12 books. To which are added, Epistles and Extracts from some of the most early of the Christian Fathers. The whole intended not only to recommend the Bible as superior to all other books, but as a moral and theological repository for Christians of every rank and degree. In four large volumes, octavo, price 1l. 4s. in boards. By the Rev. DAVID SIMPSON, A. M.

A DISCOURSE on STAGE ENTERTAINMENTS. By the Rev. D. SIMPSON, A. M.

A DISCOURSE on the late Royal Proclamation for the Suppression of Vice and Immorality. By D. SIMPSON, A. M.

A DISCOURSE on the vast Importance of True Religion. By the Rev. D. SIMPSON, A. M.

A DISCOURSE on BENEFICENCE, and the Wonderfull Remunerations of Divine Providence to Charitable Men; with a great variety of Examples. By the Rev. D. SIMPSON, A. M.

The SCRIPTURE LEXICON; or a Dictionary of above Four Thousand proper Names of Persons and Places, mentioned in the Bible; divided into syllables with their proper accents; with the description of the greatest part of them: also the explanation of many words and things in the Bible which are not generally understood. The second edition, with additions, and the Greek of the proper names, affixed to them. Octavo, 6s. sewed.

Books printed and published by Swinney & Walker.

MISCELLANEOUS OBSERVATIONS relating to EDUCATION: more especially as it respects the conduct of the Mind. In one volume, octavo, price 3s. 6d. in boards. By the Rev. JOSEPH PRIESTLEY, LL.D.F.R.S.

An ADDRESS to the INHABITANTS of BIRMINGHAM, upon the necessity of attending to the philosophy of the mind—previous to their forming a just or compleat theory of education—upon the influence of education, and its relative value; with a particular Address to Tutors and Parents.—Price 1s.

The ART of ANGLING; or, Compleat FLY-FISHER. Describing the different kinds of Fish, their haunts, places of feeding, and retirement; with an account of the generation of fishes, and observations on the breeding of carp. Together with directions how to regulate pools or ponds. Also the various kinds of baits, and the great diversity of flies that nature produces. To which are added, directions for making artificial flies. Illustrated with many new improvements in the art of angling. By CHARLES BOWLKER, of Ludlow.—Price 1s. 6d. sewed.

The History of the LIVES of ABEILLARD & HELOISA.—Comprising a period of eighty-four years, from 1079 to 1163. With their genuine LETTERS, from the collection of Amboise. By the Rev. JOSEPH BERINGTON. 2d Edition, quarto, boards, 1l. 1s.

LETTERS on MATERIALISM, and on Hartley's Theory of the Human Mind, 8vo. 3s.

IMMATERIALISM delineated, or a View of the first Principles of Things. 8vo. 1s. 6d.

LETTER to Dr. FORDYCE. 8vo. 1s. 6d.

STATE and Behaviour of the English Roman Catholics, from the Reformation to the Year 1781. 2d Edition, 8vo. Price 2s. 6d.

REFLECTIONS addressed to the Rev. JOHN HAWKINS. To which is added, an Exposition of Roman Catholic Principles, in reference to God and the Country.—Octavo, 1s. 6d.

Books printed and published by Swinney & Walker.

An ADDRESS to the Proteftant Diffenters on their memorial for the repeal of the TEST ACT. Second Edition, containing a Letter from the Rev. Dr. PRIESTLEY. 8vo. 1s.

An ESSAY on the Depravity of the Nation, with a view to the promotion of Sunday Schools, &c. of which a more extended plan is propofed. 8vo. 1s.

The RIGHTS of DISSENTERS from the Eftablifhed Church, in Relation, principally, to Englifh Catholics. 1s.

A BOTANICAL ARRANGEMENT of BRITISH PLANTS; including the Ufes of each Species, in Medicine, Diet, Rural Economy, and the Arts; with an eafy introduction to the ftudy of Botany. Illuftrated by copperplates. In 2 volumes 8vo. price 14s. in boards. The 2d Edition. By WILLIAM WITHERING, M. D. F. R. S. Including a new Set of References to Figures. By J. STOKES, M. D.

The ARTIST's ASSISTANT, in the attainment of the polite Arts; particularly in drawing, defigning, perfpective, etching, engraving, mezzotinto fcraping, painting upon glafs, and in water colours, and on filk or fatin, &c. Comprizing the greateft variety of interefting difcoveries ever given in any one publication. Illuftrated with copperplates. 8vo. boards, 3s. 6d.

READING MADE COMPLEATLY EASY; or, the Child's Pleafing Inftructor. Calculated to affift Children in the attainment of the Englifh Language, and to make learning rather an amufement than a tafk. Adorned with cuts. Adapted to the ufe of fchools or private families, being the compleateft book of the kind ever publifhed. To which is now firft added, ÆSOP's FABLES Made Eafy; confifting of words of only one fyllable. By G. DUNNING, late Mafter of an academy at Coventry. Price only 6d. Ornamented with copper-plates.

www.ingramcontent.com/pod-product-compliance
Lightning Source LLC
Chambersburg PA
CBHW020817230426
43666CB00007B/1047